# Screw It,
# I'll Take The Elevator

A man with Cerebral Palsy who
demonstrates how to laugh in the face
of adversity

By
Patrick Souiljaert

ISBN-13: 978-1982077815
ISBN-10: 1982077816

This book has been printed by
CPI Group (UK) Ltd, Croydon, CR0 4YY
**www.cpi-print.co.uk**

**Thank you to the following people for pre-ordering this book and helping me to self-publish it**

Alex Wade
Alison Taylor
Ameya
Anna-Marie
Heywood
Bhakti
Brahma
Brian Colclough
Callum W.
Stannard
Carol Wyse
Chris TR
David Carroll
Deva
Doug Eaton
Duncan Cooke
Eliisa ropponen
Gareth Bertram
Gavin Thomson
George Boullin
Gill Alton
Gillian Millar

Ian Jackson
Jane Leclercq
Jane Smith
Jason Hamblin
John Potts
Julie Brazier
Kama Dayini
Kanjara
Kathy Riley
Katie Silverson
Lynn Austin
Maitreya
Mark Birch
Mark Wisdom
Markella Mikkelsen
Mary Oswald
Matthew Hollamby
Maya Carrington
Mira
Padraig Tobin
Patrick Woodward
Paul Howard

Peter G. Williams
Peter Venis
Phillip Haslam
Pranava
Richard Drakes
Richard Goodyer
Richard Rahim
robbiecozz
Rosalind Charles
Roy Stannard
Savadhara
Simon Kennerley
Steve Norman
Steven Stark
Susan Haggas
Susan Oliver
Susan Saunders
Tim Tomlinson
Timothy Black
Wendy Wells

Patrick Souiljaert

# Contents

Patrick Souiljaert

# Thank you Steve Norman from Spandau Ballet

To cut a long story short, Steve tweeted me a few months ago to say how much he enjoyed Stairs For Breakfast and he is full of praise for me. However I think he was disappointed that Spandau Ballet aren't mentioned in my first book, whilst their 'arch rivals' Duran Duran are!

There is no question, Spandau Ballet are one of the biggest pop groups of the 1980s. I was a thirteen- year-old schoolboy when 'Through The Barricades' was in the charts. I remember hearing a small cluster of twenty-something-year-old teaching assistants chatting about Spandau Ballet, and which band member they fancied the most. I'm sorry Steve, I don't recall hearing your name.

Without a doubt 'True' is one of the greatest ballads of all-time. When I hear the saxophone in the song, I think of you Steve.

You seem like a great human being with a heart of GOLD. It was fun having lunch with you recently. I like people who I can have a laugh with, and you are one of them!

# Foreword

It is three years since Patrick asked me to write the foreword to 'Stairs For Breakfast'. In that time Patrick has published the book, sold over a thousand copies through his own efforts, appeared on TV and radio and undertaken numerous speaking engagements. Between the two books he has written more than 190,000 words all painstakingly typed with the left index finger. He has learned to sail, travelled the world and become an adherent of ascension meditation in which remarkably he is on his way to becoming a teacher.

This sequel to his first book has all the same magnetic qualities as before. Born with Cerebral Palsy because of not breathing for the first 4 minutes of his existence, his life since has been breathless in a different way. Within its covers are daily stories of rejection, tales of climbing mountains, real and metaphorical and a modern day Arabian Nights saga of one man's quest to achieve self-enlightenment, and through it, true independence.

Unlike the rest of us who take our ease of speech and mobility for granted, Patrick has to overcome these challenges every day with great effort. In this volume you can read about the frustration he encounters after a major fall in 2010 and the battles with bureaucracy that he encounters inside the NHS and in the wider world. For a man who uses crutches, I have never met a person who wants or needs support less. For him, falling over is an opportunity to demonstrate how to stand up again.

Perhaps most emotional of all, is the story woven through the pages of Patrick's search for a soulmate. After a myriad of unsatisfying encounters, including an incredible account of an evening in a Brighton casino, Patrick comes to realise that it is better to 'pull' in relationships than to 'push'. The litany of unreturned phone calls, dismissive texts and missed meetings is heart breaking but like an Excalibur sword, Patrick's determination is honed by each one.

As in 'Stairs For Breakfast', the names have been changed in the book to protect the innocent, and the not so innocent. The same forensic detail is present. The process leading up to one of the biggest decisions in his life – the departure from a secure well-paid job at a big corporation is described in gripping stages. The move into property investment and later, internet marketing is set out on the page like washing left in the sun to dry.

Fizzing from every line are the fireworks of Patrick's humour, often at his own expense. When you or I would be crying with frustration or pain, Patrick is laughing at himself and seeking the learning from the experience. What springs off the page is Patrick's photographic memory for detail.

Patrick's search for the higher plane becomes the reader's. He shares every bump, twist and landslide. When he should be lying face down on the ground, he picks himself up and dusts himself down. Your journey and his are intimately entwined. He ends the book in a better place – and so will you.

**Roy Stannard**
Friend

# Introduction

Welcome to 'Screw It, I'll Take The Elevator'. This is the second part of my autobiography.

After making the decision to take voluntary redundancy from my 'job-for-life' in 2011 I've had an amazing time. It's been a journey of self-discovery, overcoming adversity and doing the impossible.

Seven years ago little did I expect that I was going to become an author or a public speaker. It wasn't part of my plan!

It wasn't until I started networking in the property investment community and blogging about my property journey that I realised I'm not a regular independent guy. In a way that connects me to others, I now see my Cerebral Palsy as a gift and I am using it to help people in life. Public speaking and inspiring people is something I love. I often say to people, "Do something you love and that adds value to people's lives".

In the time it has taken me to write my two-book autobiography (typing it with my left index finger), I have discovered inner peace. Through meditation it is an ever increasing, unbounded experience.

As someone with impaired speech due to my Cerebral Palsy, another amazing thing I have done recently is radio interviews. Even with my can-do attitude, speaking on the radio was never on my to-do list. However speaking on the radio is something I do very clearly. I remember being slightly apprehensive on the way to my first ever live radio interview, but feeling confident after walking into the studio. Once there, I found myself in the present moment, and the interview was easy and I loved it.

After self-publishing the first part of my autobiography – 'Stairs For Breakfast' – I've created a limited company and business plan, which has enabled me to obtain a government grant to employ a full-time PA. Having worked with me for three months now, Felicity has helped me with this book.

I would also like to thank Alex Wade for his legal advice and Roy Stannard for his friendship over the last twenty years – and for all his help in publishing this book.

I also greatly appreciated all the reviews from people who have read 'Stairs For Breakfast'– and in response to the commonly asked question "When is the sequel coming out?" Here it is!

I hope you enjoy it. It covers the first part of my life up to 22nd September 2000, the day I walked out of Surf and started something new. After working at that radio station for two and a half years as a studio producer, I had achieved my goal and had nothing else to prove. My new millennium had arrived, albeit nearly ten months late.

# Chapter 1

I will never forget Monday, 25th September 2000. It was a relief to be out of Surf and doing something completely different. I was completing a full-time vocational course with the Prince's Trust in Hove, mixing with a group of people who came from numerous different backgrounds.

There were between twelve and fifteen of us on the course and we were an interesting group of people. One was Claudia, a recent university graduate who went on to work for the Prince's Trust. Another was Tom, an eighteen year old with a really positive energy in him, who had recently come out of prison.

And then there was Kwok. Kwok appears later in this story and had just started a new job. His new employer had sent him on the course for one day a week.

The nice thing about the Prince's Trust course was that everyone was equal and we all got on well. But there were one or two disruptive people, who tended to storm off or who didn't turn up if there was something better to do.

The course leader, Gemma, was very good with people, especially when dealing with the troublesome guys. Initially, she asked them individually if they disliked the course. After establishing that they were just unruly eighteen year olds, she then asked them in front of the group if they had a problem - and provided a platform to say what was bothering them.

If the challenging behaviour continued, they got sent out for a while and were completely ignored when they came back into group. This made them feel that they were missing out on something, which encouraged them to behave better in order to return. A good bit of psychology!

The twelve week course was designed to build interpersonal skills (team-working, communications etc) via doing things to help the community (including painting the outside of a youth centre which made me feel useless as the task was physically beyond me) as well as various fund raising activities

Although the course was good fun and not very taxing, I felt worthless. I remember having the same thoughts as I had when I went on the two day interview process with Scope earlier in 1999. On the one hand, I thought all the people on the course were better than me, whilst on the other thinking, 'Why am I doing this vocational course? I'm worth more than this'. My mindset wasn't good.

Some of the time I felt sick and this, I'm sure, was mirrored on my face. However, for the majority of the time on the course, I was my quick-witted self and made the group laugh with my off-the-cuff jokes. As a naturally helpful person, I would try to assist people with things like written work which in turn gave me a boost.

I didn't realise it at the time, but I inspired people and was well respected. Had I just relaxed and felt good about myself, I would have enjoyed the course a lot more. I felt under enormous pressure to succeed.

The second week of the course was spent in North Wales on an outdoor adventure week. It was an enjoyable five days, during which I remember abseiling! Kwok was with the group on that trip. A year younger than me with a similar mindset and we bonded well.

Back in the Prince's Trust office in Hove, we spent some time writing CVs and covering letters. I just adapted the CV and covering letter that Stephen Holmes had created for me in 1997. I also wrote two positive pieces on my time at Surf and my experience with IBM and included a copy of my acceptance letter from IBM.

In October, I started to have an odd issue with my car. For no apparent reason, it stalled from time to time becoming more prevalent as time went on. The car was not even eighteen months old. Over a six week period, I took the car to the Renault garage twice. On both occasions, the mechanics said, "We've connected the car to the computer and we can't find anything wrong with it." I remember replying, "There's definitely something wrong with it..."

During week five or six of the Prince's Trust course. Kwok mentioned to me and Gemma that when he finished university, he had a temporary trainee job waiting for him in the IT department of East Sussex Fire Brigade. Kwok said the fire brigade often had temporary jobs going and that he would contact Dick Jeffries, the manager of the IT department, to see if they had a job for me.

Sure enough Kwok fulfilled his promise and I got a job interview with Dick Jeffries at the headquarters of East Sussex Fire Brigade, which at the time were in Lewes.

I don't know what Kwok told Dick about me, nor do I remember much about my job interview, other than I was very nervous and Dick Jeffries offered me the job! It was so relaxed it felt more like an informal chat than a job interview.

Dick was a retired fire fighter in his sixties and in common with all of the people I worked with at the Brigade he was a very good person.

During the interview he said they were currently employing a young lady as a trainee programmer, who had started to develop a Microsoft Access health and safety database system but her four month contract was ending in a few weeks. Dick offered me a four month contract on £15,800pa to finish the database system.

I was delighted to be offered the job, whilst at the same time feeling a little unsettled because it had come about so unexpectedly. I hadn't done much at all to get the job.

However, I had succeeded in teaching myself Visual Basic 6 (VB) a year or so prior to this. VB is the programming language embedded in Microsoft Access (and all of the Microsoft Office products; Word, Excel etc).

I had about three weeks between the interview and starting the job. Whilst looking forward to starting a proper job, I had a lot of self-doubt about not being able to do it, which was really just lack of self-belief.

Starting a new job can be a nerve-racking experience. During the three weeks before I commenced the job, my sub-conscious wanted me to not do it. But I knew I wasn't going to pull out of it. It was another case of feeling the fear and doing it anyway.

I kept going to the Prince's Trust until I began at the Fire Brigade. When I started the course on 25th September I hadn't expected to be starting a job ten weeks later on 4th December.

About the time of my twenty-seventh birthday in November 2000 there was still a problem with my car. By that time it was stalling once a day.

Ten days before I started at the fire brigade, prior to a fund raising commitment due to start in the afternoon in central Brighton and which was likely to extend into the evening, I arranged to meet my friend Stuart in the Churchill Square shopping centre for lunch. I had time to do this before meeting up with my Prince's Trust chums.

On my way to meet Stuart, turning off Brighton seafront into the road which leads to the side of Churchill Square, my car stalled. After restarting my car, I went a few hundred yards up the hill, past the shopping centre's multi-storey car park, before my car stalled again. More accurately, the car conked out! The engine wouldn't restart and smoke started to escape from under the bonnet and drift upwards, ominously.

The commotion quickly gathered a crowd of onlookers. Before I knew it, somebody had dialled 999 and called the Fire Brigade!

People were telling me to get out of my car fast! I didn't think it was that bad and replied, "It's alright, it's only a bit of smoke."

While I was on the phone, telling Stuart what had happened and where I was, I heard the siren of a fast approaching fire engine. Stuart arrived just as the firemen were putting out the dying embers of my smouldering car!

I thanked the firemen and said, "You might find this hard to believe but I start working with you guys the week after next!"

Stuart and I decided to have lunch in the adjacent pub, whilst we waited for a recovery truck to take my car to the Renault garage and I remember it being a very funny lunch!

I'm not a mechanic and might be wrong here. I think all that started to smoulder was the rubber seal around the engine. Having said that, I don't even know if car engines have rubber around them! Obviously there was an underlying problem with my car. Had my car been able to travel a few more yards, I would have got it into a parking space.

After my car had been taken away, I had a good story to tell people while fund raising. That evening I went home on the bus with Claudia, who also lived in Shoreham.

The next day the Renault garage was extremely apologetic for not having spotted the problem with my car sooner. They fixed my car in double quick time, ready for me to start my job with the fire brigade.

My first day at work was not a typical day. The headquarters of East Sussex Fire Brigade were in a little compound, comprising a converted Victorian house where my IT department was based and a modern one-storey prefab building.

On my first day, I found myself allocated to one of the offices in the prefab building because that building had a disabled toilet in it!

As you can imagine, I wasn't happy about being put in this disabled box! I wanted to work with my team in the Victorian house. It took me the whole of my first day to assure them that I could use a normal toilet! Part of their concern was that the toilet in the Victorian house was quite small.

My department had a team meeting every Monday morning and on my first day Dick and Brenda (Dick's deputy) made me feel welcome and part of the team before being sent to work in the other building on my own!

On day two I was working in my rightful building containing my IT department of about fifteen people. The Victorian house had a main office with six or seven people and a few smaller offices. I was based in the office at the back of the building. Usefully, it was right next door to the toilet which was quite cosy and not very soundproof!

I shared an office with Bill and Edward. Bill was fifty-five and had recently started his desk job, which he wasn't enjoying as much as being a fire fighter, a role he had held for many years. Being slightly older than Bill, Edward was more of an IT person and my mentor. Bill told me some harrowing but highly entertaining stories about his time as a fireman.

The Prince's Trust course ended on Friday 15th December. The day before it finished the group were doing a presentation at Hove Town Hall and I took a day off from work to be part of it.

My friend Ray came to the presentation, as did Gemma's husband, Allan Moulds. I hadn't met him before but I knew Allan was the Managing Director of Burgess Hill radio station Bright FM. I did little more than say hello to Allan when I met him. Coincidentally, Ray and Allan had previously worked together on an RSL radio station years earlier.

The presentation went well and I thought Gemma had done a good job in running the twelve week course. Being in charge of fifteen occasionally unruly young people couldn't have been the easiest job in the world.

It took me about a month to settle into my job and feel comfortable with the Access database I was completing. It was a personal injury recording system and had an Access form which went into great detail.

The form had numerous tabs on it, which contained tick boxes, pull-down menus and list boxes, all of which were known as controls in the MS Access world. On one tab there were two full length images of a body (front and back). Each image had a load of tick boxes on it to specify which part(s) of the body had been injured.

Ideally, I would have liked to have added a few more controls onto the form. However, there was a limitation to the number of controls Access would allow. So I had to work out a way of capturing the additional information through writing VB code instead which the database contained a fair bit of already.

Teaching myself VB had served me well but there were still things that I wasn't familiar with. I felt under so much pressure to succeed at the brigade that certain VB functions, which I would have found easy to look up at home, were far more difficult to unlock at work. I was probably too reliant on Edward for help at the beginning.

Six mini cans of Guinness had been left in my car by someone after I had helped them with their computer. One morning in the first month when I got to work, I was feeling so sick with nerves that I decided to have a few sips of Guinness, just to take the edge off.

Sitting in my car in the little compound at work, I opened one of the mini cans and took a little sip. Not having tasted Guinness before or being a morning alcohol drinker, I just vomited it straight back up and made a dark brown circular mark on the top right side of my blue shirt.

I couldn't believe what I had done. There was no way I could go into the office with my shirt like that. I didn't have another shirt in the car. It was past nine o'clock and I lived thirty-five minutes away. I thought 'Sh*t, what do I do?' I put my jacket on and zipped it up, so that only the top of my collar and tie were visible.

Despite feeling a little hot and with Bill and Edward bemused as to why I sat in the office all day with my jacket done up, I got away with it. Needless to say, my career as a would-be morning alcoholic started and ended that day.

My first payslip was a momentous occasion. When I saw how much tax and national insurance had been taken from my gross pay I phoned the accounts department because I thought they had made a mistake and deducted too much money! I recall my net pay was between £850 and £900.

Mum said to me that as I had been living rent-free at home for the last few years, I should give her most of my wages. I thought she had a fair point, so I did.

While working at the Brigade I arranged for me, my sister Clare and my nephews Scott and Oliver to visit a fire station in Brighton one weekend. The firemen were very nice and open to allowing the two boys to sit in the front of a fire engine and trigger the sirens and then to hold a fire hose outside and squirt water. As you can imagine, being five and three years old, Scott and Oliver loved it and thought it was funny.

I was close to Scott and Oliver and often went round to see them. My speciality was making them laugh by saying funny things to them and tickling them. They used to refer to me as being 'the best uncle in the world'.

For those of you who have not read 'Stairs For Breakfast' (I can highly recommend it!), Martin had been my friend since my arrival in England from Belgium in 1984. Martin had Duchene Muscular Dystrophy (MD), which is a muscle wasting disability. Most people with MD are lucky to live past their teens. At twenty six, he was defying the odds with an iron will to live, reinforced by the fact that he was married to Janet and they had Ben who was four.

In 2000 or 2001, Martin moved out of his residential home and into a three bedroom semi-detached house with Janet and Ben in Chichester. The house was fairly small. Downstairs had a kitchen, lounge and a toilet, whilst upstairs boasted three bedrooms and a bathroom.

Directly above the lounge was Martin's bedroom. A 6' x 2' area of the lounge ceiling had been taken out and a lift installed. The lift eliminated a large chunk of either the lounge or Martin's room, depending on whether it was up or down.

Because Martin needed 24 hour care he received a grant to employ three carers. Even with these working full-time shifts, it wasn't enough to provide 24/7 care and so Janet had to manage Martin's care the rest of the time.

It was nice for Martin, Janet and Ben to be living together. They had had a long battle sorting out a house and carers.

When Martin lived in the home, there was a regular turnover of volunteer carers and Martin sometimes got frustrated with having to explain to someone new how to do things like turning him in bed. By employing his own carers, Martin didn't have that problem anymore.

As all of his muscles had virtually wasted away, there was an art to turning Martin in bed. People had to be careful not to pull his arms or legs out of their sockets. I sometimes caught a glimpse of Martin's bare chest. It was a gruesome sight, as all of his organs were clearly visible.

I used to treat Ben the same way that I treated Scott and Oliver. I found it so easy to entertain him. He used to scream with laughter, even wetting himself a couple of times! Just the thought of me tickling him made Ben go wild. All I had to do was sit on the edge of the sofa, as if I was about to stand up, and say "I'm coming to get you...!" It was so funny.

However, hearing Ben scream annoyed Martin a little. He would say to me, "Can you not do that." It caused me a dilemma because Ben loved me playing with him. I think the fact that Martin couldn't bond with Ben in the same way frustrated him.

Over the years I got to know Janet well and we talked about all sorts of stuff. I used to tell her about my efforts to find a girlfriend which included going speed-dating and slow dancing with (usually) inebriated girls in pubs. It made Janet laugh because she could empathise with me, as she understood how out of place I was.

I sometimes mentioned Rosie to Janet. I referred to her as 'the girl I fell in love with at college'. I often thought about contacting Rosie again but didn't have the confidence to do so.

There was a downside to Martin moving into his own house with Janet. Because there wasn't a nearby pub, he stopped going out so much. Although he still went out to places, (he was good at art and played wheelchair football), over the next few years Martin stayed in bed for longer periods. Some days, he didn't get out of bed.

When I went to see Martin and Janet on Saturday evenings, I would normally sit next to his bed and talk to him, while watching 'Casualty', which as you can imagine wasn't my favourite television programme. By 9-9.30pm Martin would doze off to sleep and I walked down the stairs and spent time with Janet and Ben.

In the past, when I used to visit Martin in his residential home, we went out to the pub and he stayed up past midnight. Sharing the home with other disabled people gave Martin more incentive to get up.

As time went on, he got progressively weaker. It was clear that the reason Martin survived so long for someone with Muscular Dystrophy was due to his strong will to live. He inspired me.

In 2000, I went with Martin to see the Manic Street Preachers at the Brighton Centre. It was a brilliant gig and we bumped into Emily, one of our mutual friends and classmates from school.

Around the same time, Clare, Scott, Oliver and I went to stay with Dad and his wife Madeline in France. They were living in a three bedroom first floor flat and Madeline was pregnant.

Madeline was very hospitable and eager for us to watch the video of their wedding featuring a lot of Moroccan music and dancing. It lasted for three days (the wedding - not the video!), although it felt as if someone may have filmed the whole thing.

Dad told me that he had decided to marry Madeline because he was fed up with having a succession of different girlfriends over the years and he wanted to be with someone for the rest of his life. For a person who enjoyed beer, wine, cigars, a pipe (not all at the same time!) and who had never been religious, I found it odd when he said, in order to marry Madeline, he had converted to Islam and in consequence had given up smoking and drinking.

More bizarre, however, was Dad and Madeline's suggestion that I marry her sister who lived in Morocco! This wasn't a single one-off joint proposal, but rather a series of nudges, together and individually. Each time I replied (in French), "No thank you. I would like to meet a girl, fall in love and then get married". It became embarrassing because they were quite persistent.

Most people are employed in tourism or agriculture in south-west France where Dad and Madeline live. At the time, Dad was working in a fruit picking factory doing a manual labour job (before he worked his way up and became a manager). He worked twelve hour shifts and came home pretty exhausted. Madeline worked at the same factory.

The following year, Clare, the boys and I went to stay with Dad and Madeline once more. By then they had a baby girl called Isabelle and it wasn't long before Madeline was pregnant again.

Despite the year's gap, Dad and Madeline again suggested that I marry her sister. With a sense of déjà vu, I found myself replying, "No thank you. I want to meet a girl, fall in love and then get married". I think Dad got the message earlier than Madeline. It got to the point where I tried not to be left in a room on my own with Madeline, because I knew she would bring the subject up.

The upshot of this embarrassment was that it opened a gap between my father and I based on the feeling that he couldn't really relate to me. I found the idea of marrying Madeline's sister so outlandish that after that visit to France I didn't contact Dad for about five years.

Back at work at the Fire Brigade, in the small back office with Bill and Edward, I was now making good progress in finishing off my database. Although the two of them were good guys they tended to keep their heads down and I found working in that office a bit boring.

Without offending them, I managed to migrate into the main office, where there were more people. It was a much livelier office to work in. After completing all of the development work on the health and safety database I produced a good user guide and design document to go with it.

Before my four month contract was due to end in April, Dick offered me a new contract, starting the next month with a £500 salary increase, to develop another system. Without really realising it, I had impressed the Fire Brigade.

A few days later I received an unexpected phone call from Gemma. She was phoning to let me know that she had got me an interview with a senior HR manager in a company I am going to refer to as *Shh* (I'll explain why in the next chapter).

I couldn't believe that Gemma had gone to the trouble of doing this and I was very excited about it. My job interview was in London and I had to phone the senior HR manager's PA to arrange a date and time for the interview, which I organised for the following week.

Coincidentally, after applying for a job vacancy which I had seen in the Evening Argus, I had an interview lined up with a small local software house two days after my interview with *Shh*!

Talk about two buses coming along at once! Not having had much annual leave from the Brigade yet, I took a few days off in the week of my two job interviews.

My interview at *Shh* was in the afternoon. Dressed smartly, I travelled up to London on the train and then took a cab to an impressively well appointed, very tall building. I was interviewed by two guys: the senior HR man, who liked to be known by his initials, KC, and a senior IT guy called Charles.

Both KC and Charles were really friendly and they both had copies of my cover letter and CV, my acceptance letter from IBM and the two pieces I had written about my experiences of Surf and IBM.

My interview was more like an informal chat than a job interview. Most of the conversation was between KC and I.

KC recognised what I had achieved by doing the IBM IPAT tests in 1999 and said, "Don't worry, we won't let you down", but he was far more interested to ask me about what I had done at Surf! I was happy to talk about this but I thought it strange because it didn't really relate to IT. However KC was probing my tenacity and determination to succeed in life.

After chatting for about ten minutes, KC asked:

KC: "What would you like to do?

Me: "Computer programming"

KC: "Where would you like to work?

Me: "Brighton"

KC: "Okay - I'll make your starting salary £21,000. Is that alright for you?'

Me (Speechless with a big smile on my face): "Yes, thank you very much…"

KC: "And as you've been to university I'll put you on a management grade."

I couldn't believe it.

KC: "Oh, when would you like to start?"

Me: "Erm, errr, on the first of May please."

KC: "Done!"

Then we just carried on chatting for another ten minutes or so, interspersed with me saying "I can't believe it!" every now and again.

After I had profusely thanked KC and Charles, KC's PA came outside with me and hailed a cab and helped me to get into it, telling the cab driver that I had just got a job on £21,000!

Sitting in the taxi on the way back to Victoria Station, I thought it was my biggest achievement in life so far. I knew I had a job for life. I phoned Mum, Gemma and Kwok. Mum was delighted. Gemma modestly said that it had all been my own doing. Kwok, who worked at *Shh* in Brighton, was surprised and pleased for me.

KC is one of the most genuine people I have met in life, as is Gemma. Together with Kwok, they have really helped me. However, I'm still waiting for Kwok to find me a British-Chinese wife!

For the next few days I was walking on air. I went to the interview at the local software house, for the fun of it. I think they were offering £16,000. As I was feeling so relaxed and confident, the interview went well. Towards the end of it I said to the two guys who were interviewing me, "I'm going to be honest with you. I've just been offered a job with *Shh*, starting on £21,000." The two guys told me to go for it!

Going back to work at the Brigade was nerve-racking. Being a very loyal person, I felt extremely nervous going into Dick's office and turning down the new contract he had offered me, but once I had told him about my job with *Shh*, I felt great. Dick was very pleased for me and astonished when I told him what my starting salary was.

When I worked at the Fire Brigade, I drove past Lewes Prison every day and it reminded me of going weight-training there when I was twelve!

With a twinge of sadness, I finished my job with the Brigade at the end of March. Then I went to New York for six days in April. For some reason, I stayed in a youth hostel which was a bit of a dump rather than a hotel.

Carl, who I had been skiing in Aspen with in 1999, was now living in Boston. Together with his girlfriend, he came and hung out with me in the Big Apple for two or three days. We had a good time in China Town and Central Park. We were going to go to the top of the World Trade Center but instead went to the Empire State Building. I discovered that New Yorkers weren't as friendly as in other parts of America, but the food in New York diners was great.

A week before I began my new job, I popped into the office to meet my manager and the team I was going to be working with. I was due to start at *Shh* on 1st May but I actually started on Monday 30th April 2001

After numerous job interviews in my life, the funny thing is that my last two were by far the easiest. I think I had done the hard work at Surf and IBM.

I want to end this chapter by asking you a question:

Imagine being twenty-six years old and looking for a job. You see an ad that asks, 'Are you between 18 and 25?' Would you explore that opportunity?

# Chapter 2

Disclaimer: I worked for *Shh* from May 2001 until July 2011. The reason I am not going to reveal the name of the company is because it was contractual policy not to disclose sensitive or financial information about it.

Because it is not my intention to divulge any classified information, I have changed the names of people and projects, including some of the place names I went to.

If there is a company out there called *Shh*, it's not you that I am referring to!

I was proud to work for *Shh* because they treated their employees really well. It was a good company to work for. Why then did I choose to leave the company after ten years? You know what you need to do to find out!

\* \* \* \*

I joined a team of six people. Gordon managed the team and was a project manager. He was in his late forties and had been working at *Shh* since the age of sixteen. Gordon was easy going and a laid back boss. Although, unlike the rest of the team, he wasn't a software developer, Gordon was technically proficient and good at setting up computer networks, amongst other things.

Nigel was one or two years older than me and was a relative veteran of about eleven years. Having not started out as a software developer, Nigel had about the same knowledge of Visual Basic 6 (VB) as me. He was a family man with two young kids and he was a helpful person.

The other four guys were contractors. As contractors came and went over the years, I'll mention a few of them as I go along. One of the contractors, who was there when I started, I later nicknamed 'Neighbour'.

On my first day the team moved to another part of the first floor of the building as there wasn't a desk for me where they were.

Once we moved, we occupied a bank of nine desks. The desks were in rows of three, with two of the rows facing each other. In front of each desk were desk dividers, which you could pin things onto. There was a spare desk between Gordon and I. On the other 'spare' desk were three PC/servers, piled on top of each other.

We each had a desk phone with a headset and I had a company mobile as part of my package. I had only used a headset for a short time before at the Fire Brigade. However, I found it really useful because my hands were free to type on my computer.

After having set up my desktop PC, email account and desk phone, I was eager to do my first bit of software development! Gordon cautioned, "Relax, take it easy. You need to do some training courses, have a look on the intranet."

The building we were working in was large. I think it contained about five hundred people. The main entrance to the building had a reception desk and a security guard sitting behind it.

However, my route through the main entrance involved my walking a long way through an office labyrinth to our desks. So they gave me a key to a side door, close to the disabled car parking spaces. It meant I only had to walk a relatively short distance.

There was a lift right by the side entrance door. Once on the first floor, I went through the door on the right and then it was about ten metres to my desk.

Going to the toilet took me a good five minutes which was inconvenient for someone who wanted to get on with his work. The gents' toilets were on the ground floor directly below the ladies toilets, which were by the door leading to the lift. The toilets had two heavy fire doors which were a bit of a nuisance.

When I was engrossed in writing a piece of computer programming code, this interruption was not always welcome. However, it often proved to be beneficial. I'll explain how later on.

On my second day, Gordon got me to write something simple in Microsoft Access, on one of the servers we had.

Having started my new job in a shirt and tie, by the end of my first week I was going to work in my jeans and t-shirt. Because we didn't have a customer facing job, the dress code was casual.

The canteen was on the fourth floor. Every morning at about 11am, we went up to the canteen and had a cooked breakfast! It was great and didn't feel like work at all! In the early days I also went to the canteen for lunch. I sometimes saw Kwok in the canteen. He was a project manager and worked on the fifth floor.

The software development team I was in was part of was called Quick Solutions (QS). There were QS teams all around the UK, with the main hub based in Cambridge.

It was two months before I got my first project at work. In the interim I went on some training courses and attended some work events.

One of them was a five day VB course in London, which I attended with Nigel. I stayed in a hotel near the course venue as it would have been difficult to commute every day. Nigel as a family man on the other hand, commuted to London every day.

Nigel and I got on well at work. As the contractors were far more experienced than we were, He found it comforting that we had the same level of expertise in VB.

Nigel was the type of person that when you asked him any sort of question, he would come over and help you, then go off on a tangent and end up talking to you for about half an hour!

Soon after I started at *Shh*, KC invited me to an event he was hosting in Cambridge. It was nice to see KC again. He made me feel like I was a VIP. I enjoyed it but it felt a bit weird because I was still a comparative novice with no achievements to my name. At the end of the event they played 'Nobody Does It Better' by Holly Simon.

People will know the song from the James Bond film 'The Spy Who Loved Me', but for me the song is forever associated with the event that KC hosted.

Having given most of the money I had earned at the Fire Brigade to Mum, at *Shh* I started saving for a deposit to buy a place of my own.

I felt uplifted by the first couple of months in my new job. After my emotionally damaging experience at Surf, I decided to exorcise this by joining them one Friday evening for their regular pub get together. It felt good telling them about *Shh* and how well I was doing.

When I went to see Martin and Janet, I remember Janet saying to me, "I don't know anybody else who earns £21,000". We had known each other for about five years by then and I knew she admired me.

I felt so comfortable with Janet that sometimes I wouldn't speak very clearly. She would then repeat the gobbledygook that she thought I had said and we both laughed about it!

It slowly became obvious that we liked each other but as Janet was married to Martin I kept my feelings to myself.

In June 2001, Gordon organised my first project. Gordon, Nigel and I went to Cambridge and had a couple of meetings with the project manager and various teams who were involved in the project. Nigel accompanied us because Gordon thought I might need Nigel's help on the project.

Dressed in a shirt and tie, I came away from the meetings feeling daunted. So many people were involved in the project and I didn't understand it! My honeymoon period at *Shh* was over!

Whilst one team that we met gave me a primitive template of a spreadsheet, another team gave me a printed example of a script.

The project was to develop a spreadsheet to convert data in Excel into a script which, when run in a database, would populate the data into the database.

Basically, the customer wanted a spreadsheet for people to enter a load of information into. By pressing a button on the spreadsheet the programme would scan the data to ensure it was in the correct format and then generate and save a script on the person's PC. The script could then be passed to another team, who ran the script to insert the information into the database.

It took me weeks just to understand the above paragraph! What troubled me was that the data on the printed script that I had been given didn't seem to correlate to the data in the spreadsheet.

The project involved lots of conference calls and me phoning loads of people. I had to overcome my fear of speaking to new people on the phone. It wasn't easy, especially working in an open plan office, but I overcame my fear.

For the first few weeks I struggled and thought I wasn't up to doing my new job. I felt under enormous pressure to succeed. Writing about it now makes me smile. It was a good first project to do because I learnt so much by doing it and it gave me an understanding of what it was like working for a big company.

One day in the canteen after having lunch, I was feeling so physically sick that I stood with my head outside of the window for twenty minutes. The windy day helped me to stop feeling sick.

However I had to do something about it. Having already been to my GP and tried various different pills before, I went to see Alison again and said to her, "I've got a really good job but I'm still feeling really sick at work. I can't cope anymore. I need some pills to help me stop feeling sick."

Alison gave me some antidepressants which really helped and I have been on them ever since.

At first, I thought it was terrible to be taking these but the pills help me to keep going every day. On the rare occasions when I don't take them one night, I feel like I'm hungover the next day.

I am not a naturally depressed person nor am I really depressed. I have been unhappy for many years because I haven't found someone to share my life with yet.

The funny thing is, it's only through writing these two books that I've realised why I've been beating myself up for so long. As I said in 'Stairs For Breakfast', the self-criticism dates back to the letter I sent to Rosie in 1993. Writing that book was a revealing time. The good news is, I've stopped beating myself up about that mistake.

If you were around on the 9th November 2001 and old enough to understand it, I suspect you remember where you were? I was on a training course in Milton Keynes.

The course had just recommenced after lunch when someone came into the room and said a plane had crashed into one of the World Trade Center buildings and we thought it was an accident. During a coffee break a while later, we heard about the plane crashing into the second twin tower.

Watching the TV coverage in the evening was horrifying. It resembled something from a science fiction film - but the stark reality was it was happening. My belief is that 9/11 was a day when everything changed.

I recently read an article which said some engineers believe that the twin towers collapsed as a result of them being detonated. The article included that a third building at the World Trade Center also collapsed. Whatever the truth, the world's axis shifted that day.

During my ten years at *Shh* I attended lots of training courses and meetings, particularly in the first twelve months. The novelty of staying in hotels didn't last long.

My bed at home is sixteen inches high. I had it lowered slightly after I bought it so that it is the right height for me to get dressed and undressed.

Having stayed in many hotels, only rarely have I found something to sit on that is the right height for me. The other thing I've found with hotels is that there is often a long walk from the reception area to my room, the dining room or to my car. Nevertheless, it has never stopped me from using them.

Gordon was a good boss. He quickly recognised that I was self-sufficient, with good people skills. Gordon just left me to get on with my work and I asked him for his help when I needed it.

He also gave me lots of opportunities and the freedom to learn. When Gordon asked me if I wanted to do something I nearly always replied, "Yes, I can do it..."

Another leap forward was getting a work PC for home. It gave me the flexibility to work from home whenever I wanted. This was still in the days of a dial-up connection to the internet. I found that I was more productive working from home because there weren't so many interruptions. Nigel also worked from home sometimes.

*Shh* was an agile company. It was common to work for a manager who was in a different location and working from home wasn't unusual.

Because I was on a management grade, I deputised for Gordon and covered him when he was on annual leave or out of the office. It gave me a flavour of what project management was like. Having worked with many project managers over the years and becoming a certified project manager myself, I became adept at it.

That's not to say that I like it. My simplistic view is, it mainly involves chasing up people to do things and anticipating problems before they occur. I found it tedious and boring.

Something far more interesting that I did with Gordon from an early stage was interviewing prospective new contractors. The insight I gained was that you get a good idea if someone was right for the job within the first two minutes of the interview.

However, I remember one guy who impressed us until he was asked, "When you're writing code, do you include many comments with it?" Because he replied,"No, I don't bother writing any comments", he didn't get the job.

Later on, I'll tell you about the time I told a contractor that he had to leave the company immediately!

The fact that I started at *Shh* on a management grade caused Nigel to have a slight resentment towards me. I could understand how he felt. Nigel had worked at *Shh* for eleven years and had always remained on a technical grade. To try and help the situation, Gordon included Nigel in some of the contractor interviews we did.

Dennis was one of the contractors in the team when I started at *Shh*. He seemed like a normal forty year old bloke. He mentioned having dated a number of women locally and so started online dating where he met a woman who lived in America.

In September Dennis decided to leave *Shh* and move to America. Before he left we took on a replacement contractor called Mick and Dennis invited the team to a farewell party he was hosting.

Dennis left work on a Friday and the party was the following evening.

Thinking there would be loads of people at the party, including people from work, I turned up at a flat in Hove to an extremely bizarre party. It consisted of me, Dennis and four transvestites!

I found it funny but didn't stay for long. I knew it was time to leave when one of the transvestites blew me a kiss from across the room!

After the weekend when I told people at work about the party, it backfired on me. Most of the people in my team joked that I liked transvestites. It gave me an insight into who in the team really respected me.

Gordon disappointed me. If it wasn't him who started the joke, he certainly carried on with it for months, if not years. It made me wonder how much Gordon respected me.

I think because I didn't have a girlfriend, I was an easy target to make fun of.

A few years later after Gordon had left a group of us met for a beer and I said to Gordon that I felt that he didn't really respect me. I think he was a bit surprised because he replied, "I respect you a great deal, when I hear people moaning about life, I use you as an example and say to them, used to work with a guy who has Cerebral Palsy and walks with crutches. I watched him struggle into the office everyday and do a full days work. He never complained about life."

I've heard it said that IT can be a competitive environment and working in an all-male environment amplified this. My experience of working in a team of four or five experienced contractors over the years showed me that they didn't compete amongst themselves, but I did find many of them selfish.

Take Neighbour for example. He was the same age as me, with a wife and struck me as very materialistic. All he seemed to care about was himself, his wife and the latest gadgets he was buying.

Although I didn't particularily like most of the contractors, I got on alright with them at work. When it came to software development, the contractors were expected to give Nigel and I a hand when we got stuck with something. I found it good to have people to bounce technical ideas off.

Mick was one of the contractors I got on well with, because he respected me. In his late thirties and a family man, he lived in Hove and had joined from a job where he was commuting to London every day. Mick took quite a big pay cut to work locally. Over the four years at *Shh*, Mick and his wife had two kids.

By October 2001, I understood what I was doing at work and was making good progress. However, the slow progress was the number of people involved in the project. It seemed as if nobody knew for sure all of the information that needed to be captured in the spreadsheet or the database field names needed for the script.

People kept changing their minds about the required specification, which meant I kept having to rewrite bits of code!

I finished the project in November and the customer was pleased with it. The spreadsheet ended up being quite massive. It had seven worksheets, with some of them having more than twenty-six columns.

My second project was another spreadsheet doing the same thing as the first one, but based on another set of information.

Gordon gave me this good advice, "Before you start any of the development work, do the design document first and get everyone involved in the project to agree to it."

It took some time and hassle to get the design document signed off, but once I had done so, it only took me three weeks to do all of the development work. Having learnt a lot from the first spreadsheet, I wrote the second one in a much more concise and proficient way.

Once I had completed the second spreadsheet, the customer casually said, "It's alright, we don't need it now. We've decided that we're only going to use the first spreadsheet"!

Another thing Gordon taught me early on was to over-quote how much time it would take to do a piece of work. He said, "You never know what issues you're going to come up against. Estimate how long it will take to do the work - and then double it."

Although I never excessively over-quoted, this practice allowed me to deliver the work in under the time I said it would take me. Also I included some extra features in the applications that I developed.

This is known as over-delivering in under the time quoted. It is an extremely good habit to adopt in whatever line of work you're in because it delights customers.

Towards the end of 2001 the family business was sold. It had been plodding along since the dispute between Mum, Liz and John in 1998. The business was no longer in profit. Subscriptions were down due to the early nineties recession being over, leading to a reduction in people interested in working abroad compared to when the business started in 1991. However, I think if the three partners of the business had pulled together, they might have kept it going in profit.

Around that time, the mandate of the business bank account had been changed and any cheques now needed two signatures, one of which had to be Mum's.

Once the sale of the business had gone through, its list of creditors started to be paid. This came to light when Stuart the database programmer, who was still friends with Mum at the time, received a cheque that hadn't been signed by her!

Stuart informed Mum, who understandably went a bit ballistic. She phoned the bank and went to see the business manager, who admitted the bank had made a mistake by failing to note that the mandate had been updated.

John must have hit the roof when he received the phone call from the bank manager, informing him that all of the transactions which had already been processed had been reversed and all of the cheques had been cancelled. I was proud of what Mum did that day. I would have done the same thing.

Also towards the end of that year, Clare became pregnant.

In the first three months of 2002 I started my third project. Working with a new customer, it was to develop a totally different spreadsheet from my first two projects. Although not so many people were involved in this one, which made it easier, I didn't really understand it at first.

I started it at the same time that Gordon went on holiday and so I had to do some of his work as well. Before he went on leave Gordon said to me, "Get Nigel to help you with your project if you want it."

I could really have done with Nigel's help while Gordon was away. Over a fruitless couple of days of asking him if he could help me, it was obvious that Nigel was not playing ball and this led me to take the formal step of emailing him for his help.

Feeling frustrated, I walked over to Nigel's desk.

Me: "Please can you help me? I could really do with your help..."

Nigel [doing something on his PC and not looking at me]: "No."

This is where my frustration and inexperience got the better of me. I made a mistake.

Me [a bit too loudly]: "Why won't you help me? Gordon said to ask you to help me."

Nigel: "I don't appreciate you shouting at me. You were parachuted into the team and the only reason you got given your job is because you're disabled."

I felt so shocked and hurt that I just walked back to my desk. The other four guys in the team didn't say anything.

My dispute with Nigel didn't stop me doing well with my project. However it was a defining moment regarding my working and personal relationship with Nigel.

At the end of the day I sincerely apologised to Nigel for shouting at him. It took some time but I was able to rebuild a working relationship with him. However, for the next three years or so Nigel seemed to resent me.

As someone who didn't like dealing with confrontation, Gordon didn't want to get involved: all he would ever say was, "It's six of one and half a dozen of the other."

Returning to my technical work, the third spreadsheet I developed was to represent the capacity of a router. The spreadsheet contained lots of figures and calculations across several worksheets. Figures automatically updated themselves when information was entered onto the spreadsheet.

The client wanted the spreadsheet to show, at a glance, how full a router was. I came up with a traffic light colour scheme. The figures on the summary page went through various shades of green, amber and red. I also made the spreadsheet look very aesthetically pleasing.

It was a fun project to do. The client was so pleased with what I had developed that I got commended and received some CD vouchers!

Over the years, I did so many things in Excel (by writing VB macros) that I once said, "I can make Excel do anything, apart from make coffee!" And I still believe it.

I got on well with Gordon most of the time but there was one instance we had to agree to disagree. Working on the first floor, it was when he said he was going to order an Evac Chair for me - a chair you can strap someone into and slide down the stairs in cases of fire.

My initial response was, "It's a waste of money because I will never use it". Then we had this kind of ongoing 'argument':

Me: "I can walk down the stairs."

Gordon: "No, you can't."

Me: "Yes, I can!"

Gordon: "It's against health and safety."

Me: "If there is ever a fire I will walk down the bloody stairs. You cannot force me to use that thing..."

Gordon ordered the Evac Chair anyway. When it arrived he wanted me to try it out but I refused. So Neighbour volunteered to sit in it (all six foot of him) and he got pushed down the stairs in it.

Health and Safety sometimes irritated me. I did understand it, but often saw the funny side of it instead.

Every six months everyone had to do a series of online courses. It basically involved answering a series of obvious multiple choice questions. I remember a question from the fire awareness course made me laugh. It was along these lines:

If you discover a fire what should you do?

A) Tell other people in your office about it.

B) Dial 999.

C) Try to put the fire out yourself.

D) Evacuate the building.

E) Sound the fire alarm.

Another question was along the lines of:

True or False - on hearing the fire alarm you must evacuate the building?

The correct answer was True - but it wasn't strictly true.

Every Monday at around 11am the fire alarm was tested. The alarm would go off three times - with a gap of about twenty seconds between each one.

Having had CP since my birth, I class myself as a bit of a CP expert. However I don't know why this happened every Monday:

My body jumped every time I heard the first alarm but never jumped the second or third time.

I used to think, 'The first alarm is about to go off any second now - don't jump.' But no matter how hard I tried not to jump, I always did on hearing the first alarm test.

I am interested to understand why.

Away from work, in the first three months of 2002 a few things happened close together.

At the beginning of January, I decided to start looking for somewhere else to live. Surprisingly it only took a few days to find. Mum spotted a two bed ground floor apartment for sale, less than two minutes around the corner from where we lived. I had looked into buying somewhere in Brighton or Hove but it was out of my price range.

To say Mum and I never got on would be untrue as we have the same sense of humour. In an ideal world, I'd love us to be close and sharing jokes. Being a visual person, Mum enjoyed looking at properties and interior designing, whereas those two things don't interest me much. I just know I prefer things to look modern.

The flat looked really good for me because it had an allocated car parking space next to the communal entrance. The property was in a complex of apartment blocks, which included a swimming pool, jacuzzi, gym and a restaurant/bar.

When Mum phoned the estate agent, he said that an offer had just been accepted on the property. The next day I asked him about the property, told him about my circumstances and said that I was in a very good position to buy it quickly.

The following day Mum phoned the estate agent again. The agent said to her, "I was just thinking about you...!" He continued "The vendor is a bit apprehensive about the current buyer because they don't seem very committed to buying the property..."

Mum wasted no time in going to see if the flat was suitable for me. She said it was, so I went to see it with her.

The communal entrance had a step, which wasn't a problem and apart from its internal décor, the flat was really good. So I offered to buy it for the asking price of £50 short of £100K. It was as easy as that!

I knew house prices were rising. A bonus with my purchase was that it included a garage. As it's unusual for a property in this area to have an allocated parking space as well as a garage, I knew I could easily rent the garage out.

The funny thing was I made the offer to buy the property the day before I went on holiday to see Jake. I left without knowing if my offer had been accepted.

I flew to Maui, Hawaii via Vancouver with a Canadian airline. Interestingly, rather than crossing the Atlantic and America/Canada, the plane flew up to the North Pole and then down to Vancouver.

Once I got to Hawaii I was eager to know if my offer had been accepted. It had been and within a few days Mum found a local conveyancing solicitor called Roland, who happened to live in the same complex as my flat.

It was good to see Jake again and for the first few days we got on like brothers. I was supposed to be in Hawaii for two weeks but my mind was preoccupied with buying my flat. I wanted to get home to ensure the purchase of the property was going through. As before, I changed my returning flight and only stayed in Hawaii for a week.

My flight back to Vancouver left Maui in the evening. Annoyingly, that morning, Jake and I went out on a boat with a few of his friends, where I met a really nice girl who was disappointed that I was leaving that day. I wished I had stayed in Hawaii for two weeks!

Back at home, I went to meet Roland. Other than a few signatures, the only thing that I had to sort out was a mortgage. I knew that the monthly payment on a repayment mortgage wasn't going to be more than £600, which I could comfortably afford. However on paper, my income limited the available mortgages that I could go for.

At *Shh* I had twenty-six days of annual leave per year. One thing I was never very good at was taking my leave evenly throughout the year. Often when it came to January, I still had loads of leave to take before the end of March.

Six weeks after getting back from Hawaii I was due to fly to Australia. I had planned to meet JP in Sydney for two weeks and I had bought the plane ticket before going to Hawaii.

I was concerned that I wouldn't be able to afford to buy my flat and Australia. I decided to get a full refund on my ticket to Sydney. In hindsight I wish I hadn't cancelled that trip. It would have been a blast and I still haven't been to that part of the world.

I continued to see Martin and Janet every few weeks. Martin wanted to play in a wheelchair football match in Maidenhead one Saturday. As he didn't have many players Martin asked me and another old mutual school friend, Neil Dillon if we would go along to form a team.

The same day Janet wanted to go to a farewell party in the evening. The farewell party was at the Greyhound dog racing stadium in Hove and was for a volunteer who had worked for years at Martin's old residential home. I offered to go with Janet and to drive her home, so that she could have a drink in the evening.

What transpired was a long but good day. Having added Janet onto my car insurance, I left home at 7.30am and got to Martin and Janet's at 8.15. Martin went to Maidenhead with one of his carers driving his van, with Neil and two electric wheelchairs, whilst I went in my car with Janet and Ben.

It was really nice spending time with Janet and Ben and being driven in my car. The electric wheelchair football was fun too as a one off experience. We spent most of the day in Maidenhead then drove back to Chichester, before driving with Janet to Hove in the early evening. The dog racing was busy and enjoyable. Afterwards we went to someone's flat in Brighton for a while.

The time was past one o'clock in the morning when I drove Janet home to Chichester. I took the opportunity to float an open-ended statement to see what she came back with.

Me: "I'm never going to find a girlfriend or a wife."

Janet: "Yes you are."

I didn't pursue the matter any further and Janet wasn't drunk. We knew what we were saying to each other.

For a few years after that moment I carried on going to see Martin and Janet. Superficially, I was going to see them both but secretly I wanted to spend more time with Janet. We got on so well and used to laugh a lot.

So many times over the years I thought about telling Janet that I wanted to be with her and Ben. I was incredibly tempted. But I couldn't do it because I knew it would hurt Martin.

In the latter half of March 2002, the purchase of my flat was completed. I felt a bit daunted but excited to own a property. I had a variable rate mortgage and the monthly payments were £525. I bought Roland a bottle of champagne and we became friends.

I didn't move into the property until mid-April. In the meantime, handyman Eric ripped out the 1988 bathroom suite and built a wet-room shower. I researched the most reliable manufacturer of white goods and found the best prices for them online.

Today, over eleven years later, my Bosch fridge freezer, washing machine and tumble dryer haven't broken down.

My bathroom is neat and simple. It's got a nonslip floor and a tiled wooden bench style seat under the shower. The bench is the right height and width, making it easy for me to sit down and stand up from.

A few days prior to moving into my flat I was feeling a bit apprehensive but once I moved in it soon became my home. Physically life became harder because I had to do everything myself. However the pros far outweighed the cons.

At last I was away from Mum. The freedom and space felt great and I started to go out more.

I took the smaller bedroom because the big one has an en-suite shower room. I had the idea that I would get a lodger at some point.

Having never really cooked before, I made the decision that I was going to eat healthily so I taught myself. I'm no gourmet chef but I cook various vegetables and pasta dishes, fish, lamb - and buy a hot chicken from the supermarket. I like whizzing around the store on an electric scooter.

When I first moved in I was concerned about not having my hamstrings stretched anymore. Having had Clare put my gaiters on me most nights for the last five years, I didn't know how my hamstrings were going to be stretched. It's amazing how the mind and body adapts; I just naturally learnt not to bend my legs when I sleep.

I taught myself to cut my finger and toe nails for the first time and hired a cleaner, who still comes once a week for two hours.

Over the next few months Eric replaced the kitchen floor, oven and hob. I had the flat painted white and got new grey carpets. People often comment how nice my flat is when they come and see me.

Mum enjoyed sourcing the oven, hob and carpet for me - and we even went to Ikea together. However I felt these sessions with Mum often ended with her using me as an emotional punch-bag. On another occasion, we were going to go to Ikea but only made it a mile up the road before having an argument and turning back.

Around April 2002, I received an email informing me that I had been nominated, by KC, to be one of the people to go and represent *Shh* at the Queen's annual garden party. I felt absolutely honoured and thanked KC. I felt I hadn't done that much at *Shh* yet. The fact that I wasn't selected to attend the garden party at the end, didn't matter to me.

It's probably just as well because I may have joked with the Queen that she should go and live in a council house to see how the other half live!

Employees at *Shh* were assessed every three months. At the start of each quarter, I agreed what work goals I would complete over the next three months. At the end of the period I then had to provide evidence, in writing, of how I had achieved my goals.

In addition to outlining the work we had done, there was also a common set of about eight interpersonal competencies, which included Delighting Customers, Communication, and Trustworthiness. Employees had to give examples of how we fulfilled each competency in our work.

I found it a real bind having to write up this evidence every three months. I had completed my goals but writing my evidence took me two or three days each quarter.

However, I wanted to produce good evidence because these quarterly grades contributed to our annual pay rise and bonus. I was motivated to do well and either achieved 'Good' or 'Very Good' grades. Achieving a grade of 'Satisfactory' wasn't on my agenda.

In early June 2002, Nigel and I went to Cambridge for a two day team-building meeting with other employees in Quick Start (QS). We had a good time. There were more than a hundred people at the event. It was nice to meet people that I had spoken to on the phone. Without being anything other than my normal self, people seemed to take to me.

With some excitement, I was waiting to get my first ever pay rise and bonus at the end of June. While at the two day event, on my way to the canteen with Nigel and Arnold (the head of QS), I innocently asked Arnold if he had any idea how much my pay rise and bonus were going to be. He said he didn't know. However, Nigel found my question very funny and couldn't wait to get back to Brighton and tell Gordon of my little faux pas.

Gordon had a quiet word with me and said it wasn't quite the thing to have asked so openly.

However it didn't seem to have done any harm. At the end of June, I received a £2k pay rise and a bonus of £1.5k. I was thrilled. How much of a pay rise people got was partly dependent on where you were in your pay scale. Because I was at the bottom of my pay scale in my first year with plenty of headroom for improvement, there was less potential for uplift in subsequent years. However my bonus was normally pretty good.

At some point in 2001 or 2002 another contractor Giles, joined our team. He worked for a project manager based in the North of England called Ken. Ken was a humorous guy and sometimes came to Brighton. Whenever I saw Ken in Brighton or at a QS meeting I would often laugh out loud. He was the type of person who was always fooling around and performing practical jokes on people.

Giles sat at the desk between me and Gordon, opposite Neighbour. He was a couple of years older than me and very much like Neighbour; married with no kids and very self-centred. Giles was also a very analytical person. Before he made a decision about anything, he would have to research it first and consider the options from every angle.

Neighbour and Giles got on well because they were both into distance running. They regularly went out in the evenings separately and timed their runs. In the office the next day, they would study Google Maps and conduct a retrospective virtual competition as to who had run the fastest!

Giles ran the London marathon a couple of times. On the second occasion, he collapsed during the race due to dehydration. Afterwards, he was *not* happy about having made such a schoolboy error!

Although I wasn't particularly close to Giles, I knew how to get on with him.

One thing I felt uncomfortable about at work was not being able to make coffee. The kitchen area was too far away for me to comfortably walk to, let alone carry a travel mug back from. In consequence I was reliant on others to make me a drink. It wasn't a good feeling. I didn't like asking someone to make me a drink because it wasn't their job to do so. So I waited for someone to offer.

It came to a head one day when Gordon was out of the office. Whoever decided to make drinks did so whilst I went to the toilet. As I was walking back to my desk I saw that everyone else had a cup of tea or coffee apart from me.

I don't recall there being any particular friction in the office that day. Standing at my desk, I said, "Whoever has just made the drinks, it's really good of you to have made me a coffee."

To which Giles replied "Don't worry Patrick, next time I make a coffee I'll make you one."

It undermined my opinion of Giles. It was a horrible situation to find myself in.

It made me feel like I was a second class citizen. For someone who has always been able to build good professional relationships, it hurt me that most of the people I worked with didn't respect me.

However I knew what I had to do. That evening, I bought a 1.5 litre flask and from then on, I took a flask of coffee into work every day.

It did annoy me that I had to make and carry a heavy flask into work every day, but I overcame the problem.

For others the inability to make a drink at work wouldn't register on their radar. But it caused me real discomfort.

Capitalism can be a killer. Most of the time I found ingenious ways of making it work. I was inspired by John Potts (JP) who in late 2001, quit his job in the City after working for a few years at British Airways and then for Price Waterhouse Cooper (PwC). He went travelling around the world for a year. I remember JP telling me that he was working with egotistical, competitive people. He said it wasn't his scene and he had had enough of the rat race.

Although my antidepressants helped me from not feeling sick at work, I also suffered from insomnia. Because I was not getting to sleep until about 2am I was arriving in the office at about

10.30am. Gordon didn't mind but I felt obliged to stay at work until 6.30pm.

By that stage I was taking sandwiches into work and not going up to the canteen for lunch anymore. I just ate my sandwiches at my desk and didn't have much of a lunch break. It was my choice. I was motivated by my work and was a hard worker. Although I was doing well and people were pleased with me I felt it wasn't enough and I could do better.

When I bought my flat I thought that it would be good to pay off my mortgage early. However, I was tied into my mortgage for the first two years and it didn't allow overpayments to be made. Part of the reason for my limited choice of mortgage was because I had never borrowed any money before. I hadn't built up a good credit rating.

So I began the credit card game! I got a credit card with a long interest free period and used it for things like my hob, oven and carpet and paid the minimum amount every month. I became skilful at using credit cards to my advantage without paying any interest or fees on them. It didn't take me long to acquire an excellent credit rating.

On one occasion when I phoned and activated a new credit card, the customer service woman I was speaking to asked:

Lady: "Would you like us to transfer some money into your current account, interest-free for 12 months?"

Me: "How much money can I borrow?"

Lady: "£3,700"

Me: [thinking 'Cash ISA, cash ISA!']:"Are there any fees?"

Lady: "£98"

Me: "I'd like to think about it, can I phone back in a day or two?"

Lady: "Yes, that will be fine."

I found the best cash ISA, borrowed the £3,700, paid the £98 fee and put £3,600 into the ISA. At the end of the twelve months I terminated the ISA, paid off the credit card and closed it. It had been a bit of fun making £138 profit!

If I had activated the credit card via an automated phone system, would I have been offered the £3,700? It's always good to speak to people.

Thinking fast sometimes coincided with moving fast. One thing I haven't mentioned so far is that I used to be a bit of a 'boy racer' driving my car. I think it was partly due to not being able to walk very fast. When I got in my car, I felt equal to everyone else and I enjoyed being faster than them.

Over the years I did have a few minor accidents which were my fault. However, I had a slightly cavalier attitude and wasn't careful enough when it came to doing simple things, like pulling into the driveway or parking the car, causing me to scrape gateposts and walls.

Because I didn't pay car insurance on the Motability scheme, every time I bumped or scraped my car, I just got it fixed on my insurance and paid the excess. This approach to driving caught up with me.

In 2002, a couple of months before my car's three year contract expired, I received a letter from Motability. The letter said that they were unwilling to let me have another car at the end of my current contract because of the number of insurance claims.

The thought of not having a car really scared me. It would have been disastrous. I had to get Motability to reverse their decision.

I knew I could drive well and safely, I just needed to drive slowly and be more careful. I had a plan.

I phoned Motability and said that I had a real problem and asked to be put through to the head of the company. It took a few phone calls but I persisted until I was put through to the right person.

When I got through, I explained to the ultimate decision-maker, a woman called Mo, why I was phoning and outlined my predicament. I asked Mo if she could help me as I had a solution to the problem.

I offered to have my driving re-assessed by an instructor. If I was deemed to be a safe and a careful driver, would she let me have another Motability car. She agreed - and that is what happened.

I spoke to Mo a few times. She was very nice and couldn't have been more helpful. I sent her a bouquet of flowers to thank her. When she phoned to thank me for the flowers, she said she thought at first the flowers were from her husband, who was called Patrick! This tickled me because on the note with the flowers I wrote, 'Thank you for all of your help with my new car.'

This was a positive development because it frightened me into completely changing my attitude when driving. I now stick to the speed limit, which is easy with cruise control, and I am extra careful. My last accident was in 2008 and it wasn't due to carelessness.

In summer 2002 Clare gave birth to Charlotte. I remember holding Charlotte in my arms soon after she was born. Feeling emotional, I said to her "Hello sweetheart, how are you?"

Mum was there and said, rather harshly, "Don't call her sweetheart, you sound like Del Boy." This annoyed me as I should be able to use whatever term of endearment I wish with my niece.

Last time I saw 'Only Fools and Horses', I don't recall Del Boy having a Cerebral Palsy accent!

Shortly after Charlotte came into the world, Dad, Madeline, Isabelle and new baby boy Pierre, came over for a long weekend. Not having spoken to Dad for a year or two I wondered how we would get on. When we met at Clare's house we got on surprisingly well.

After finishing my third spreadsheet project at *Shh* I managed with Gordon and Nigel, a realtime system called Job Builder. Having done some work on it already I knew it well.

Job Builder was an automated gateway system. Customers submitted jobs to it and Job Builder then gathered data from various other systems and passed each job onto another system.

Job Builder processed about a thousand jobs a day. It had three Oracle databases and eight servers. Like a busy motorway, everything ran smoothly until something crashed, which instantly created a logjam of jobs.

When something crashed, it was a case of identifying where the problem was and then either rebooting one of our servers or notifying the owners of one of the other systems. The owners would routinely say "we're rectifying the problem now" and then it was a matter of resubmitting the failed jobs.

Job Builder wasn't complicated to manage. It involved SQL (managing database records) which I enjoyed. I also wrote a couple of VB apps to automate manual data feeds and to alert us via email and text messages when jobs started to fail.

My main project responsibility which I developed for the next three years was Login Manager, a user/password authentication 24/7 system that held about ten thousand user accounts.

If you think back to the early days of the internet and the laborious process of dialling up to access your email or the net, a box would appear for you to enter your username and password. Login Manager was similar to that pop-up box.

The system consisted of two servers/Oracle databases and was written in VB and PL/SQL which was the programming language built into Oracle.

When I started working on Login Manager, I managed the VB side of it, whilst Mick (an Oracle developer) took care of the PL/SQL side. I then gradually took over all of the PL/SQL as I learnt the language. I like learning new skills as it broadens my mind.

Having developed three Excel spreadsheets it was good to move onto two more substantial systems. It was just what I needed to keep me stimulated.

After a few weeks of starting on Login Manager and speaking to the client, Amanda, I went to Cambridge to meet her and discuss what enhancements were needed on the system.

The good thing about Login Manager (and Job Builder) was the fact that it was a QS application. It meant Amanda was also a colleague. She managed the QS helpdesk which consisted of a team of three guys.

When I met Amanda for the first time I discovered she was a voluptuous lady and quite a bit taller than me. Physically, I felt like a midget compared to her. However, being of a similar age and intellectual status, we connected straight away.

After our meeting about the work needed on Login Manager, where we spent most of the time laughing and joking, Amanda said the second best thing anyone has ever said to me.

It was a large building and it was quite a long walk to my car and aware that I had my laptop in my rucksack to carry, Amanda asked "Would you like me to give you a piggyback back to your car?"

It made me laugh out loud before saying, "Thank you for offering but I'll be alright." In hindsight I wish I had replied "Yes please" to see what she would had done.

We enjoyed a brilliant working relationship over the next two and a half years or so. Amanda was someone who liked instant messenger. Quite regularly in my open-plan office a joke from her would arrive and I would burst out laughing!

I have always been quick-witted but if anything Amanda was quicker witted than me. I enjoyed the challenge of keeping up with her. She was a flirtatious, earthy person but you knew where the line was with her and you didn't cross it.

Gordon also got on well with Amanda but other guys found her intimidating, as she was very confident and could be abrupt. I remember Mick telling me he was a bit apprehensive of her!

Over the years I visited the team in Cambridge quite a few times and got to know them all well. As it was the main hub of QS it was bigger than the other QS teams around the UK.

I did some work with Doug who was a very experienced software developer with an exceptional memory for passwords and names. He once remarked, "Your surname contains all five vowels of the alphabet."

I considered changing my surname to Soul when I was younger. At first I thought it would be cool if people said things to me like, "Hello Mr Soul, how are you today?..", but then I realised it would be an own goal. Any woman whose first name began with an R wouldn't marry me!

Working on Login Manager, I often received calls or emails from developers who had written a new application and wanted to incorporate Login Manager into it. I created a webpage containing the DLL file people needed and step-by-step instructions on how to install and configure it. So when developers contacted me asking to use Login Manager, I just emailed them the link to the webpage.

Most people came back with, "Thank you very much, got it set up and working". However, others would respond with a query, "I've installed the DLL file and it doesn't work..." It was always because they hadn't followed some of the steps correctly in setting it up. I found it interesting that some software developers had difficulty following logical instructions.

The reason I nicknamed one of my colleagues 'Neighbour' is because he lived in the house on the other side of the fence to me. He lived so close by that I could walk out of my complex and into his house.

After moving into my flat I wasted no time in becoming known in the on-site bar. There I met my friend Steve Bell and became friends with his wife Jill and daughter Tammy.

Unlike me, Steve is an artistic person. He used to be a secondary school art teacher and has always played a variety of musical instruments. The reason Steve and I get on so well is because we are both people persons and share the same values and sense of humour.

Neither of us will forget the time we went to a party at someone's house. I was in the back garden when a woman, ten to fifteen years older than me, approached me and asked:

Lady: "What do you do?"

Me: "I'm a computer programmer and I work for *Shh*."

Lady [looking perplexed]: "no...really, what is it that you do?"

Me: "I really am a computer programmer - and I do work for *Shh*."

Lady [still unconvinced]: "no, honestly, what is it that you do?"

Me [becoming bored] "What can I say? I *am* a computer programmer..."

At which point Steve walks by.

Me: "Steve, help me out here. This lady doesn't believe me that I'm a computer programmer and that I work for *Shh*."

Steve [without hesitating]: "No, he works at the post office, licking stamps..."

Steve [pausing for a second] "...and on Sundays he works at the supermarket, stacking shelves. But he only stacks the middle shelves because he can't reach the top or bottom shelves."

Lady [smiling, as she pinched my cheek]: "Ahh, I knew it." [then she walked away]

Obviously, I didn't know Steve was going say what he said. It was absolutely hilarious!

On another occasion Steve and I were having a beer with our friend and neighbour Adrian.

The three of us decided to come up with what would be the most inappropriate job for me to do. After obvious suggestions, such as, waiter, surgeon and car mechanic, our favourite one was when Adrian suggested "Air traffic controller!"

I know I can't talk, but Steve is originally from Dundee and I still don't understand some things he says due to his strong Scottish accent and the arcane regional phrases he uses.

My solicitor Roland and I became regular cinema buddies and were both interested in politics. Although we were friends of around the same age, I liked Roland in small doses as we were quite different.

Roland had a good heart but could be self-focused and this sometimes translated into his financial philosophy and attitude to money. Roland was also a devout Christian and I found him to be on occasion quite innocent. Compared to Roland, I was a hell-raiser!

Whenever we went to the cinema, we talked about the running of our self-managed estate or how we both wanted to find a girlfriend and get married. Despite this, we always seemed to end up talking about religion or politics, two things we didn't agree on!

Prior to Roland moving back to his hometown I got us tickets to be in the audience when 'Question Time' came to Brighton. We also went to see Gordon Brown speak on cancelling third-world debt.

Another politician we went together to hear speak was Michael Portillo. At the end of his speech, I had a good five minute conversation with him about politics and he seemed like a decent bloke. Whenever I think of Michael Portillo I always have the urge to call him Michael Portaloo!

When Roland and I went on 'Question Time' I took advantage of a once in a lifetime opportunity. It was after the Iraq war when Tony Blair was still Prime Minister and the Health Secretary was Patricia Hewitt, who was one of the 'Question Time' panellists.

At the end of the programme, I went up to Patricia Hewitt and after saying "Hi, I'm Patrick, it's nice to meet you..." I stood face-to-face with her and clearly said:

Me: "I've always been a Labour voter but I am very, very disappointed with Tony Blair."

Patricia Hewitt [abruptly], "Yes, well I'm sorry to hear that. I've got to rush off now."

And off she rushed. It was funny.

Roland found it hilarious and wanted to have a photo with David Dimbleby.

Roland tried to sign me up after he joined the Conservative Christian party. He knew he was never going to succeed in doing so.

I've always respected peoples' religious beliefs but some Christians haven't seemed to have respected mine. Why are some people intent on trying to convert others to their religion?

Despite having had Jewish maternal grandparents, I've never really been religious. I've debated with Christians on many occasions on whether or not there is a god.

However, over the last few years I've changed my opinion. As an analytical person, I cannot either prove or disprove if God exists, which means that I am now open-minded,

It was a surprise to hear in late 2002 that Ray was part of the bid team who won the licence for a radio station in Worthing. I don't remember a radio licence for Worthing being advertised and I only have a vague recollection of Ray being part of a bid team. Unlike the earlier Brighton bid which had seen Ray and his team, including me, working full time on the application process, this time the bid was conducted out of hours and people kept their day jobs.

Shortly after the licence was awarded, Ray was appointed as MD to run the radio station called Splash FM.

I remember Ray asking me if I would like to work at Splash full-time. Appreciating the offer, I thought about it and said, "No thank you". I was already lined up to produce the sport show on Saturday afternoons and I had a good job at *Shh* where I was still relatively new and which I considered had better job security.

In December 2002 JP returned from his trip around the world, but only for three weeks. JP had liked Latin America so much that he got a job in a travel agency there. It didn't take him long to learn Spanish and to open up his own travel agency – 'Happy Gringo' - in Ecuador. Having just had a look at the website, the company now has twenty-three employees. I knew JP would do well in life.

Into 2003, Janet gave birth to Karen. Martin was doing well and he continued to inspire me.

Just over a year after I moved into my flat, my annual maintenance bill jumped from roughly £1,000 to £1,500. It prompted me to join the Board of Directors of the leasehold company who manages the estate. It may sound like a grand position but it's not. We're an unpaid group of leaseholders who have a meeting every so often to discuss the complex and the work required for its upkeep.

Roland was eager for me to join the Board because he said I wouldn't stand for any nonsense!

Anyone who has been part of a committee will probably know how difficult it can be to get anything agreed upon and done. When I first joined not everyone on the board respected me. However, after Adrian became chairman and started managing the complex, the place has never looked so good and maintenance charges have never been so low.

I often think of our board meetings as bored meetings!

Something I really like about living here is going to the Jacuzzi. However I've only been in it a handful of times over the years because the benches are too high for me to easily get changed. It's something I need to sort out.

In November 2003 I had a 30th birthday party at the onsite bar/restaurant. Lots of people came to it including KC and his wife. It was good seeing KC again. He spent ages playing games with Scott and Oliver which kept them entertained!

A couple of days prior to the party, Mum moved in with me for a few days. It annoyed me because rather than asking, "Can I move in with you for a few days?" she said, "I've got to move in with you, I've got nowhere else to live."

In part at least, this was about her controlling me, because she could have stayed with Clare and Rupert.

Mum didn't have a job anymore and she had sold her house which had lots of equity in it.

In hindsight, I wish I had come to an arrangement with Mum and taken over her mortgage. The house would have made a great multi-let property; it had four double bedrooms, two bathrooms, a big kitchen and lounge and the dining room could have been easily converted into a single bedroom. However, I wasn't into property investment at the time.

In April 2003, two weeks before Splash FM launched on 5th May, I took two weeks of annual leave at *Shh* during which time I spent recording songs onto the play-out system at the radio station.

Located on the first floor of the Guildbourne Shopping Centre in the heart of Worthing, I was ripping songs onto the computer in the middle of what looked like a building site.

Operations Director Ted, John Roberts and a gang of workmen were constructing the office and studios! It was a slightly surreal environment but great to be part of.

Most of the song titles and artists had already been entered onto the RCS play-out system so all I had to do was rip the songs from CDs and set the start/end, intro and segue markers.

The thing I remember about the launch party was meeting Leo Sayer. The amusing fact about him is that I am taller than he is! I haven't met many people who are shorter than me.

There were a few familiar faces about the place when Splash started.

My friend Fergus who I knew from school was part of the launch team. He had been doing hospital radio for years and had joined Splash through knowing Ray and Ted via Hospital Radio and was producing local football material for the sport show.

Ted himself who was one of the directors of Splash and in charge of all things technical.

Phil, who I knew from Spirit FM, was another former hospital radio volunteer and was working full-time at the Benefits Agency and then walking across the road at 5.30pm to present the evening show at six.

Seth who I knew from Surf days.

And of course, Ray.

Working on the Splash FM sports show was a similar experience to the one at Spirit FM. I was recording sports feeds from IRN. As I was based in the News studio, I was recording the reports onto the news computer system called Burli. As Burli wasn't installed in the on air studio, I had to play the reports live on air.

The News Editor William presented the sport show. He introduced the reports and I played them out. As a report played out I told him via the talkback system how long it was and then when there were 20 and 10 seconds left of the report. It was easy and I mastered it after the first week. The first show did have its moments, however.

I can use a computer mouse perfectly well, except not on the day of the first sport show. I didn't know what the Burli keyboard shortcut was to fire a report, and not having worked in radio for a few years, I was a bit nervous and not pinpoint accurate in starting the reports with the mouse. By the second show, I was spot on because I then knew the keyboard shortcut to start the reports. By preference, I would always use the keyboard rather than a mouse.

I also recall on the first show teaching William how to use RCS in a couple of areas including how to skip a song.

One of the things I liked about the show was its reliance on teamwork and a lot of verbal communication.

Being around the same age and liking radio, we worked well together and became friends. I got the impression, however, that William was presenting the show out of obligation, rather than choice. His wife Heather popped into the station during a few Saturday afternoons. They were a nice couple.

On music-led stations, I've always thought the term 'sports show' is a bit misleading. It was predominantly a music show with at least ten songs per hour which included some sport.

There was a vast contrast between working at Splash and Surf. At Splash the studios were well equipped, had talkback and were built for people to use sitting down. Unlike other small commercial stations, Splash had a production studio and a third studio - the news booth.

There was a lift, the office was a good environment in which to work and I was well respected.

When I started at Splash I worked voluntarily. I didn't mind showing people what I could do at first. Then after the beginning of the football season in September, I got £25 a week for producing the four-hour sports show. I felt valued.

When the station began in 2003, little did I expect that I would be doing the sports show for the next nine years. Being technically able and with a natural flair for radio, I loved working on the sports show and was extremely good at it.

After the start of the football season Simon Cox (aka Coxy) joined as our Brighton & Hove Albion reporter. Coxy was, and is, a great Albion supporter who went to every match.

During each game I phoned Coxy every fifteen minutes and recorded a 20 second report from him. He had obviously done radio before because his reports were superb, entertaining and funny. Even when the Albion were losing, Coxy's reports were great because you could hear and share his emotional pain.

After every game William had a live two-way conversation with Coxy. He was such a passionate supporter that sometimes William and I were apprehensive that Coxy was going to swear. He never did.

I think Coxy was also a bit of a Lionel Richie fan. I will never forget a couple of the things he came out with.

When the Albion won three-nil on one occasion a very excited Coxy came up with, "It was once, twice, three times a lady into the back of the net...". And after another win, "They'll be dancing on the ceiling tonight in Brighton."

I went into Splash to get reports from Coxy when the Albion had a weekday evening game. Phil presented 6 to 9 PM and John Roberts did 9 to midnight.

Sometimes John pre-recorded (voice-tracked) his show. On those occasions John left me a couple of pre-recorded links to use to introduce Coxy's reports and after 9 PM I phoned and recorded Coxy from the on-air studio. This enabled me to play the reports between two songs segued together.

I liked keeping the show sounding live. The links which John had pre-recorded would be similar to this, "Brighton are in action against Chesterfield tonight. Watching the game for Splash FM is Simon Cox - What's the latest Coxy?."

I would ask Coxy to start his reports by saying, "Yes, hello John..."

It was a bit of fun on a weekday evening!

Splash FM attracted fiercely loyal fans and listeners. I remember in the first year at an outside event in Worthing Ray being approached by Barry, Elaine and son Darren who wanted him to sign a book they had with them. The book had no connection with either Splash or Ray but he obliged anyway. They turned up to most events and were typical of the tribal loyalty that the station attracted.

William and Heather invited me over to their house for dinner one Saturday evening and to stay overnight in their spare room so I could have a couple of drinks. Heather cooked something nice and we watched a film. This was on the 13th December 2003 and the next morning we saw on TV that Saddam Hussein had been captured.

At the end of 2003 William left Splash having got a job at a London station. Phil presented the sports show from then on.

William and I stayed in regular email contact for a few months, chatting about radio. During this time we went with Heather to see comedian Tim Vine at the Komedia club in Brighton. I had seen Tim Vine at the Komedia a few years before and I find him very funny as he uses my kind of word-play humour.

I paid for the tickets and after the gig, went out of my way to give William and Heather a lift home to Worthing. William and I carried on emailing each other for a while until life overtook us and we lost touch.

# Chapter 3

The next two chapters are structured differently to the rest of my book. They contain the following main sections:

- Family - 2004 to 2007
- Radio - 2004 to 2007
- DJing at The Warwick - 2005 to 2008
- Meeting women - 2004 to 2009

In April 2003 Rupert, Clare and the boys moved to a bigger house on Shoreham Beach and rather than selling the old house, they rented it out.

Over the next few years Rupert bought a few buy-to-let houses locally. He also had a lot of work done on the house the family were living in.

I felt Rupert was a materialist. There's nothing wrong with being materialistic - it's just not me. My view is that materialism can initiate a vicious circle because it reduces the life-span and novelty value of items and encourages more spending, some of which can be unaffordable.

Money does not buy happiness in the long term. Having been part of the property investment community since 2010 I know a lot of rich people. It's not what they have that makes and keeps them happy - it's what they do. This is the key to becoming successful.

Wealth is a relative thing of course. Some of the poorest people in the world consider themselves to be wealthy.

After Mum sold her house in 2003, she rented a penthouse apartment for a few months at Brighton Marina before living with Clare and Rupert for a while. It seemed her grandkids became Mum's purpose in life.Over the next few years Mum became a bit of a nomad. She spent spells living in Brighton,

Hove, Lancing (a village west of Shoreham), France and did some voluntary work in Africa. She became flatmates with Angie, an alcoholic depressive thirty-something year old in Hove. Mum also met Vince, who lived in Ireland. They may still be together - I don't know.

My mother was like a boomerang. She kept coming back to see me to offload her 'problems' and use me as a councillor. As the only one in the family still talking to her, I wanted to help her. Trouble is, it felt as if Mum would always come armed with difficult news, which made me feel sick and caused me ongoing vomiting. I spent hours writing Mum a series of emails over a period of months, trying to make her see sense, take responsibility and make up with my Aunt Liz and Uncle John. I advised her that counselling would do her good and she should accept Rupert.

In one email I wrote, "You used to be such a positive person. I remember you used to listen to your Zig Ziglar tapes. Do you remember that time?"

However, all my efforts were in vain because Mum never took any responsibility for herself. Instead she said, "I haven't done anything wrong...I don't need any counselling,.."

This continued in a vicious circle until late in 2010. Repeatedly, Mum and I would have an argument and not speak for weeks and months. Then, thinking that the argument was a thing of the past, Mum would get back in touch with me. Each time I thought 'I must try harder to help her' but she didn't follow my advice and make any effort to help herself.

Mum often wanted my help to do something simple on her laptops. Over many years I had tried to show her how to do things on the computer but her response was always "You're the computer programmer - you do it". I found it such a defeatist attitude and very frustrating. In the end it was easier to do what Mum wanted me to do on her computer than to have an argument about it.

I love my mum and my wish for her is to find peace and happiness, essentially she's a very good person but my impression is she lets the past affect her daily life. The past cannot be changed and the present moment is all that exists. Clare and I were on good terms. Usually, I went over to her house one evening a week, to see the kids and for dinner. The children went to after-school activities on most days and Rupert was often at work in the evenings.

Something odd happened on one occasion when I arrived to see them. As I walked into the lounge Oliver came over to me. I thought he was going to kiss me hello but he took everyone by surprise.

Oliver put his hand on my chest and pushed me, which made me fall over backwards. I didn't hurt myself but it made Scott burst into tears of fright. Oliver went into a corner sobbing with embarrassment. I think Oliver, aged about five at the time, just wondered what would happen if he pushed me.

Until Scott was eight and Oliver six, I was a bit soft with them. I wanted to be a fun and easy-going uncle, who made them laugh. I didn't want the persona of a relative who regularly told them off.

I remember looking after the boys one evening at Clare's, whilst Clare went out somewhere with Charlotte. I was such an easy-going person with them that whilst sharing the sofa I let them take turns with scissors to cut off a bit of my hair!

Clare came home, saw what the boys were doing and said to me:

Clare: "What the hell are you doing letting them cut your hair?"

Me: "They've only cut a little bit of hair..."

However it made me realise what I was doing was wrong. After my barbarous act I toughened up with Scott and Oliver. I was still a fun uncle but they soon learnt that they couldn't misbehave around me. And they respected me more because of it.

Over the years I took Scott and Oliver to the cinema, out for meals at places like Pizza Hut and McDonald's. They sometimes stayed at my flat at the weekend and I let them stay up late! They saw it as a real treat. I liked being called "The best uncle in the world".

I also bonded really well with Charlotte - but she was a bit too young for me to take her out. She liked me tickling her!

Clare is a very good Mum and has devoted her life to her children. She worked part-time, teaching an autistic girl nearby - and taught horse riding at the weekend before Charlotte was born.

Coincidentally, Clare got to meet Ted from Splash FM quite independently of me. They met each other at a school fete. Ted lived on Shoreham Beach with his wife and two kids and it made sense for Clare to share the school run with them for a few years.

Clare would always respond if I needed some help. For example, when I needed to fill in a form I took it round to her house and she would complete it. Clare was very handy!

Sometime after 2007 I had an appointment to see my GP. At the end of the session she asked:

"How's your Mum?"

Me: "I haven't spoken to her for a few months. I think her problems are due to her breakup with Liz and John, and probably even further back than that."

It wasn't until early in 2011, after I got into property investment and started learning about different types of people, that I realised what the root of Mum's problem is.

On a lighter note, I often said to Clare she should listen to Splash rather than Southern FM. I found Southern so formulaic. I referred to it as wallpaper radio because it was bland and in the background.

Having said that, I haven't been much of a commercial radio listener for years. To me, listening to radio ads is dead time in an otherwise busy life.

I remember the time I went over to Clare's and we had a conversation that ran like this:

Clare: "I heard you on the radio the other day!"

Me: *"What? When?"*

Clare: "Yeah, it was on Friday evening, I was on my way home and I just happened to put Splash on and during a song you said, *"Alright Coxy...how's it going?""*

Me: "Bloody hell, I didn't know about that. I phoned Coxy to get another report from him. Seth was covering the show and he must have forgotten to put the News booth fader down after I played Coxy's previous report."

Clare: "I thought it was hilarious! You're always telling me to listen to Splash and the one time I do I hear you on it!"

I didn't find it funny!

From January 2004 Phil and I worked well together after he started hosting the sports show on Splash. We were both passionate about making great radio and we brought a good mix of skills and knowledge to the programme.

I haven't met anyone who knows as much about sport as Phil does. By contrast, I come to it as a non-sports fan but with a good ear for entertaining radio.

When I started working with Phil he always rushed home at the end of the sports show. He was living with his girlfriend Sara in Littlehampton and her four kids - one of whom was Ross, who she had with Phil in 2003.

At the weekends, I was becoming quite well known in the onsite bar near my flat. I went out with groups of people into Shoreham and Brighton, where I met a few women. Having always driven everywhere I don't mind being the designated driver and giving people lifts.

I met a married couple in the onsite bar who were about my age. It was obvious that they were on the verge of splitting up and I liked and got to know the wife quite well. I was quietly disappointed when the couple separated and she got a new job and moved away.

The reason I always drive when I go out has partly to do with an experience in the onsite bar shortly after moving into my flat. After getting somewhat inebrehated, two guys walked me back to my flat and left me lying on my sofa. Shortly afterwards, I needed a wee but was too drunk and dizzy to walk. So I crawled to the bathroom but couldn't stand up to go to the toilet. I proceeded to vomit on the floor and then fell asleep in the bathroom!

After cleaning the mess up the following day, I decided drinking heavily wasn't for me.

Back at Splash in Spring 2004, sadly our reporter Coxy left the programme after The Seagulls were promoted to the Chamionship League. The cost of the broadcasting rights to have a live reporter at the Albion games were too high to make it viable. Splash wasn't a Brighton station and the live reports were something of a luxury, although great radio.

Instead to reinforce our local credentials, Rob Cocozza and Mark Sanderson covered Worthing FC and Worthing United respectively. I phoned them each game and recorded a preview, half-time and full-time report from both.

Mark had done some radio before and his reports were good. I don't think Rob had as much experience because his reports sometimes seemed a little nervy and his intonation wasn't always right. Nevertheless, Rob appreciated my coaching and his reports got better and better.

Another excellent contributor on the sports show was Phil's school friend Andy Lutwyche. In addition to being a secondary school maths teacher, Andy played for Worthing FC and Worthing Cricket Club at the weekends. Phil chatted live on-air with Andy after his games. As two witty people, the pair were easy on the ear.

Andy is naturally funny. He would say to me "Do you know anything about sport yet? I don't know how you can produce a sports show when you clearly don't know anything about sport!"

To which I replied "Do you know anything about binary yet? I don't know how you can be Head of Maths when you clearly don't know anything about binary!"

Also very funny, albeit more off-air than on, was Dave, who worked for a sports news company and provided short bulletins for Splash, via ISDN throughout the week and on Saturday afternoons. Phil and I spoke to Dave every Saturday for years but we never met him. Radio can be like that.

When it came to the Premiership, our practice was to play goal updates.

I realised that rather than ending the IRN Premier football reports sharply, straight after the reporter had finished, it was a good idea to let the recording continue for a second or so to catch the crowd atmosphere at the football ground. Asking Phil to fade out the reports sounded slicker than reports ending sharply and the show benefited from it.

Equally, there was often a bit of crowd atmosphere at the beginning of reports before the reporters started speaking. This enabled me to start playing each report early, before Phil had finished his link into the report. Doing this gave a live feel to the reports.

Starting a report whilst Phil was still introducing it, took experience and so it wasn't something I did when I started on the sports show in 2003. Phil and I worked so well together, we were like a well-oiled machine. I knew what Phil was going to say into each report.

When it came to working in a radio studio I was a perfectionist, playing things out on-air with pinpoint accuracy.

I was in my element doing the sports show with Phil and often said, "There's nowhere else I would rather be on Saturday afternoons between two and six".

When people at the station told me that I was doing a good job, I replied "Thank you, it's teamwork".

Possessing poor co-ordination and a speech impediment, I like the irony that I was doing something that required high levels of accuracy and good verbal communication. I was also proud of the fact that not many people in my position were working in radio, doing my job.

I always knew that I could do it - and I was highly motivated by the desire to prove it. I would love to work in radio again.

My timing was also excellent when it came to doing other things. If I had a report to play out and Phil had a segue of two songs to play first, rather than sit and wait in the studio, I started the Burli computer recording of the IRN feed to capture any new goals. I then went for a wee and to make a fresh pot of coffee but never got the two things mixed up!

It wasn't unusual for me to walk back into the studio with seconds to spare before playing a report out. I knew how much time I had. Sometimes, I played reports standing up. I was in my element and felt like I could do anything.

In the first hour of the show I did the bakery run downstairs in the Guildbourne Centre - I was very fast!

It felt great generating respect from others for my work at Splash. One of the people in this category is Mike who was the programme controller (PC) for the first few years at the station. I know he thinks highly of me, calling me 'Mr Stix' (which I quite like). In return I respect Mike, he's a good bloke and I see him at Splash events once or twice a year.

However I've never quite worked Mike out. He's always tended to talk at me, almost as if he thinks I'm slightly deaf, rather than talk to me.

Mike often greets me by saying, "Hello, Mr Stix-O-Stix-O-Stix. How are we today?"

In more recent years he has changed this to, "Hello Mr Stix, how many properties have you bought this week?!"

It was rare for me or Phil to have a Saturday off but when Phil did, Mike presented the sport show. The only time I recall Mike speaking to me normally was just before he did a link into a report and on the talkback he said, "Right, are you ready?"

I didn't feel totally at ease when Mike did the show because he watched and listened to everything I did like a hawk and could be critical of me. I didn't take it personally because Mike was like that with other people who did stuff on-air.

The first show Mike and I did together wasn't the best, but I was more relaxed when he covered subsequent shows.

Over the years most of the presenters on the station covered the sports show. They all saw what I did and developed a high opinion of me.

One person who really didn't know how to talk to me was one of early salesmen. Phil told me about this conversation:

Salesman: "Phil, what do you say to Patrick when you don't understand something he says?

Phil: "Pardon."

Salesman: "What do you say to Patrick when you don't understand something he says?

It made me laugh!

I later met the salesman's wife at a barbecue and I had a perfectly normal ten minute conversation with her.

Someone I regularly spoke to on Saturdays was Jennifer, one of the journalists at Splash who used to do the Saturday morning news shift. Being a conscientious worker, Jennifer often worked in the afternoon writing and preparing things for the following week.

One weekend the air-conditioning in the studios broke down. Phil was ok as he had a temporary fan in the main studio. However it was so hot and stuffy in the news booth that I took off my jumper and t-shirt. At football half-time I went into the office to get some fresh air.

As I opened the door and stepped into the office, Jennifer glanced up at me and from where she was sitting half obscured by a desk, she thought I was completely naked! It gave her a shock and it was a first as I've never had that effect on someone before!

I've always thought there was an air of mystery surrounding Jennifer because she never revealed much about herself. All I really know about her is that she's got a long term boyfriend, likes cheese and is into collecting handbags.

For all I know, Jennifer could also be into swinging and Tupperware parties.

Now as you know, I'm not someone who likes being put in a box but it's got me wondering - is a swinging and Tupperware party where people are put in a box?

I've emailed Jennifer the above and her response is "very good, I quite like Tupperware".

I was always keen to do more things at Splash. A few times I helped when the station did an outside broadcast - by babysitting the RCS play-out computer in the main studio. This was in case the computer or the line being used for the outside broadcast went down. On a couple of occasions it did. In those instances I switched the output to come from the RCS computer in the studio whilst Ted fixed the problem at the outside broadcast.

I also helped other people by doing production stuff at the weekends. It was all good fun.

In the early days at Splash the opportunity came up to buy some shares in the station. So I did! Although I'm a minor shareholder, I've got radio in my blood - and I like it!

Over the years a few volunteers came in to help on the show by phoning local football clubs to get the scores.

When Ryan Lainchbury turned up Phil and I thought he would make a good cover for me.

If and when I'm in the position to employ people I would like to hire Ryan. He's got great people skills, is conscientious and doesn't take himself too seriously.

Having said that, it took me years to train Ryan up! He can be lightheaded and a bit forgetful - and he turned up rather sporadically on Saturdays.

Despite this, I trained Ryan to be a perfectionist like me. Every time he covered me, Phil said that Ryan did an excellent job. I found it very pleasing.

Ryan was good fun to have around on Saturday afternoons. He was often more entertaining than Phil!

As Splash was based in the town centre on the first floor of the Guildbourne Centre, it didn't have any off-road parking. The closest I could park was in Ann Street which was a cul-de-sac leading to the Centre where there are two disabled spaces, often occupied. It took me about seven minutes to walk to Splash from the disabled spaces.

As the sports show was four hours long and the disabled spaces were often occupied, I had a problem as my disabled badge only entitled me to park on double yellow lines for up to three hours.

I overcame the issue by going to Worthing police station and explaining the problem to the guy who was in charge of on-street parking. It resulted in an informal agreement. I could park for as long as I needed anywhere in Ann Street, so long as my car wasn't causing a danger or obstruction.

In May 2005 Phil went through a messy breakup with his girlfriend Sara leading him to move back home to his parents in Lancing.

This was when Phil and I started going to The Warwick. With an entrance in Ann Street, The Warwick is a popular pub in Worthing with a twenty-five year plus clientele.

After he split up with Sara we frequented The Warwick most Friday and Saturday nights, which I continued to do, with and without Phil, until about 2009.

The pub has the capacity for about two hundred and twenty people with a DJ on Friday and Saturday evenings, when there is often a queue of people waiting to get in.

After the sports show on Saturdays we went to a restaurant before going to the pub where we regularly stayed until closing time at 2am when I gave Phil a lift home to Lancing.

Phil and I talked about everything under the sun, sharing as we do similar opinions on most things in life. We often spoke about radio and people.

Phil told me about his previous relationships and that he had got together with Sara for the wrong reasons. He said he was happy being single and had neglected his friends when he had been in relationships.

Phil and I became regulars in The Warwick where a few things happened. I met a number of women, Phil and I became DJs there and Phil met his wife Kim.

To begin with we sat chatting and observed what the DJs were playing and the impact it had on the dance floor. We referred to some of the DJs as being "all over the place". For example, they would play an eighties song, followed by a sixties song and then something that was currently in the charts. Without proper sequencing, this song by song approach attracted people on and off the dance floor.

We observed that to get, and keep, people on the dance floor you need to play fast, high tempo songs and stick to the same genre of music for at least a few tracks.

I had never thought about DJing until the Summer of 2005 when Phil became a regular DJ at The Warwick. When I saw what Phil was doing I wanted to do it!

As Phil knew my capabilities, he was happy for me to help him. It involved cueing up a song on CD whilst another one was playing and choosing what to play, of course! It wasn't difficult. The hardest thing was doing it standing up, before I got a stool.

We would DJ from 9pm until 2am. People often didn't arrive on the dance floor until 9.30-10.00 o'clock. Once they did, it was easy to keep them there.

It wasn't long before Phil was leaving me to DJ on my own for half an hour or so. I got a real buzz from it, especially when playing stuff that got a good reaction from the crowd and the dance floor was full.

I created a collection of CDs with songs for us to play at The Warwick and called them Pat-Trax.

Over the years various managers, staff and bouncers passed through The Warwick. They all liked and respected me. I also got to know the other DJs, some of whom had taken the easier option of playing sets from their laptop.

After seeing the software they were using to DJ, I bought a laptop and the software. Although it took a bit time for me to transfer hundreds of songs onto the laptop and to set a cue point for each song which was a marker to start playing the song from, it was worth it.

I remember Phil saying, "I'm going to try the laptop but I'm going to keep on using CDs". By the end of the evening he decided that CDs were a thing of the past! It was so easy. The songs were separated into folders, denoting the decade they were from and I had created three folders for dance songs. To select and play only required pressing a couple of buttons!

One evening when Phil and I were DJing, Ryan popped up to the DJ booth to say hello. As we were in the middle of an Eighties set, Ryan looked through the songs in my 1980s folder and excitedly said, "Ooo - play 'Freedom' by Wham!" Having never roadtested it, I played the song. It cleared the dance floor!

Phil kept the laptop during the week to put new songs on it. The DJing software only cost £25 and it enabled Phil to mix and beat-match two dance songs together (something I don't know much about).

I'm not a massive fan of dance music, but I loved doing an hour's set of heavy-ish dance anthems such as 'Insomnia' by Faithless and Darude's 'Sandstorm'.

Phil and I had it down to a fine art. We ended up having roughly eight hundred songs on the laptop, from the Sixties through to current chart stuff,

The funny thing was, we could never predict what genre of music would go down well from one night to the next. Sometimes it would be Seventies and Eighties, other nights it was Dance and current Chart music

I remember doing a Nineties Indie set ('Place Your Hands' by Reef was often a crowd-pleaser). When Phil came back from the toilet he said that the whole pub was buzzing.

That night the then owner of The Warwick was there (a rare occurrence), and from afar, he put his thumb up at me while I was DJing. It was the only occasion I received any form of communication from him.

Because I didn't want to keep visiting the toilet, I often made one pint of lager-shandy last the whole evening!

At Christmas time 2005 at about 2.30am, I was giving Phil a lift home when I got pulled over by the police. As he was slightly inebriated, I said to Phil, "I'll handle this".

Policeman [standing at my car door with the window open]: "Hello Sir, I'm just carrying out a spot check. Can you tell me where you've been tonight?"

Me: "I've been DJing in The Warwick pub in Worthing."

Policeman: "Have you had any alcohol this evening?"

Me: "Yes, I've had one pint of lager-shandy over the last six hours."

Seeming a little perplexed, the policeman looked over to Phil.

Phil: "It's true. He has..."

It was funny.

When I bought and set the laptop up, I named it Pat-Lap. After I started calling my car "The Patmobile", Phil commented "You're building a little empire!"

I'm thinking of writing a book on the genres of music and songs I like - and calling it Pat Sounds.

(Remember the Beach Boys?)

In 2007 Jim and Harry became the new managers at The Warwick. I liked them and one Friday evening around Halloween, shortly after 9 o'clock, I had a call from Jim asking if I was available to DJ that evening as the DJ they had booked hadn't shown up.

I jumped into my car and headed to The Warwick. Jim went with me into Splash to get Pat-Lap.

It wasn't long after that evening when Jim and Harry decided to use Phil and I as resident DJs at The Warwick. They said it was because we knew our stuff and we were reliable.

Phil chose to do Friday evenings with me and I DJed on Saturdays on my own. It was a fun and easy way of earning £100.

After seeing my laptop, Jim and Harry got the owner of The Warwick to buy one for the pub so that they could use it to play music from during the day.

I copied my songs and some freeware play-listing software onto The Warwick's laptop. I said to Jim and Harry that they could have my songs as long as I remained DJing at the pub.

On New Year's Eve in 2007 Phil was booked to DJ at The Warwick (as he had done the year earlier). However Phil had eaten something that disagreed with him and was ill at the last minute. So I did New Year's Eve solo at The Warwick

It was a blast. I had a recording of Big Ben leading up to midnight which I back-timed perfectly with the help of the speaking clock. Jim put the big screen TV on mute and Harry did the countdown on the microphone.

In the meantime, after nine years of going to visit Martin and Janet every few weeks, in July 2005 (shortly after Martin's thirty-first birthday) I felt I was on the verge of falling in love with Janet. Because of this, I decided to halt these visits as they were too painful for me.

Since I started writing this book, people have been inspired by what I am doing. One person asked me, "Will there be any dancing in your book?" "Yes, there will be some dancing in it" I replied.

I feel I could write a book solely about me meeting women. It is something I have put an incredible amount of energy, effort and time into - trying to find someone to share my life with. It's something I haven't done successfully.

In every other aspect of my life I class myself as a successful person, because I achieve everything I put my mind to.

The Warwick was where I started meeting lots of women. When I started going there with Phil in 2005, I became very confident about walking up to someone I liked the look of and starting a conversation with them.

In 'Stairs for Breakfast' I mentioned the difference between 'pushing' and 'pulling' someone. This is something I learnt about fairly recently in 2011.

Pushing is when you will do almost anything to impress somebody. Most people see it as a real turnoff because it's a sign of desperation.

Whereas, pulling is when you attract someone or more than one person without meaning to do so.

How many times have you heard, "You'll find someone when you stop looking" or, "You'll find someone when you least expect it"?

If you are looking for the love of your life, stop. They will be waiting for you when you start doing things you love.

In The Warwick era, I was doing everything I could to try to impress women. I was 'desperate'.

However I prefer the term 'too eager' because criminals are desperate. I'm a gentleman.

I was going out to meet women, wearing my 'I can achieve anything I put my mind to' attitude and thinking, "All I've got to do is meet one woman who can see that I'm a great guy".

In four years I met over fifty women who gave me their phone number at The Warwick. I had all their numbers in my phone and yet I found it demoralising.

The reality I face in life is, when it comes to attracting women, I've got a smaller 'pond to fish in' than able-bodied men because I look and sound severely disabled.

A lot of the women that I come across are apprehensive of me. This is mainly due to my speech. If my voice wasn't affected, people would think 'He just can't walk properly'. But due to my voice, some people who don't know about CP, think, 'Oh, he can't walk property and he can't talk properly. I don't know what's wrong with him and it scares me.'

To try to overcome this issue, when meeting women at The Warwick and at social events, I let them know I wasn't stupid by mentioning I was a computer programmer and used a lot of self-deprecating humour to make them laugh and engage them in conversation.

It's easy to explain how I met so many women at The Warwick. I repeated the same pattern every weekend. By going up to and talking to women, a good number would ask me to dance with them. By the end of the evening, we would swap numbers and I phoned them the next afternoon. Many of them wouldn't answer their phone so I left a voicemail with a version of, "...It was nice meeting you last night. It would be good to speak to you, hope to talk to you soon. Take care."

Most of them didn't respond or just wanted to text me. I ended up having lots of text conversations. I'm not anti-texting but it's hard work and when it's the only form of communication there's no intonation and I found messages can also be misunderstood.

I know what my strengths are and dancing isn't one of them. When I try to dance I look like a severely disabled guy on crutches doing odd moves. I hate dancing. Apart from anything else, it requires me to use an enormous amount of energy.

It took me a while to understand why so many women asked me to dance with them. There are two reasons. Firstly, it was a way of them interacting with me, without them having to say much to me. Secondly, women saw me as a charity case and dancing with me made them feel good about themselves, as if they were doing something noble.

The only person I felt comfortable 'dancing' with was Janet, the time we went clubbing in Brighton.

I don't remember most of the women that I met at The Warwick as it's a blur. However, some I do remember:

There was 'the Bob Marley t-shirt girl' about my age and I met her on a night when Phil and I were DJing and I was wearing my Bob Marley t-shirt bought in Los Angeles in 1995. She liked my t-shirt so much that at the end of the evening, when all of the other punters had left the pub, she asked me if she could try it on. I agreed, in exchange for a bit of her hotdog!

For some reason, The Warwick were selling hotdogs at the end of the evening and they had none left for me.

In the middle of the pub, she took off her blouse, I took my t-shirt off and she put it on for a minute. It was a poor exchange as the hotdog tasted crap! She came back to The Warwick a few times with her boyfriend.

When I next went to Antigua, I bought a Bob Marley t-shirt and kept it in the glove compartment of my car for when I next saw her at The Warwick. When I tried to give it to her, she wouldn't accept it. It felt disappointing because I didn't mean anything by it. I just saw the t-shirt at the market and thought she would like it.

Months later she texted me, saying she had spilt up with her boyfriend and had got a job in another part of the country.

I met a student nurse in her mid-twenties, who told me she had worked with people with CP. She was really nice and we had a good laugh on the night we met. She called me Frankie - I had my hair gelled back at the time and she said I looked like the jockey Frankie Dettori.

I gave her a lift home. When I phoned her the next day, she didn't want to know me. I think I displayed too much eagerness in wanting to see her again.

At The Warwick I met all sorts of women including a memorable goth and someone else whose perfume smelt like toilet cleaner. I spoke to a woman called Rachel a few times in the pub and a couple of times on the phone but I found her patronising and insincere.

Someone who wasn't shy in coming up to the DJ booth and who was about ten years older than me and a bit scary was the woman whose opening line was:

Woman: "I've got a son like you..."

Me: "In what way?

Woman: "I was raped when I was young. My kids have been taken into care...I miss my babies...and now they want to section me."

Woman: "I like you...and would like to have sex with you."

She was a bit full on physically as well.

I said to Phil "Help me...!"

I felt sorry for her, which made me feel sick.

In preparing to write this chapter I spoke to Phil, as I couldn't fully remember when things happened. One person who neither of us will forget is Kate, who Phil says I met in September 2005.

It was a Friday night when Phil and I were in The Warwick as punters. Normally we stayed until closing time at 2am but we were both feeling tired and I was slightly hacked off because I had already met several women to no avail. So at about 1am we decided to go home early.

Shortly before leaving I remember saying to Phil "I'm never going to find a girlfriend here." "Yes you are" Phil replied.

When we decided to leave:

Phil: "I'm going to the toilet, I'll meet you outside, mate."

Me: "Okay."

As I stood up and turned facing the bar, a woman, about my age and height, said to me:

Kate: "Hello handsome..."

This was a unique response!

Me: "Are you taking the piss?"

Kate: "No!"

We stood chatting for a while. Unlike other women, she seemed really interested in me and wasn't patronising. After about ten minutes Phil came back in to see what I was doing. I introduced him to Kate and carried on chatting to her.

Another five to ten minutes of us chatting went by before Phil said, "Come on mate, let's go..."

I said to Kate "I've got to go now because I'm giving Phil a lift home."

Kate: "I'll walk out with you to your car."

As we walked out of the pub, and the short distance up the road to my car, Kate asked Phil "Where's your car?"

Phil [pointing to the multi-storey car park]: "In the car park."

When we got to my car, Kate followed me round to the driver's side whilst Phil sat in the passenger seat.

As I started to get into the car Kate had other ideas!

She pinned me up against the back door of my car and started French-kissing me. It went on, and on, and on! It felt lovely.

We were snogging each other for twenty to twenty-five minutes. Kate was *so* nice - and she wasn't a bad kisser either!

Afterwards, I got into the car and Kate went round to the other side, opened Phil's door to say something to him and she then leaned over Phil while we had another snog!

When most of the kissing was over:

Me [slightly fearing she would say no]: Can I have your number?"

Kate: "ABSOLUTELY."

We swapped numbers and another kiss.

Giving Phil a lift home he said, "I'm really happy for you, mate". He also said that while he was waiting for me in the car, he became very familiar with what was written on the back of my tax disc!

I didn't get much sleep that night. My mind was absolutely buzzing. I kept thinking 'I've finally found someone who accepts me.'

After speaking to Phil about it the next day during the sports show, I phoned Kate on Sunday and left her a voicemail. She texted me back a few hours later in the evening.

What followed were four days of intense text conversations. Kate and I were texting each other so much that I got a bit of RSI in my index finger.

I kept thinking 'She accepts me. All I've got to do now is get her to realise that I'm a lovely guy.'

I kept texting her things like:

"I've got so much love and affection to give."

"I'm the nicest guy you'll ever meet."

"Please give me a chance."

"Why won't you give me a chance?"

I also phoned her a couple of times and got frustrated when she didn't answer my call.

Kate's reason for kissing me when we met was that she had drunk a lot of wine and was inebriated, although she hadn't seemed that drunk to me. In our text conversations she mentioned that she had recently had a miscarriage.

I couldn't understand why she didn't want to give us the chance of getting to know each other.

I was so eager. Had I known about pushing and pulling, it might have turned out differently. However, it's in the past and it doesn't matter anymore.

Writing about how I used to be is making me cringe. I find my eagerness embarrassing.

At the time I felt so distraught that I hardly ate anything in five days.

On the Thursday night Kate and I agreed to stop texting each other. The next evening Phil really helped me when we went out for a meal.

He said that Kate had used me because she was vulnerable following her miscarriage. Phil went on to say that he had personal experience of someone who had a miscarriage.

Phil said something I'll never forget, "A miscarriage is painful emotionally but you do get over it, whereas you need to cope with your CP for the rest of your life."

I haven't been a fan of Christmas for years because I tend to think of it as a time to spend with 'your other half' and as a family occasion.

However, I liked Boxing Day because there was always a sports show on Splash and with most of the Premiership teams in action, it made it an extra special programme to do.

Christmas 2005 was memorable for the wrong reasons. Mum, upset with Clare and not seeing her grandkids, decided to spend Christmas in Africa, doing voluntary work for a few months. This in turn made Clare upset on Christmas Day because Mum had decided to not spend it with her family.

On the afternoon of 23rd December 2005 I was by the fish counter in my local supermarket. Spookily, as I got my phone out of my pocket to call Clare to ask her if I should buy anything fishy for Christmas Day, Janet phoned me:

Me: "Hello?"

Janet: "Hello, it's me, Janet"

Me: "How are you?"

Janet: "I'm okay. I've got some bad news...Martin has died."

The shock of it took my breath away. It caused me to hyperventilate slightly and I couldn't talk for a few seconds.

Janet: "Are you okay?"

Me: "Yeah...I'm *so* sorry. Can I do anything to help?"

Janet: "It's okay. He died towards the end of November."

Janet went on to say that Martin's funeral was going to be in the first week of January because there had been an inquiry into his death. She said Martin's oxygen machine had stopped working on the way back from a day in London with Graham (one of his carers) and Graham who was driving the car, noticed there was a problem a few minutes after the oxygen machine stopped.

It was a tragic accident. Martin had one of those car conversions where the roof at the back of the vehicle is higher than at the front to accommodate someone in a wheelchair. Martin had some loud music on (probably Oasis) and Graham was driving along the dual carriageway.

Janet seemed a bit distant on the phone and we didn't have a long conversation. I found it a bit odd that she hadn't called me sooner. She said she would call me with the funeral details when she had them.

I then phoned Clare, asked her about the fish and told her about Martin. She said to go round to her house.

Before going over to see Clare, I went home to phone Martin's parents and spoke to his Mum. I told her how sorry I was about Martin and how it had come as a real shock to me. She appreciated my call and was surprised that I had just found out about his death.

Over Christmas and New Year, I felt compelled to make a CD compilation of some of Martin's favourite songs, including Nirvana's acoustic version of 'The Man Who Sold The World'.

The only photo of Martin I could find on the internet was of him and Janet on their wedding day so I used it as the front cover of the CD and at the funeral, I gave a copy of it to Martin's parents and one to Janet. Martin's parents appreciated the CD.

Janet acted very strangely towards me at the funeral. She brushed the CD aside and avoided me like the plague throughout the whole event. I couldn't work out why.

I sat right at the back during the funeral service next to Linda Smith, the mother of Richard and Justin, who both had MD - and were my friends at school. Linda was a bit teary during the service so I tried to comfort her.

Not having been to many funerals, I felt sad but also found the whole thing slightly surreal.

After the service during the foodie bit I talked to Martin's son Ben, when I said, "I'm really sorry about your Dad", he replied, "it's okay, it's just one of those things". At this point Janet's Mum came and introduced herself to me:

"Hello Patrick, I'm Norma, Janet's Mum. It's so nice to meet you, Janet's told me all about you. You are an amazing guy."

What Norma said surprised me. We spoke for a few minutes and then she said, "You must come and stay with us in Corwall sometime."

After mingling with some other people, I spoke to Norma again - and asked her:

Me: "How has Janet been coping since Martin died?"

Norma: "Lee [one of Martin's carers] has been a great comfort to her. They are probably going to end up together."

Hearing that was like a dagger going straight through my heart and, metaphorically at least, I fell to the ground. I understood then why Janet was acting so out of character towards me.

The next few months weren't easy.

Towards the end of January 2006 after phoning Janet a few times at home and there being no answer, I got through to her and arranged to go and see her at the end of the month.

I don't think Janet had a mobile phone. I remember her saying years earlier, "before mobile phones came along we managed perfectly well without them".

Half an hour after our call she phoned me back:

Janet: "I thought I had better tell you that I've gotten together with Lee."

Me: "I know, your Mum told me at the funeral."

Janet: "Oh."

When I arrived to see her in the evening, Janet and I chatted for a while. She was her normal self with me again, but I felt like I was in bits, trying hard not to show I was upset about her and Lee. I wanted to tell Janet how I felt about her. After a while Janet asked me if I would look after Karen whilst she went and picked up Ben from scouts.

Karen had just turned three years old and was amazing. For the twenty minutes that Janet was gone, I kept Karen enthralled by throwing a McDonald's balloon up in the air.

It made me realise the difference between Janet's kids' upbringing and Clare's. When Clare's children were three, it would have taken more than just a balloon to keep them amused.

Because Ben and Karen didn't have the latest gadgets, perhaps it made them less materialistic than some other children. Ben and Karen valued human interaction more and they knew me.

Strangely, when Janet and Ben returned, Janet ordered Ben to go straight upstairs to bed. She didn't want Ben to come and talk to me for some reason. Ben said hello to me as he walked up the stairs.

After Janet put Karen to bed, we chatted for a bit and she told me more about how Martin died.

She said that Graham pulled over in a lay-by and spent ages trying to get Martin's oxygen machine working again. It must have been a horrendous experience for Graham.

I was not going to say anything about Janet and Lee but a short while later I couldn't stop myself:

Me: "I am surprised about you and Lee..."

Janet: "I would rather not talk about it."

It made the atmosphere uncomfortable and it was time for me to leave.

As I walked out of the house to my car, I knew it would probably be the last time that I saw Janet.

I sat in my car outside the house for a few minutes. I felt absolutely distraught. So many emotions were fighting for attention. On the one hand, what an awful way for Martin to die after he had defied all the odds for someone with MD, living to the age of thirty-one.

On the other, after being friends with Janet for nine years, I hadn't expected our friendship to end. Although I had never told her that I loved her, we got on *so* well that there is no doubt in my mind that she knew how I felt about her and the kids, and she knew what I had hoped would happen.

For years, I had thought about telling Janet that I loved her and wanted to be with her on so many occasions.I never imagined that Janet would get together with one of Martin's carers.

Over the next few weeks, in my distressed state, I called Janet a number of times before she finally answered the phone. I decided that, somehow, I was going to tell her how I felt about her. I knew it was probably fruitless but I had nothing to lose.

It was on a Tuesday evening, towards the end of February, when Janet answered the phone. She didn't want to talk to me:

Janet: "I'm busy packing everything up, as we've got to move out of the house on Saturday."

It was my last opportunity - and I wasted no time.

After putting the phone down, I wrote Janet a letter.

I said I was very upset about Martin dying and I knew she was with Lee now but I wanted to share my feelings for her.

I then continued to write that I had never felt so at ease and comfortable with someone as I did with her. I even wrote that I liked the way she made fun of what it sounded like, when she didn't understand something that I had said.

Ending the letter I said, "I had hoped that one day, I would become like a Dad to Ben and Karen. I would give absolutely anything to be with you all".

I sent the letter and I had done all that I could.

In the second half of March I phoned Norma. One of the first things she said to me was "Janet and Lee have just got married." It felt like another dagger in my heart.

I asked Norma if Janet had said anything about the letter I sent to her and I told her that I had hoped that Janet and I were going to end up together. She said she didn't know anything about my letter.

For the next four months I didn't want to get out of bed. I was dragging myself up in the middle of the afternoon.

At the end of February 2006 the last few people in our old office including me, moved into the new *Shh* office in Brighton. There was a great deal of change at *Shh* at the time and I was mechanically working on a tedious clerical project, which didn't stimulate me at all.

I was forcing myself to work at home on the pointless project I was stuck on at work. After telling my manager Debra I wasn't right for the role and listening to her saying I was doing a good job, rather than finding something else for me to do, I didn't feel that she was in a position to complain about my low productivity.

Another reason why I didn't feel like going into my new office was, since the disbandment of QS, I wasn't part of a physical team in Brighton. Effectively, I was working in my own.

The desk I was allocated in the new office was the closest one to the lift - and I was sitting with a group of women in their forties and fifties, who were always nattering. Also my desk and chair were right next to the all-in-one printer/photocopier/scanner machine which was often breaking down!

With about a hundred people working in an open-plan office, I was constantly in the way of people going to the printer. I kept having to pull myself on my chair into my desk, for people to get past me. It was very annoying and not the best desk for me to sit at. To add insult to injury I rarely used the printer!

I stayed in bed mourning the loss of Martin, but I was much more upset about 'losing' Janet and this in turn made me feel disloyal to Martin. I thought about the years of opportunities missed to try and get together with Janet.

The pain I suffered in those four months was different to the pain I went through after my friendship with Rosie ended in 1993. Unlike Rosie, I had done nothing wrong when my friendship with Janet ended. Janet really hurt me.

What kept me from getting up was the loss of belief that I was going to find the love of my life.

Also, having been very close to Ben and Karen since birth, I felt it unfair on them to not see me anymore. But that's what happens in life. I did think about trying to stay in touch with them through Martins' parents but I felt it was best not to do so.

Phil was the person I shared everything with - and he helped me.

We met for a beer in The Warwick on Tuesday evenings after he finished his radio show at nine o'clock. Every week we had the same exchange and it became like a running joke.

Phil: "Have you been into work this week yet, mate?"

Me: "No not yet, maybe next week."

Matt and Vicky were managing The Warwick at the time. Vicky was nice, she was a bit worried about me being so down and we became text buddies. She texted me filthy jokes!

Normally, I never told Clare or Mum about all of the women I met (and got rejected by), but I did tell them that I had been hoping that Janet and I were going to end up together.

During those tough four months, I was going over to Clare's for dinner once a week but I think she didn't realise how low I was. I simply didn't know what Clare could do to help me. Mum was in Africa at the time which was probably a blessing because I don't think she would have made me feel any better.

All I felt like doing was the Splash sports show on Saturdays, DJing with Phil in The Warwick at the weekends and having a beer with him on Tuesday evenings.

One Saturday evening in May 2006 when Phil and I were in The Warwick as punters, Phil met Kim. She had been out for a meal with her work colleagues and had popped into the pub afterwards. Phil and Kim were both a little drunk and they had a bit of a snog and started seeing each other from that point.

In June, I managed to pull myself out of my emotional hole of despair and went into my 'new' office for the first time since early March.

One of the people that I got on well with in the office was my friend Kwok, who was sitting in a group of six project managers about fifteen feet from my desk. I often chatted with Kwok and got to know the people he was working with.

In the late summer of 2006, the girl who was sitting next to Kwok left the company. It was an ideal desk for me to have. So I went through the bureaucratic process of requesting to be reallocated to that desk.

It took another three to six months before I was allowed to move to a desk fifteen feet from where I was sitting and be out of the way of the printer!

When my desk move request seemed to be stuck 'in the system', I kept phoning and emailing people up the chain of command until my request was approved. I was in the supermarket late one afternoon when the phone rang and I was told, "Yes, you can now move." My persistence had paid off. I knew it would.

In mid-September I decided to phone Norma again. It wasn't a long call. The first thing she blurted out was, "I've just come back from seeing the new baby girl."

On the three occasions that I spoke to Norma she said something which really hurt me.

Not having received a reply from the letter I sent to Janet, I mentioned it again to Norma. She replied bluntly, "Janet's got a new life now, you must carry on with yours."

When Norma said that, all I wanted to do was to get off the phone as quickly as I could.

That was the last time I spoke to Norma and it occurred to me that Janet was probably pregnant when I went to see her at the end of January. The reason why Janet stopped Ben from talking to me was in case he blurted out, "Mum's having a baby". I reflected that Janet *was* wearing a baggy jumper that evening!

I don't know how long it took me to get over Janet because it happened gradually. Having overcome so many tough things in my life, Janet was by far the hardest and it is a testament that I can get over anything in life.

In January 2007 Phil and Kim got married. Andy Lutwyche was Phil's best man and it was a good wedding. I know because I witnessed it! I also managed to fall down a hill at one point!

In my defence, it had been raining and the grass was slippery and I have got CP. Falling over is part of my life and I instinctively know how protect myself in order not to get hurt. The only thing to do when I fall over is to stand back up.

At the wedding, I recall Phil's Mum saying to me "If it wasn't for you, I don't know how Phil would have gotten over Sara." It made me feel very humble because all Phil and I did was talk about all sorts of stuff at Splash and at The Warwick.

The funniest thing at Phil's stag night was his Dad who got a bit drunk. I'm not sure what he rambled on about when I gave him a lift home but he was hilarious.

A few months after the wedding Phil and Kim bought a house and now they have three children. Having known Ross from when he was a young age, I'm pleased for him as he's part of a loving family and he calls Kim 'Mum'.

Phil's desire was to work in radio. So it wasn't long after he started presenting the evening show when Splash launched in 2003, that he quit his job at the Benefits Agency.

He also went into partnership with a guy he knew and opened a record shop in Littlehampton. Phil spent a few years working in the record shop during the day and presenting the evening show on Splash.

When Phil got the opportunity to work full-time at the radio station he sold his half of the record shop to his business partner. He then worked full-time at Splash presenting a daily show and scheduling the Station's music.

Life is about seizing opportunities to do things you love.

Going to The Warwick, meeting so many women and then being rejected by each of them, took its toll on me. It's like being in a boxing match and being constantly knocked down with each rejection and then getting back up and continuing fighting. After each knock down it became a little harder to stand back up.

However I never gave up and nor will I. What keeps me going is my belief that I am going to meet the right person for me. Without that belief, I couldn't keep going.

It became harder going to the pub every weekend just to meet women. At the time I thought, 'I'm not going to meet anyone sitting at home' and I kept thinking, 'All I've got to do is meet one woman who can see that I'm a nice guy and who can see past my crutches and funny voice.'

I usually met someone at The Warwick who I had a meaningless kiss with.

The other thing I used to think, after every rejection, was, 'I'm not nice enough' so I did everything I could to negate this including buying drinks and giving them a lift home.

In The Warwick I bumped into Zoe, who I went to school with, and another Zoe who was on my college course.

I was on the lookout for a girlfriend everywhere I went.

After having a meal out with Phil where an Eastern European waitress was extremely flirtatious with me, I plucked up all of my courage the next day, went back to the restaurant and asked her if she would like to have a coffee with me. She thanked me and said she was very flattered but that she had a boyfriend.

Although it was disappointing, I was pleased that I seized the opportunity.

I often spoke to Ray about my desire to find someone to share my life with. As a practising Christian, Ray believed that Christian woman would see past my CP and suggested I go to church with him and his family on Sundays. The invitation was extended a number of times so I went on a couple of occasions.

While walking to Splash one Saturday lunchtime in the Guildbourne Centre in 2009, a woman about my age came up to me:

Emily: "Have you got Cerebral Palsy?"

Me: "Yes."

Emily: "So have I,"

She was shopping with her Mum and we chatted for a few minutes. Emily mentioned that she worked in the leisure industry and she seemed to be really impressed with me.

I found her inspiring because she was very active and didn't let her condition stop her. The only outward sign of her CP was a slight limp.

The last thing Emily said to me was: "I'll see you around and will take you for a drink next time I see you."

No more than a minute later after we said goodbye, I started kicking myself, metaphorically speaking of course! I wish I had replied, "No, I'll take you for a drink! What's your number?"

I became determined to find Emily. The following week, after I had phoned three places where I thought Emily might be working, Ray suggested sending an email to the Letters' Page of the local newspaper. I thought, 'It's a waste of time, nobody reads the Letters' Page in the local newspaper' but I thought it was worth a try. So I sent a short email and it was printed.

Two guys phoned me as a result. One knew Emily's parents but didn't know where they lived. The other guy gave me her parents' address.

One of the most nerve-racking and desperate things I've done in life was when I knocked on Emily's parent's front door holding a copy of the Letters' Page with my email in it. I could feel my heart pumping and my legs were so stiff, I could hardly walk. But it was something I had to do.

Her Mum opened the door and recognised me. I explained why I was there and gave her the Letters' Page. She invited me in and was impressed by my efforts to find Emily. She said Emily was at work but she would ask her to call me. Walking out of the house I felt really pleased with what I had done.

Emily called me and we had a good conversation. We were going to meet up but I think I seemed too eager in my subsequent text messages because Emily didn't get back to me.

Having made so much effort, I felt really deflated. I didn't know about pushing and pulling but after my email was printed in the newspaper five people asked me if I had found Emily! It surprised me that people do actually read the Letters' Page in local newspapers.

Early in 2008 when Phil and I turned up to DJ one Friday evening, we were surprised to learn that Jim and Harry were no longer there and they had been replaced with Kirsty. It was a shame but Kirsty was a good manager and we got on well with her.

My tenure as the Saturday night DJ came to an end in shocking fashion in May when, just after I had played my last song at 2am, Kirsty came up to the DJ booth with tears in her eyes, and sacked me.

She said it was because the owner of the pub wanted someone who could use the microphone. Sacking me wasn't an easy thing for Kirsty to do and she was extremely apologetic and in tears. I felt sorry for her so I gave her a hug and told her not to worry about it.

It wasn't an easy thing for me to get over because it was blatant discrimination. I wrote the owner a very diplomatic letter but he never replied to it.

Ironically, 'Warwick Avenue' by Duffy was in the charts at the time. It's not a bad record but her track 'Mercy' is better.

I continued to DJ with Phil for a couple of months until, one evening I deleted everything I had put onto The Warwick's laptop.

One of the bouncers came up to the DJ booth just as I deleted the last folder. After I had explained my actions he asked me to leave the pub and I was barred from The Warwick!

I was well aware of the probable consequences of my action. I had reached the end of my tolerance for going to The Warwick every weekend and meeting so many drunk women there.

I got a real buzz both from working at Splash and DJing at The Warwick. However, I much preferred working in radio because it was more creative and it relied on teamwork.

After I was sacked and barred from The Warwick, I joined City Socialising (CS) in Brighton, a social networking website that organises local group meet-up events.

I was going to CS events (pub meet-ups, parties, restaurants) two or three times a week. I was doing exactly the same thing as I had done at The Warwick, which was meeting (and then being rejected by) drunk women, some of whom got me to dance with them.

All I can say now is, at the time I didn't know any differently. Another thing I've learnt in property investment is doing the same thing over and over again and expecting a different result is madness.

Writing about the five years I spent going out, specifically searching for a girlfriend, I find it hard to put into words the colossal amount of physical energy I used. Talking with people while standing up and dancing takes enormous stamina for me.

Even more draining was the emotional energy it took after every rejection I encountered. I always bounced back despite this and carried on. It has to do with something about my mindset, which I discovered in 2011.

Another activity I did in 2009 was online-dating. One evening, shortly after I joined the website, I got chatting on the site's instant messaging system to an Eastern European woman who lived in Worthing. She was my age, had a little boy and was divorced from an Englishman.

Our conversation lasted for over two hours and it was going extremely well, until it became clear that she was keen to meet up for a coffee. I hadn't told her yet that I had CP. I did so in the most gentle and positive way I could, including, "...it doesn't stop me from doing anything in life."

To which she replied "I've had a hard life and want to enjoy the rest of it. I don't want to be held back. I'm sorry." And she went offline.

I then spent another two hours writing her a positive email, explaining how I don't let anything hold me back in life, only to discover when I tried to send it via the website's email system that she had blocked me from sending her messages. She was obviously an experienced online-dater!

Another person I met on the dating site was a Ghanaian woman of my age, doing a Master's degree in Brighton. I told her about my CP from the start and we spent three months emailing each other, during which time I sent flowers on her birthday and Valentine's Day, which she appreciated. We spoke on the phone a couple of times and arranged to meet. Then at the last minute, she said that she wasn't ready for a relationship.

The couple of people I told about my online-dating experiences said things like "You haven't tried very hard…" I don't think they realised how much physical time and effort I put into the process of writing emails and how much emotional pain it caused me.

# Chapter 4

This chapter includes the following sections:

- *Shh* - 2004 to 2009
- Radio 2007 to 2009
- Antiguan holidays 2004 to 2008

Ever since I started at *Shh* in 2001, they always seemed to be restructuring things and, as one voluntary redundancy programme closed, another one would open - at least in the part of the company that I was in. Gordon often thought about applying for voluntary redundancy.

Also, two or three years after I joined the business, they started gradually moving teams of people out of our office into other offices.

Managing and developing Login Manager and Job Builder was for the most part good fun. It involved working with lots of people (database administrators aka DBAs and server guys) who managed the upkeep of the databases and the servers they ran on. The people I liaised with respected me because they knew I was good at my job as well as being a conscientious person.

In 2004 I remember having a long phone conversation with Jimmy, one of the DBAs I worked with, about mortgages! Having recently re-mortgaged my flat, I was really interested in mortgages! Jimmy was a really good guy; he went out of his way to help me when I needed something doing on a database, which was out of my scope.

People who don't know the difference tend think that a database programmer and a database administrator are the same job. They are not. Here's a good way to define the difference between the two roles: think of a database as a baby - a programmer is the parent of the baby, whilst an administrator is the midwife or doctor.

I re-mortgaged my flat with a mortgage that had no limits on overpayments and in 2004 I started making monthly overpayments on my mortgage.

One of the things I hated doing most working on 24/7 applications at *Shh* was deploying enhancement updates to the applications on the live servers.

It first involved having to submit a bureaucratic Update Request (UR) online, in order to gain approval to deploy an update!

A UR was an absolute pain to complete and to get approved. It involved supplying copious information detailing why the update was needed, the exact steps involved in deploying the update, a back-out plan, and a list of the teams involved who individually had to approve the UR.

It took me ages to write a UR. Once submitted, it was left to faceless people sitting around a table once a week to approve or reject URs. If anything was missing or slightly incorrect the UR would get rejected and you had to go through the whole process again.

URs were like having an insurance policy. However I found them extremely irritating - especially when it was just to upload a file onto a server which would not cause any kind of outage to the application. URs often turned a two minute job into a two week job. I admit that, occasionally, I just didn't raise a UR!

As more and more people were relocating to other offices, our team got moved to the other side of the first floor. Annoyingly, my new desk was considerably further to walk to than my old desk.

I went through the formal procedure of requesting that our team be moved. It took three months for us to get the authorisation but it was worth it as my new desk was even closer to the lift!

Normally, when it came to going on courses, I was the one who booked the course and Gordon authorised it for me. However, when I asked Gordon if I could go on an advanced Windows course, for some reason, he was the one who booked me onto it, whilst I booked a hotel.

The nearest course was in Stockport, near Manchester. I contemplated flying up to Manchester or going by train but my course was four days long and having to get taxis to and from my hotel would have been a real hassle.

So I decided to drive to Stockport which also made it easy to go into Manchester in the evenings.

After the six hour drive, I arrived at the hotel in Stockport at about 11pm, only to discover that the hotel had been overbooked and they didn't have a room for me. The hotel staff recommended another hotel nearby.

The hotel they recommended was in fact a small pub with three bedrooms downstairs. It was the best place I ever stayed at for work as it wasn't far to walk and the food and staff were great!

At the end of the first day of my course, I phoned Gordon:

Me: "You will never believe it..."

Gordon: "What's up?"

Me; "I'm on the wrong bloody course! I'm on a course all about IP addresses!"

Gordon: "Oh - can't you transfer onto the Windows course?"

Me: "No, that course was last week!"

Gordon: "Oh well, just enjoy the course you're on then!"

Four days of learning how IP addresses are constructed was quite interesting - but I don't remember any of it now!

Manchester was good fun too. I went into the City three times. One evening, I ate in a dingy basement pancake house which had orange walls. The pancakes were good though!

Gordon, Nigel and I attended an overnight QS meeting in Bournemouth. On the way back from Bournemouth we stopped off in Chichester for something to eat. Nigel and I were walking to the café after Gordon had dropped us off and was parking the car, when we saw Liz Matthews walking towards us. She was one of my Second Year tutors at Brighton University in 1995! We chatted for a few minutes and I discovered she was now lecturing in Chichester.

Not having seen Liz since my university days it was a chance in a million to bump into her like that. It's what's known as the

Chaos Theory. With billions of people running around the world, people who know each other can randomly bump into each other somewhere unexpected.

In the first half of my time at *Shh*, I leant some HTML and built a simple website. HTML is not difficult to understand but it is very tedious and I don't know why someone would choose to write raw HTML. I always thought building websites was too arty-farty for me.

However when one of the guys who worked on the QS helpdesk in Cambridge wanted to get into web design, I quasi-mentored him to build a website for Login Manager. As we worked well together, it was fun and a win-win situation for both of us.

Working on Login Manager, Amanda and I had a brilliant working relationship. We were on the same wavelength and got to know each other well. We mostly communicated via instant messenger.

I told her about meeting and being rejecting by a load of women. To which she replied, "Well, there's nothing wrong with the way you flirt!" Amanda told me that she was going through a divorce and some other really personal stuff. She said she needed "constant stimulation in every sense", to which I replied, "You're too much for me to handle!"

When Amanda felt down sometimes I phoned her up. She was one of the easiest people to make laugh. In my slightly comical manner I said things such as:

Me: "Hello, what's happening? Oh no - you're not going to start laughing again, are you?"

It immediately started her off laughing - so I carried on:

Me: "Why is it that every time we speak all you do is laugh? Do you find my voice funny?!"

Amanda [laughing] "No..."

Me: "Come on, let it all out. You know you want to..."

Me [when Amanda quietened down]: "Is that it or have you got some more left in you?! [which started her off again] Oh no, here we go again..."

Me: "You're just a laughing machine, aren't you..."

Me: "I haven't got all day...I have got work to do, you know..."

It was very funny and could go on a while.

My happiest time at *Shh* was when I was working with Amanda.

Life can be odd sometimes. For over two years Amanda and I got on so well and laughed a lot. Then, one day during one of our humorous and flirtatious instant messenger conversations, I typed a short sentence without thinking about it. It was so easily done and I instantly wished I hadn't typed it.

I don't remember what I wrote but I hinted that I fancied her. Amanda asked me to clarify what I meant.

Sitting in my open-plan office, it was a very surreal moment. I could feel the blood draining from my face and I felt like shouting out "Help me - I've just messed things up with Amanda."

In the absence of a reply Amanda typed, "Well?"

I felt under pressure and so with my tail between my legs I wrote, "Although I know it will never happen, I would quite like to be with you."

I had never seriously thought about getting together with Amanda. Intellectually we were well suited but physically we were unalike. She was a giant in stature compared to me and she lived hours away. She also wore a lot of make-up and was a bit materialistic for my taste.

However, Amanda had a good heart. Without thinking, I felt sorry for her as she was going through a messy divorce and I wanted to help her.

Over the next few days, I profusely apologised and reassured her that I wasn't attracted to her. I was so persistent in asking Amanda if we could go back to the way things were that she blocked me on her instant messenger account!

At some point Amanda came back with, "Anyway, you said that I was too much for you to handle."

It's funny writing about it now because the error of my ways are blindingly obvious. I was so naive and eager back then.

When Amanda cut me off from instant messenger, this hurt me even more and I really beat myself up for messing up. After about a month, she unblocked me and we rebuilt a good working relationship, but it was never as good as before.

That is what I don't like about instant messenger, text messages and sometimes even emails. It is so easy to write something without thinking about it and being misunderstood when communicating without facial interaction or verbal intonation.

One of the contractors who came and went from our team in Brighton was Richard. He was a great bloke, with good people and analytical skills, and having travelled the globe, he reminded me of my friend John Potts.

Another contractor was Bob, who we hired to replace somebody who was leaving. Bob started on a Monday after Gordon departed on holiday. Covering for Gordon, I didn't have much to do with Bob because he was shadowing the contractor who was leaving.

On the Wednesday after Bob started, I received a call from Jo at the agency through which Bob was contracted, who had left a voicemail on Gordon's mobile. Jo informed me that Bob was unwilling to sign his contract.

Shortly afterwards, Gordon phoned me from his holiday in Spain. He advised me: "Have a word with Bob and see if he's got a problem. If he still won't sign his contract, he's got to leave immediately."

First, I phoned Jo back and told her about what I was about to do.

Knowing what I had to do, I was feeling a little nervous. As Bob was a well-built biker, I thought he might hit me!

Adrenaline pumping, I walked the two rows of desks to where he was sitting.

Me: ""Bob, can I have a quick word with you please."

Bob: "Yes, sure."

He followed me back to my desk and I took my time in sitting down. Bob stood beside my desk and looking him in the eye, we had this very calm exchange.

Me: "I've had a call from Jo and from Gordon, and I understand you haven't signed your contract yet...?

Bob: "My wife handles all such matters, and when she tells me not to sign a contract, I don't sign it."

Me: "If you're unwilling to sign your contract, I need to ask you to leave immediately."

Bob: "No problem. I'll pack my things up and go now."

Me: "Thank you very much."

And with that he packed his stuff up, picked up his helmet, said goodbye to the team and left.

A few minutes later I phoned the security guard on the front desk downstairs, to check that Bob had left the building and I told him not to let Bob back in! I then phoned Jo.

It wasn't a standard afternoon at work. I was pleased with how I handled the situation and the rest of the team seemed to respect me for the rest of the afternoon. Gordon phoned me toward the end of the day and asked me about it.

Later in 2004 Charlie turned up one day out of the blue and decided to sit himself at the desk next to Nigel. Having previously contracted for *Shh* before I joined the company, Charlie was working for a QS manager elsewhere in the country. Nigel and Charlie appeared to be best buddies.

For some reason, Charlie took an instant and absolute dislike to me. For the few months he was sitting with us he was rude and verbally abusive towards me. I don't know what he said because he wouldn't tell me, but Charlie said something extremely derogatory about me one morning before I got into the office.

Charlie was the most arrogant person I've ever met. He had an air of superiority, as if he was the best software developer that ever lived. Even Neighbour and Giles thought Charlie was a pillock.

He wasn't one who suffered fools gladly, which is why I found it strange that Charlie got on so well with Nigel. Nigel must have really helped him out at some point.

Having learnt a lot about people and their psychology since 2010, I now understand why bullies and emotional controllers act the way they do. They are people, who inwardly, feel powerless and worthless. In consequence, they feel the need exert authority outwardly.

Bullies thrive on provoking reactions. The way to stop a person from bullying you is to not react to them. It's as simple as that.

Back in 2004, I hadn't been enjoying my job for a while. I don't recall it being due to me messing up with Amanda but this might have contributed to my unhappiness.

I was fed up with working with people who didn't seem to respect me. I didn't see why I had to put up with the atmosphere that I was enduring from Neighbour, Giles, Nigel and Charlie.

Gordon was shocked when I told him I would like to find another role in *Shh*.

Gordon: "Is it because of Charlie? I'll tell him that he can't work with us, if it is."

Me: "It's not just him."

I didn't know what role I wanted to do but I wanted to work with spreadsheets and people. In speaking to a few people, they advised me that it sounded like a role in finance.

After emailing KC's PA, I went to see KC. It was good seeing him again. Over a coffee, I explained my unhappiness and asked him if he could find me some sort of financial role, involving people and spreadsheets. He said he would have a look around and see what he could find. I don't remember KC ever getting back to me.

When I went to see KC he said to me: "You've got a job for life here but maybe at some point, you might want to do something else and decide to leave."

Towards the end of 2004, Charlie left *Shh* and got a permanent job in another part of the country.

Coincidentally, not long afterwards, Nigel also left *Shh*. Charlie got Nigel a job working for him. This really surprised me. I thought Nigel would work for *Shh* until he retired and didn't think he had the confidence to do anything else. Nigel sold his house in Brighton and moved his family to where his new job was.

In early 2005, the part of *Shh* I worked in underwent a major restructuring as they started to outsource technical work. The transformation included disbanding all of the QS teams around the UK. It took place gradually and wasn't totally unexpected, but for a few months people felt in limbo.

After thirty-six years with the company and having contemplated it for a couple of years, Gordon took voluntary redundancy and left *Shh* at the end of March 2005.

Having worked with Gordon for four years it was strange to see him go. However, I didn't feel at all dependent on him. Gordon had given me a lot of freedom and opportunities to take things on, but I felt he didn't totally respect me. He often had a jibe at me because I didn't have a girlfriend.

Around the time that Gordon left I was busy packaging up (writing documentation for) Login Manager and Job Builder. The two applications were due to be outsourced and I had to hand them over to Doug, as the QS team in Cambridge were funnelling all of the apps for outsourcing.

Handing over Login Manager didn't bother me too much. In the two and half years of working on it, I had learnt all that I could from it and I had become bored of it. More of a shame was the fact that Amanda and I naturally lost touch.

Along with massive restructure and outsourcing, was the introduction of 'the bench' and of the three month assignment model.

Gone were the days when people were part of a permanent team. Instead the new regime dictated that people would go onto a three month assignment or project and work for an assignment manager for the duration of the assignment.

If you were any good and while there was still a demand for you, three month assignments turned into rolling assignments.

A few weeks after I had handed over Login Manager and Job Builder to Doug's team, it was decided from above that the information that Job Builder contained was too sensitive for the application to be outsourced. Rather than giving Job Builder back to me, the gits kept it for themselves to manage.

It meant that I was project-less and in consequence I was assigned to the bench where there were many other employees who had handed over their projects for outsourcing.

An internal website containing available assignments was updated daily, which employees who were on the bench could apply for. The other purpose of the bench was to retain staff to do roles which were in demand. While on the bench, people had a bench manager, whose role it was to help people find an assignment or to expedite retraining.

There was a prevailing expectation that people could relocate elsewhere in the UK to do a three month assignment. However that expectation didn't seem to apply to me.

My first stint on the bench lasted over six months. At first, not having much to do was good fun. But after about three weeks, it became more and more demoralising. Most of the available assignments were clerical or location specific.

To get a good appraisal every three months, I just had to be seen to be proactively looking for an assignment. This led to me applying for assignments that I knew I wouldn't get.

The other change which took place in late 2005 was that my Brighton office was being closed down.

Another faceless, contactless manager decided to allocate me to an office in another part of Brighton. To get to the new office I was going to have to go on the seafront road, doubling my journey to work to forty minutes.

However my bench manager was an excellent guy. He didn't find me an assignment but with the prospect of the more distant office, he had no issue when I asked to become an 'occasional home-worker'. It meant I got free broadband and a home phone line and could work from home whenever I wanted. I was doing this already but having broadband made it much easier.

Towards the end of 2005, I attended a *Shh* health and safety workshop day, where I met a lady. In chatting to her we had the following exchange:

Me: "I'm looking for a technical assignment using spreadsheets."

Lady: "Jodie who works for me is doing a project involving spreadsheets. I'll tell her about you."

Over the next day or two I received a call from Jodie, who arranged to come and see me in Brighton.

For the next six months, I found myself stuck on the most boring and pointless project I ever did at *Shh* and which caused me slight repetitive strain injury (RSI).

It was a clerical project, auditing computers which hadn't logged onto the network for over six months. From a register we could see who each computer was allocated to, then emailing them to complete an online survey!

The survey was to ascertain if they still needed the computer and encouraging them to raise a disposal order for it. Each computer in the company had a service contract and by raising a disposal order for a PC it cancelled its service contract, thus saving the business money.

Some people had more than one PC. In my case, for example, I had a laptop and a test PC server in the office and a desktop PC at home. There was also an old laptop sitting in the cupboard at work. Jodie nearly had a fit when she saw the four PC servers piled on top of each other on the desk next to me.

Her opinion was, 'it's one computer per person'. However, she didn't have a software development background and didn't realise the need to have test servers. I did dispose of the four PC servers next to me as well as the laptop in the cupboard.

I knew Jodie and I weren't going to get on well when she came to see me on day one. When she mentioned she was a golf fanatic, it was my cue to tell her my infamous golf joke:

Me: "I've never played golf before but think I would score quite highly at it because I've got a good handicap!"

Jodie didn't even crack a smile. She responded, "Err, yes, well, anyway, on with the project..."

I think it's safe to say that I'm unlikely to get on well with someone who doesn't find my golf joke funny.

I believed that the project wasn't cost effective. There were three of us on it and I calculated the cost of having three people on the project far exceeded the money being saved by the number of service contracts being cancelled.

In my first week on the project, I emailed Jodie, "Why don't you just cancel the service contracts of all the computers which haven't logged onto the network in the last six months and then reinstate the contracts individually when someone phones up the support desk, needing help with one of the PCs in question?"

My idea would have saved *Shh* thousands of pounds.

Jodie's response remains one of the most baffling things anyone has ever said to me. She replied, "It doesn't work like that."

Jodie thought the project was the most important thing since sliced bread and she probably didn't appreciate me implying that it was pointless.

From the age of twelve, I realised that it is people who make the world go round, and over the years I have achieved a great deal just by speaking to someone who has got authority and common sense to make my ideas happen.

Every day at *Shh* everyone received at least one or two corporate emails. I received so many that I didn't bother reading most of them. The email we were sending to people, asking them to fill in a survey, looked like a less official version of these corporate emails. We didn't have the authority to force anyone to do anything.

A lot of people we emailed didn't do anything. Most of my time was spent typing replies to idiotic responses people emailed us. Excel was being used as nothing more than a data sort and cleanse filter.

After three weeks on the project I had had enough of it. I sent Jodie an apologetic email, explaining that I physically wasn't up to doing the project as I was suffering from RSI and I wasn't enjoying the project. I asked her to let me go back on the bench, as I had only processed nineteen PCs that week.

Jodie replied "You're doing great Patrick, that's nineteen computers that I haven't got to deal with." And she told me to not do so much typing!

I was so astounded by her patronising and irresponsible reply that I lost any motivation for the project.

After spending years managing and developing two 24/7 systems, having done project management, deputising for Gordon, interviewing contractors and much more, it was demoralising.

In hindsight, I wish I had refused to do any more work on the project as it would have removed me from this pointless project sooner.

This is the point in 2006 where I didn't feel like getting out of bed for four months.

I don't know how I stayed on the project for six months before going back on the bench.

After Gordon left *Shh*, the only people remaining from my QS team were Mick, Giles and Neighbour. Shortly before I moved to my new office, Mick and Giles didn't have their contracts renewed and left the company. Neighbour moved to one of the other offices.

Life in my new office became enjoyable when I moved desks and sat next to Kwok. I was sitting with five project managers who all respected me. They regularly made coffee and I often helped them to do things on their PCs.

The kitchen was close enough to make myself a cup of tea which I carried back to my desk in a travel mug.

Sitting on the other side of Kwok was Jack, who I also got on very well with. I often told people "Do you know Jack is twenty years and one week older than me and he started working at *Shh* before I was born!" It became a running joke.

The new office was smaller than the old one. It was a rectangular building, about thirty metres long, with stairs at each end and a lift in the centre of it. There were about a hundred people on the first floor of the open-plan building. I became well known in the office. People often came and chatted to me.

At some point, James, a health and safety guy, decided to do an assessment on how long it would take me to evacuate the building.

Amazingly, James was happy to let me walk down the stairs! Unlike most buildings, where there are two standard flights of stairs, the ground floor of our office was a warehouse area with a high ceiling. It meant there were three standard flights of stairs between the first and ground floor.

James timed how long it took me to get out of the building and I treated it as if it were a personal challenge! Had I gone too fast, I would have fallen over and it would have been a health and safety disaster!

As I made my way to the stairs and hurried the fifteen metres past people sitting at their desks, they looked at me as if to say, "What are you doing up here?!"

Me: "I can't talk now, I'm on a mission!"

As I arrived at the stairwell, I was a bit out of breath.

James: "Have a little rest. The stairwell is fireproof for thirty minutes."

I thought: 'In the event of a fire, I'm not going to put your theory to the test!'

It was important to me to walk down the stairs as fast as I could, whilst doing so in a controlled manner, so as not to fall. The handrail on the left hand side helped.

I walked down each flight of stairs in thirty seconds and made it out of the building in under three minutes. I was really happy with that result, as was James.

I went back up in the lift. It felt worth the forty minutes it took for my asthma to dissipate.


In my ten years at *Shh* James was the only person who 'allowed' me to tackle stairs. It felt like everyone else there wanted to wrap me up in cotton wool.

It's amusing to reflect how in 2001, Gordon was adamant that I couldn't walk down two flights of stairs! It's not unusual to get a different answer when asking two people the same question.

As I am still in touch with some of my old QS colleagues, we occasionally meet up. Some years ago we met in a busy Brighton pub for a Christmas meal. As there was nowhere to sit we stood around for ages having a beer.

With my legs feeling tired, I was struggling to walk up the stairs to the dining area. Having already had a slight difference of opinion with Gordon as to whether I could get up the stairs. I had negotiated the second step but hadn't yet got into my stride, when Gordon REALLY pissed me off:

Gordon: "Patrick, you can't climb the stairs."

Had it not been for Gordon, I would have walked up the stairs.

What he said made my whole body tense up and made me feel like having a massive argument with him. However, not wanting to create a scene, I kept my composure and we went somewhere else to eat.

I know that I inspire Gordon but the same cannot always be said about him.

Back in 2006, my second stretch on the bench lasted several months. During this time I went and had another coffee with KC. He advised me, "There are a lot of changes happening at the moment. Be patient and wait and see what happens."

I nearly got myself an exciting permanent technical role. Having come across a guy who gave me two phone interviews, he said, "You're good and I would like you to join my team. I just need to get the funding approved to take you on." A week or so later he phoned me back and said, "Sorry, I can't get the funding authorised..." It was a disappointment.

My second bench manager wasn't as good as the first one. He decided it would be a good idea to send me on two five-day courses to do a technical role which involved travelling around the UK.

Me: "I don't see myself travelling around the UK somehow."

Bench manager: "Don't worry, we'll find you a desk-based role."

Out of the thirteen people who went on the two courses, only four or five got a role as a result of the training.

A few weeks after the courses, my bench manager found himself on the bench (it wasn't anything to do with me)!

On the courses I met my friend Ernie, who is one of the funniest people I ever met. Every time we subsequently spoke on the phone, hilarity ensued. I must give him a call!

If you are familiar with the TV programme 'Grumpy Old Men', Ernie should take part in that show!

As a London resident, Ernie told me about the time he received a ticket after being caught on CCTV driving in a bus lane. He had gone into the bus lane to let an ambulance get past him. However, rather than going into the bus lane and stopping while the ambulance went past, he drove in the bus lane until the ambulance had gone past! Ernie wasn't a happy chappy about that ticket incident!

My second assignment materialised in 2007, when Doug recommended me for the role. Doug was working for Cath but was scheduled to move onto another project himself. My assignment was an application support role. Unlike application development, the role didn't involve much hardcore programming.

Cath worked in a long rectangular building in Cambridge. I went to meet her and to take over the support of five applications. I thought highly of Cath when she said to me:

Cath: "I've never managed someone who's disabled before, I hope I do a good job."

Me: "I'm sure you will do fine. I'm not worried about it."

I worked for Cath for about two and a half years and we got on well. In fact, Cath was the best manager I had at *Shh*. She was two years older than me and, no, I didn't fancy her.

As well as meeting Cath, I spent three days in Cambridge going through the applications I was taking over. There were four from a contractor who was leaving the company and a VB application which Doug was doing. In going over it with me Doug said, "Don't worry, I'll finish off writing the app before handing it over, all you'll need to do is support it."

It felt a bit daunting taking over five apps which I knew little about. However, shortly after I took them on, two of the web-based systems got decommissioned. One of them didn't have any users and the other one didn't appear to be online and nobody could find where the server was!

Over the next two and a half years I handed over the remaining three apps to other support teams. Cath was good, she let me get on with my work and I contacted her when I needed her managerial assistance.

The VB app which Doug handed over to me before he moved onto another role, didn't work! As Doug was a highly experienced and in demand developer, he had a high workload and it sometimes caused the quality of what he did to suffer.

To make matters worse, I couldn't even debug and step through the source code properly to see what the problems were. When stepping through the code, it crashed out at a certain point, producing a cryptic error message. I knew the problem was something to do with my PC but I didn't know what it was.

This is where no longer being in a team of developers falls down. The only help I had was Google and I became very good at Googling the solution to error messages. However, this spurious error message took me five frustrating days to find the solution for. When I found it, my week of frustration turned into a eureka moment! I needed to install onto my PC a VB component specifically for Doug's application.

In the meantime, my first conference call with the customer was a bit hairy because they were expecting Doug's application to work! On the call I said, "I'm having a bit of a problem getting the app to run on my PC at the moment, but I'm working on it..." I got the impression everyone thought, 'Does this idiot know what he's doing!'

However, once the missing component was installed, I quickly debugged and fixed the problems. I then went onto make several enhancements to the app and the customer was very happy with me.

Another system which I was supporting was a completely over-engineered MS Access 97 database. I had never done anything on it when I got a call from one of the women who used it expecting me to fix it post-haste.

When I initially tried to log on to the system I discovered that I hadn't been given the correct password to access the machine the database was on! The group of women who used that database weren't very computer literate and at one point I thought I was going to have to drive to Wales to change a password!

Instead, I found someone in the Welsh office who was computer literate enough to talk through changing the password and this produced another eureka moment!

The database was used twice daily for data-entry and it had a button which emailed the data to a distribution list. The users reported that the system was running so slowly that it was unusable.

When I looked in the Access 97 database, it had many thousands of records going back years and the users didn't have the facility to delete any data. In deleting many old records, I made several women very happy!

The third system I had was a website with an Oracle database. The customer was a good bloke and I spent most of my time on this app. I learnt ASP (a web-based language) from it and made a lot of enhancements to the system.

While working for Cath, I heard that Amanda had left the company. I found her on Facebook, we had a nice chat and she said she was getting remarried and I wished her the best.

Sometime In 2007 Kwok took voluntary redundancy from *Shh* and then easily found a more fulfilling job in London. He had become very bored and de-motivated at *Shh*.

In a way, it was a shame to see Kwok leave *Shh* but I got on well with the other people I was sitting with, especially Jack. He often asked me to assist him with something on his PC. I didn't mind helping him, but took the step of installing PC Anywhere on his computer. It meant I didn't need to go over to Jack's desk every time he wanted my help. I just connected to his computer from my laptop.

Roger was another person who was very funny in the office. After 6pm, when most people had left the office, Roger frequently came over and chatted to me and Jack. I got into the habit and the challenge of seeing how long I could keep Roger engaged in a conversation. It was good fun and made the three of us laugh. I recall my record was forty-two minutes one evening!

Every week for the five or six years I worked with Jack, I brought one or two packets of biscuits for the team I sat with.

Jack often thought about taking voluntary redundancy but said he wanted to do so in 2013 which marked his 40th anniversary at *Shh*.

Jack is a family man but after 6pm his funny mindset would often surface.

While working for Cath, I was called upon to spend two weeks in Cambridge. It was to go through Login Manager, handing it over to two guys who came over from India. Fortunately, I got a couple of months' notice, because it took nearly that long to get the use of a mobility scooter authorised.

I needed a scooter because the distance in the long building Cath worked in necessitated it. My idea was to hire a scooter for two weeks and store and recharge it overnight in the main reception building, where I could park my car. It was a simple idea but, of course, I had to overcome several health and safety objections.

After finding a company who could hire out and deliver a scooter to Cambridge, Health and Safety said I wouldn't be able to use the scooter because I wasn't insured to use it, so I got some public liability insurance.

Then Health and Safety said it wouldn't be safe to keep the scooter overnight in the 24/7-manned reception area because it could get stolen! Another objection was that it wouldn't be safe to plug the charger into the mains!

I just kept going until I got to someone with authority and common sense who said, "Yes, you can do that." Another eureka moment! Cath was very supportive of my endeavours.

I really enjoyed spending two weeks in Cambridge, working with the two Indian guys and scootering around the place! It felt good to easily get to where I had to go - and the canteen. I drove home at the weekend and did the sports show on Splash.

Having worked with several Indians over the years, they are amongst the nicest, hardest working and most respectful people I have worked with. Given the choice, I would much rather work with Indians than some English IT people.

After I looked into whether voice-activated software would make it easier for me to do word processing, Cath thought it would be a good idea for me to be assessed to see if I needed any special equipment in the workplace. Other than finding out more about voice-activated software, I didn't feel I needed any special equipment.

Nevertheless Cath was keen for me to be assessed and accordingly, a bloke from an external company spent a morning with me in my Brighton office, asking me a load of questions. A week or so later, I received a twelve-page document from him.

I was shocked when I read his recommendations. His report implied I was far more disabled than I am and that I should have all sorts of equipment that I didn't need! His recommendations included a special office chair and something to put my feet on underneath my desk. I have known from a young age that the best sitting position for me is upright, with my feet flat on the floor.

It took me two hours to highlight all of the misleading information in the document. I sent it back to him. He apologised and said he would correct it. I never heard back from him again!

When Cath said the report would go onto my HR record, I contacted HR, told them the report was a load of rubbish and ensured they didn't attach it to my file. I emailed the highlighted document to Clare because I knew she would find it funny!

The only recommendation that I tried using after much persuasion from Cath, was for me to order a left-handed keyboard.

At a cost of £98 the left handed keyboard was cheaply made. The 'clickiness' of the keys was so loud it disturbed the people I was sitting with in the office!

After about half an hour I reverted back to using my other keyboard. It would have taken some time to get used to using a left handed keyboard and having used a standard keyboard at home, and several of them at Splash and elsewhere in the world, it would have been more trouble than it was worth.

I have often found in life that it's easier to learn to use standard things, rather than adapting everything around me. It makes the world accessible. It's like stairs - they are everywhere and the fact that I can use them, enables me to get anywhere.

Cath and I did have one difference of opinion, but in retrospect I really appreciate her nagging me to try to use voice-activated software. I didn't do so. I had the attitude, "I've got more important and proper work to do."

Writing about it now, tapping away with one index finger on my keyboard, I regret not taking that opportunity and investing the time to learn how to use voice-activated software. I think it would make my life considerably easier. It's something that I would like to learn to use. It takes time to set up and train.

It's a bit late now that I'm writing a book!

Our difference of opinion came one late Friday morning after I mentioned that I had worked late, on my own, in the office one evening. I mentioned it, hoping it would help with my appraisal. However it completely backfired on me.

Cath: "You can't work in the office on your own."

Me: "Why not?"

Cath: "What happens if you fall over and knock yourself out?"

Me: "Don't be silly, I've never fallen over and knocked myself out. I've hardly ever fallen over in the office [due to the magnetic force holding me up at work!]. I can get myself back up when I fall over. It doesn't worry me."

Cath: "I don't want you working in the office on your own anymore."

Our conversation continued for a short while until I agreed with her. I felt Cath had slightly overreacted and she was creating an issue unnecessarily. However, we agreed that we had reached the end of the matter.

At work I hardly ever took a lunch break, I just ate sandwiches at my desk. Every three to six months I met Stuart for lunch in Brighton. Stuart often gave me some fatherly advice.

As arranged, after my conversation with Cath, I went and met Stuart for lunch. Returning to the office that Friday afternoon, I was feeling in wind-down mode ahead of the weekend. I wasn't expecting an email from Cath, which said:

"I've been thinking about you working late in the office and I'm not happy about it. This is what I want you to do, phone me on my mobile when you are working late and then phone me again once you're in your car and about to leave the office."

Cath's email made smoke come out of my ears! What also annoyed me was it was the implication that she didn't care what might happen after I got into my car – or about me falling over at home. Technically, when working from home, my flat was also my workplace!

After reading her email, I phoned Cath and left her a curt voicemail. Realising I wasn't happy, it didn't take her long to call me back and she reiterated, "...I want you to phone me when you find yourself working on your own in the office, and then phone me again once you're in your car."

My auto-response was, "nobody else in the office needs to phone their manager when they are on their own - that's discrimination."

Cath was so shocked and upset, she said, "I'm only trying my best" before putting the phone down on me.

When I phoned her back she wouldn't talk to me. She emailed me something along the lines of, "I'm going to report you to my manager for accusing me of discrimination."

We had always got on really well and what happened was so odd. I thought I had done nothing wrong, but nevertheless felt so guilty.

Cath didn't speak to me for days, until she had organised a conference call with her manager, herself and me, when I apologised for implying discrimination had occurred. I got the impression Cath's manager thought it was all a storm in a teacup.

Following the call, Cath and I put the matter behind us and we restored our very good working relationship.

In 2009 when I had handed the last application I was supporting to another team, I had no more work to do for Cath. However *Shh* had a new rule which prevented disabled people from going on the bench. For a few months, until October 2009, I found myself doing boring clerical stuff for Cath.

In hearing that a new software development team was being formed, containing some people who used to be part of QS, I spoke to Doug and Tom who both worked for Arnold. Doug and Tom were in favour of me joining their new team but I wasn't invited to do so.

Between 2004 and 2008 I went on holiday to Antigua and stayed at the same all-inclusive resort twice. On both occasions I met loads of people and became well-known around the resort.

It amazed me how, pretty much effortlessly, I attracted Caribbean women. Seeing me in my wheelchair inspired them that I had come on holiday on my own. Engaging them in conversation, I spread the word that I was a computer programmer, drove a car, had my own apartment and that I would like a Caribbean wife. I was relaxed and found it so easy.

On my first visit to Antigua, after spending some time with one of the women who worked at the resort and before I had a chance to tell her not to do so, she phoned her ex-husband and asked him if he could take over the bringing up of their young son, so that she could come and live with me in England! It freaked me out a bit.

When I took a public minibus into St John's (the capital of Antigua), it was if the locals on the bus had never seen a white man in a wheelchair before!

At a t-shirt stall in St John's, I met the most physically attractive Caribbean girl that I've ever seen. In her mid-twenties and despite being a bit tall, she was half-cast and stunning. However, looks aren't the most important thing for me. I chatted to her for quite a while before asking her if she would like to marry me! She said she had a baby boy and would think about it!

I bought a Bob Marley t-shirt from her for the girl I knew from The Warwick. We also emailed each other for a while and her messages were always short and in uppercase.

On my second holiday in Antigua, a few years later, she was still working on the same t-shirt stall. Rhetorically, she asked her young son if he would like to live in England. In a spirit of helpfulness, she introduced me to her friend nearby, who was also a nice person but who appeared to be in need of an orthodontist!

I hadn't planned to go back to the same resort (or even Antigua) but my choices were limited to a Caribbean all-inclusive resort which was wheelchair accessible and not too spread out.

With spatial awareness not being my strong suit, trying to find a suitable resort using the internet isn't easy. I also found phoning travel agents and asking for a resort which "is not too spread out", a bit meaningless!

On several occasions I have said that if it wasn't for the heat, I would like to live in the Caribbean. I find Caribbean people so warm and friendly. When it comes to the ladies there it's like being a kid in a sweet shop!

On my first Antiguan holiday I read 'The Healing Code' by Dermot O'Connor. After being told by his doctor "You've got Multiple Sclerosis (MS) and only months left to live. Go home and deal with it", Dermot, by changing his diet and his mindset, overcame MS and then opened a clinic to help people overcome life-threatening illnesses.

The book I read on my second trip to Antigua was the autobiography of radio DJ Johnnie Walker which is full of anecdotes. The one about the Greyhound bus is hilarious. Johnnie Walker is also an inspirational person because against the odds he overcame cancer.

Not long after reading his autobiography I met Johnnie Walker on his book tour at the Komedia in Brighton.

The memory still makes me laugh. When I arrived at the Komedia Club, Johnnie who was coming out of a café opposite and seeing me getting out of my car, crossed the road and asked me if I needed any help. I felt like saying "Johnnie Walker - it's a pleasure meeting you. I've been listening to you for years, I've read your excellent book and I'm here to hear you speak." However I became a bit starstuck and just replied "No, I'm alright thank you."

As arranged, I met up with Ray inside the Komedia. It was good meeting Johnnie and his wife Tiggy after the show. Years earlier, Ray and Johnnie had worked together on the Brighton Festival FM RSL station.

At the beginning of 2007 Clare and Rupert started planning to move to France. Clare said she didn't like her hectic life here. One of her gripes was the school-run in the mornings and the queue of traffic waiting to get off Shoreham Beach. I suggested to Clare that they moved closer to the school!

Around about the same time, I had the idea of moving myself. After looking at a bungalow or two I very nearly put my flat up for sale. However, I didn't do it because I realised that living in a bungalow (with a bigger mortgage) wouldn't make me any happier. I made a good decision because my flat is a real asset to me now.

After nearly four years of being on-air, Splash was sounding good but the overheads required to keep it sounding like a top flight station meant it was hard to make the kind of profit margins that the investors demanded. In early 2007 Ray stepped down as managing director of the station. I felt sorry for Ray because he had worked hard.

My view of the situation was, being a people-person, Ray cared a lot about the people he hired and he treated them well - but I think some staff were on too higher wages, which affected the station's profitability.

Ray said he left Splash after the Board pressurised him to make staff changes which he didn't want to make.

Before starting to write this book I spent three years working incredibly hard, trying to find the right property investment strategy which suited me. I felt like I was a headless chicken running around and I didn't get very far.

It taught me that if you don't have a plan and aren't focused on what it is you want to achieve, it's unlikely you'll get very far.

After Ray, Clive came in and had a go at being the MD of Splash. I didn't have much to do with Clive but I found him to be a little obtuse and an odd character. I only saw him at a few social events but he knew what I did on the sports show.

On the few occasions I saw Clive, pretty much the only interaction I had with him was a greeting, "Alright mate…", followed by a tap on my shoulder. I found him patronising.

How is it possible for someone who had spent a career working with people in radio not to know how to talk to me? I guess part of the answer is that Clive probably hadn't come across someone like me before.

After they had looked at moving to south-east France, Clare and Rupert decided to buy a house in the little countryside village where Dad lives, in south-west France.

In summer 2007 Clare and Rupert sold their big house on Shoreham Beach. Rupert bought a smaller house twenty minutes away and they moved to France.

Rupert's idea was that he would alternate every few weeks between working in England and spending time in France.

Before moving, Clare said her only hesitation about moving to France was leaving me here on my own, but we both knew it wasn't a reason for her not to move. It was quite emotional seeing Clare and the kids leave England.

They moved into rented accommodation before completing on the purchase of their new house. After they moved into it I went to visit them in November 2007.

It was a fairly small three bedroom house with lots of land with the potential of extending the property. The three kids learnt French and settled into their new school quickly.

Not having seen or spoken to Dad for a few years, I wondered how we would get on, but we got on fine. His eight year old daughter Isabel really surprised me. Having only met her twice before, Isabel thrust herself into my arms and gave me a big hug. Five year old Pierre was also pleased to see me. What did they know about me?

Dad and his wife Madeline now also had a one year old girl called Cécile, who in her baby-walker seemed a bit apprehensive of me walking with my crutches.

Given Clare's motivation to move to France to cut back on the school run, I found the new shuttle arrangement hilarious. In the little village they lived in there was only one school, spread over three sites. When it came to picking up the kids from school, parents would first go to the first school, pick up their youngest children, drive to the middle school, pick up child number two and then drive to the last school.

The kids had a two hour lunch break, with Clare's and Dad's kids coming home for lunch so Clare did this demanding school run four times a day! Her day seemed to consist of the school runs, cooking lunch and helping the kids with their homework.

As Dad was now retired and Madeline worked, he did the school run with his kids. With Clare and Dad always early for things, they saw each other waiting at the first school every day! Charlotte and Pierre were in the same class. Some people found it confusing that Pierre who is slightly younger than Charlotte, is her uncle!

When I went to France Clare asked me to set up her broadband and wifi which had taken ages for the components to arrive because there's a waiting list out in the French sticks.

Rupert had recently bought Clare a new laptop. It had Windows 7 which I had never used before and it was all in French! With me not being very good at reading French, I can get by 'un petit peu', and Clare not being very technical, we managed it together

Clare was reading the French installation instructions. I knew what to do but couldn't find what I was looking for. I was asking, "I'm looking for the 'Control Panel'. What's 'Control Panel' in French?!"

When I thought we had set it up correctly, I became frustrated that it wasn't working. I got Clare to phone up her internet service provider, who had to do something at their end to fully activate her account. 'Et voilà'! It worked!

Back in England, not long after Ray had left Splash, I started getting parking tickets in Ann Street on Saturday afternoons. The management of on-street parking in Worthing had been taken over by the Council who in turn outsourced the parking ticketing to a third party.

Phoning the lady at the council, who was now in charge of parking, I knew she wasn't going to be an easy person to deal with. In fact, she was the most unhelpful person I have ever come across. She had no empathy for my situation at all.

When I told her that I could only walk up to fifty yards and I produced a four hour show on Splash and that the two disabled spaces in Ann Street were often occupied, she replied:

Miss Jobsworth: "You can park in disabled spaces for as long as you like but you can only park on double-yellow lines for up to three hours."

I subsequently had loads of email correspondence with her. The situation became even more ridiculous when a skip containing building debris was parked on the double-yellow lines in Ann Street for two or three months. After the skip had been there for two weeks, I queried it:

Miss Jobsworth: "The skip has got a license from the council to be there."

Me: Can I have a license from the council to park my car on double-yellow lines in Ann Street?"

Miss Jobsworth: "No."

At one point I had seven parking tickets! This is when Ted, as a Director of Splash, helped me by having a meeting with Miss Jobsworth. As a result, Miss Jobsworth let me off four of the tickets and I had to pay the other three.

It didn't make much sense to me that she cancelled some of the tickets and not all of them. Nor did it make much sense that they had a meeting about me - and how far I can walk - without me being there.

Instead, Miss Jobsworth suggested that I parked in one of the disabled spaces in Chapel Road opposite the Guildbourne Centre. It was a bit further for me to walk but I managed it. However a few weeks later the council moved the disabled spaces a hundred yards down the road!

In over six months of emailing Miss Jobsworth she never acknowledged that I could only walk up to fifty yards. She always suggested I park in a disabled space further away.

It was then really funny when I phoned her the second time. She completely misunderstood something I said and accused me of calling her "a pain in the arse"!

During the same conversation we had this exchange:

Miss Jobsworth: "If I let you park where you want I would also have to let everyone else..."

Me: "If someone has a genuine need to park somewhere, where they are not causing a danger or obstruction, you should let them."

I contacted council leaders and my local MP but they weren't any help.

I overcame the problem in a conversation with Brenda, the Guildbourne Centre manager, who suggested I park down the little alleyway, leading up to the Guildbourne Centre. She gave me a key to unlock the padlock on the metal barrier to the alleyway. I was able unlock and then lock the barrier myself but it required some energy.

From then on every Saturday, I first checked if one of the disabled spaces were free in Ann Street, before driving round to the alleyway and phoning Fergus (at Splash), or Brenda and asked if one of the security guards could unlock the gate for me.

Brenda is one of the nicest people I've ever met.

In May 2008 Allan Moulds became the new MD of Splash. For those of you who haven't gotten bored of my book yet, you may remember me mentioning Allan when I briefly met him at the Prince's trust presentation in December 2000. He's Gemma's husband and also the MD of Bright FM in Burgess Hill.

The reason why Allan became the MD of Splash is because Splash became part of Media Sound Holdings (MSH - the company which owned Bright). The people who had shares in Splash became shareholders in MSH, together with the shareholders of Bright.

What impressed me when Allan took Splash on was he took the view of, "this is the business plan and this is the budget - which presenters can we afford..?"

Virtually all of the Splash freelance weekend presenters were axed, as well as some of the Bright staff. I think Allan also replaced some of the Splash salespeople. He did what had to be done to turn the station into a profitable business.

I was called in to see Allan and I knew what he was going to say beforehand. He said, "Splash isn't in profit and the business can't afford to pay you - but I will pay you travelling expenses." I agreed to do the sport show voluntarily, on the condition that my £25 per show was reinstated once Splash was in profit. In the meantime I received a tiny amount of petrol money.

Later on, I recall Ted saying to me that when Allan took over, Ted got Allan to listen to the sport show one Saturday.

In June 2009 Paul Williams was hired as the group programme controller of MSH that owned Splash and Bright.

The first time I met Paul was funny. I walked into the office on a Saturday afternoon, said hello to him and then I fell over in front of him! It didn't seem to faze him and we laughed about it.

I've got a lot of time for Paul because he's got no ego and doesn't take himself too seriously. In covering the sport show a few times, Paul was one of the best people to work with. The same is true about Rob Lamond.

Six to nine months after the merger happened, Splash and Bright started programme sharing. Both stations retained their own identity, local news and traffic bulletins, what's on guides' and so on. The mid-morning and the evening show were networked on both stations, presented by Paul and Phil respectively. Most of the weekend programmes were networked, including the sports show.

Splash was in profit after about a year. However it took eighteen months for my £25 to be reinstated. With Allan not wanting to pay out a penny more than he has to, Paul helped in getting my pay restored.

In summer 2009 MSH acquired two other loss-making Sussex stations - Sovereign and Arrow, broadcasting to Eastbourne and Hastings respectively.

Then in August 2009, Paul Williams brought Chris Copsey (aka Coppo) back onto the radio. After having done the breakfast show on Southern FM for about fifteen years and then being sidelined by the station, before letting go of him, Coppo hadn't done any radio for a few years.

For no apparent reason one Saturday evening in the first half of 2008, I had a little nose bleed when I was at a pub in Shoreham. Wiping my nose with a couple of tissues I had on me, I thought 'How strange?' When I woke up the next morning there was a little bit of blood on my pillow. I thought "What's going on?" but thought no-more about it.

I went to see my friend Steve Bell and his folk band on a sunny Sunday afternoon, who were playing in another pub in Shoreham. When I arrived at the pub I could hear that the band were playing the in back garden, so I walked around the outside of the pub and down a few steps. As I reached the back garden I could see the band playing straight ahead of me and quite a few people.

It was at that moment that the bloodgates opened - as blood came pouring out of one of my nostrils. It caused the band to stop playing and for its audience to look round at me. Talk about making an entrance!

Steve and his wife Jill came rushing over to me. I felt slightly embarrassed and wanted to make light of the situation.

Steve: "Are you okay?"

Me: "Yeah, I'm alright."

Jill: "You're not alright. You've got blood gushing out of your nose..."

Me: "It will stop bleeding in a minute..."

But it didn't.

Steve: "Has this happened before?"

Me: "No. Never."

Somebody else came over and said, "I've called an ambulance."

Than the pub landlord, Imogen, who I had never met before came outside. She was very concerned about me and comforting. Blood was going everywhere and was mopping up as best she could. I kept apologising to her and saying "This has never happened before!"

After about fifteen minutes a paramedic turned up in a car. The guy took one look at me and said, "You need an ambulance" before he called for one. It took another fifteen minutes for the ambulance to arrive, by which time my nose had stopped bleeding!

I had never seen so much blood in my life. The front of my t-shirt was drenched with the red stuff!

While waiting for the ambulance, I asked Steve to get the Bob Marley t-shirt from the glove-box in my car and I took it with me to Worthing hospital. It turned out to be a good thing that 'Bob Marley t-shirt girl' didn't accept my gift from Antigua!

On the way to hospital I was laughing and joking with the paramedic in the back of the ambulance. She said it looked as if I had been in a fight.

People were staring me, being covered in blood, as I was wheeled into A&E. I said to them "You should have seen the other guy!"

I laid on a bed in A&E for over three hours. During this time I was looked after by a nurse who cleaned all of the blood off of me. My t-shirt had so much blood on it I told her to throw it away and I put my Bob Marley one on.

One of the doctors came to see me three times and looked up my nose. Despite me repeatedly saying to her "I've never had a nose bleed before. I'm a bit worried about it, what's wrong with me?" On the third occasion she concluded "I can't see anything wrong with you" before she sent me home in a taxi. Knowing that something wasn't right, I felt really frustrated.

I asked the taxi driver to drop me off at the pub, where I got into my car and went home. Within two hours of being at home, the bloodgates opened again. I went into the bathroom and sat on the stool at the sink, looking in the big mirror.

Blood was pouring out of my nose once again, I thought "What do I do? What do I do?' I phoned Steve and Jill, who both came over. Jill took one look at me and said, "You need to go to hospital again" and she called 999 for an ambulance.

I kept thinking and saying "My nose is going to stop bleeding in a minute..." but it didn't. When the ambulance hadn't arrived after half an hour and my nose was still gushing with blood, I became really stressed and began to worry that there wasn't much blood left in me!

Jill phoned 999 again and said the ambulance was on its way. When the paramedics finally arrived, they said they had come from the other side of Brighton. As they sat me in a chair and took me out of my flat. I commented "My bathroom looks like a scene from a very bloody horror film." My nose stopped bleeding on the way to Worthing hospital.

Not having been in an ambulance since I fractured my skull, when I was a child in Belgium, I had now been in two ambulances in the space of a few hours.

I arrived at A&E about 11pm and the same thing happened. However, before they sent me home in a taxi at 5.30am, I vigorously walked up and down the ward a few times, hoping it would make my nose bleed again, but it didn't.

The taxi driver who drove me home was a miserable old git. Despite me telling him the ordeal I had been through over the last fifteen hours, he really wasn't pleased when I was one pound short of the taxi fare.

The moment I stepped out of his car my nose started bleeding.

It was now 5.50am and not having eaten or slept at all overnight, I felt completely emotionally drained. As I unlocked the communal entrance to my block, I felt like collapsing. I didn't know what to do. I made myself a cup of tea before lying down on my bed.

My nose had stopped bleeding by 7.30am. Having not spoken to Mum for months, I reluctantly phoned Mum and she arrived at about 8.30.

Seeing the state of my bathroom, blood in the kitchen and in my bedroom, Mum wasn't sure what to do. Whilst I remained lying on my bed, she went into the lounge and phoned her flatmate for advice. They decided that a letter was needed from my GP practice, in order for Worthing hospital to take the matter seriously.

For some reason, Mum wanted to ask me something in the lounge. I said I didn't feel like getting up and walking around, but she was insistent that I went into the lounge. As I walked into living room the bloodgates opened again!

Mum quickly put the phone down as blood was going everywhere. She helped me out to her car and we went to the GP surgery, where Mum quickly got a doctor to come outside and witness my nose gushing with blood in the car.

Luckily, my nose was still gushing when we arrived at Worthing A&E. Mum went into A&E and quickly got a nurse to help me out of the car.

With my nose still bleeding we didn't have to wait long in A&E. I was seen by the head of the Ear, Nose & Throat Department, Mr Ent.

Mr Ent was brilliant. It didn't take him long to identify that I had a burst blood vessel and he knew how to fix it. After my experiences with A&E I felt relieved - and tired.

A couple of people cleaned my nostril, by putting some liquid up it and cauterising it. They then put what they referred to as a tampon, up my nostril!

Normally, they would then send people home for twenty-four hours but, because I use a lot of energy when I walk, Mr Ent decided to keep me in hospital overnight.

Mr Ent was disgusted that A&E had sent me home twice. He said, "What they should have done is phoned the on-call ENT consultant. I'll make a complaint."

When I got onto the ward and as I didn't have Cath's number on me, I phoned Jack at work, explained the dramatic events of the previous eighteen hours, and asked him to call Cath for me.

That day and the next, Mum really helped me. Not only in taking me to hospital, but also doing an immaculate job in cleaning up the blood that was all over my flat. I find it hard to describe how much blood there was - but it was everywhere. It wasn't an enviable task.

Later that day Gavin walked into the hospital ward. Having not seen each other since working together at Surf, we were both surprised to see each other there. He had come to visit the guy in the bed opposite mine!

With the tampon up my nose, it felt a bit weird when Gavin asked me how I was! We chatted for a few minutes and he said he was really enjoying working at BBC Radio Sussex.

In writing my book, I've realised that I would love to work in radio again - especially for the BBC.

The next afternoon, Mr Ent removed the tampon from my nostril and I was free to go home.

Now, I don't recommend sticking a tampon up your nose. It wasn't that painful when they inserted it but it caused a sharp pain when they pulled it out. It felt like the inside of my nose had been ripped out.

Mum was there to take me home and made me a really nice omelette before she went back to Hove. I had a relaxing rest of the week off work. It was rare for me to be off sick.

In returning to the office the following week, I phoned Cath and explained how much blood there had been and said:

Me: "I've got a sick-note from the hospital to send to you."

And for comedic effect I added "It's got a bit of blood on it but it's alright..."

Cath: "No, no, you don't need to send me the sick-note. I believe you."

One of the things I've often found difficult in life is finding a good pair of shoes for me to wear, especially since I started wearing steel toe cap boots in 1996. Some boots are easier to put on than others and I like ones which have got metal hooks at the top, as I can hook my curly laces around them.

For a few years I bought the same boots from a high street shop and when the shop stopped stocking them I purchased the boots on the internet.

It was all well and good until September 2008, when I thought I had bought the same make and model as I had been purchasing over the last couple of years. However when the boots arrived in the post, I realised that they were the same make but a different model.

The boots were much heavier and bulkier than the ones I normally wore and on the third day of wearing them I had a horrific car crash.

I was driving down a side street in Shoreham at 5 to 10 mph, heading towards the High Street. On approaching the give way markings at the end of the road, I went to brake with my left foot. However, the front of my left boot had gotten wedged in between the two metal rods which ran from my hand control underneath the steering column, and attached to the accelerator and brake pedals.

My boot was stuck and I wasn't able to brake. I felt helpless, as if there was nothing I could do. I didn't stop at the junction and crashed into a car coming from the right in the High Street.

It felt like the accident had happened so quickly and I didn't have much time to react. Having always braked with my left foot, I wasn't used to pushing the hand control with my right hand to brake.

The car I crashed into contained a couple in their twenties or thirties, who had two young kids. Luckily nobody was hurt and the couple were nice about it. Nevertheless, I felt so incredibly guilty and small. It was one of the worst experiences in my life.

The police arrived and the car I crashed into was so badly damaged that the police weren't able to push it out of the way. The car was causing a queue of traffic until a recovery lorry arrived to pick it up. In comparison my car had superficial damage.

Both sets of grandparents of the family I crashed into turned up. I thought about calling Mum who now lived in Brighton but felt that she would criticise me and make me feel worse. The police asked me if there was someone they could call for me but I said I didn't have anybody.

Sitting on the nearby bench, waiting for the recovery service to check my car was road-worthy, I felt so incredibly alone and guilty. It made me repeatedly retch in front of people.

When the recovery service arrived, they popped my bumper back into place and put some duck tape on it.

At home that evening, I really felt like talking to someone about the accident. I didn't know who to call. I phoned my friend Fergus because I felt nobody else would care.

The next day, still feeling awful and as if I had lost all of my confidence, especially the ability to drive. I knew I had to go for a drive. So I did. I felt okay driving around town and up to 40 mph. However, I had no confidence driving on a dual carriageway. It petrified me.

The other problem I had was a terrible feeling of guilt and the thought that I could have injured someone in the crash. Needless to say, I didn't wear the heavy and bulky boots again. Wearing my normal boots didn't give me much legroom in the car, but they weren't long enough to get trapped between the two metal rods.

I gave the bulky boots to Ray, for one of his sons. At the time Ray was working with Colin who ran a personal development training company. I had a session of therapy with Colin and I overcame the guilt I was feeling.

Nearly a year later, in August 2009, I was finding life very difficult. I wasn't happy personally, I was doing boring clerical work for Cath and I still felt terrified driving on dual carriageways and motorways, I hadn't overcome my accident.

It was a psychological problem. At the time of the accident, I felt I wasn't able to brake, like I had no 'exit strategy' with no option but to crash. Driving on dual carriageways and on motorways, I had developed a fear that I wasn't in control, as if I was perpetually going to crash. On the motorway, I was kind of okay driving at 50 mph in the slow lane because I had the hard shoulder as an exit strategy. However I had no confidence going into the middle or fast lane.

In trying to overcome my fear, I had a couple of therapy sessions with Colin. Those two sessions of therapy cost me hundreds of pounds and didn't have any lasting effect. However, Ray told me I was being too hard on myself and that I should be kind to myself.

I went home and booked a holiday to Thailand!

Patrick Souiljaert

# Chapter 5

In September 2009 I took a ten day holiday in Thailand, spending three nights in Bangkok and seven in Pattaya. I flew to Bangkok via Qatar, which included waiting for a few hours in the middle of the night at Doha airport, for my connecting flight.

Arriving in Bangkok early in the morning, I slept in my posh hotel for a few hours, before venturing out into the streets of the capital city. My hotel was in an urban area of Bangkok, where there were construction and road works happening. As there were no pavements, I found myself, in my wheelchair, going along the side of a three lane highway! Dodging cars and trucks heading towards me didn't bother me because I was on an adventure.

Before leaving for my holiday I bought some black leather gloves, specifically for wheelchair users, to avoid getting friction burns from my tires.

Wearing my gloves in the twenty-eight degree humid heat, on my first push-about in Bangkok, I somehow still managed to acquire a blister on my left thumb.

Conveniently, opposite my hotel was a bijou restaurant. I had a nice meal there when I was tired of pushing myself around on the first day. Thailand is so cheap. You can have a good meal for £1. I also found Thai people extremely hospitable and friendly.

The restaurant wasn't busy and it had a large massage room at the back of it. Hence after I had eaten I went for a massage for an hour. When in Thailand...!

The massage room had six mats on the floor, with a curtain around each one. I was only expecting one person to give me a massage but three women turned up. I didn't find it relaxing because they were talking to each other in Thai and laughing a lot.

However, whereas the two youngest women in their twenties only spoke Thai, Crystal looked about my age, spoke good English and was the most attractive of the three.

I went back the next day and asked Crystal if I could have a massage just with her. She asked me if I could climb stairs and took me up a wooden spiral staircase, to a room at the top of the building, where she gave me a really good and relaxing massage for ninety minutes.

Crystal had a good heart and was smart, saving up to start her own business (but not as a masseuse). She thought I was inspirational going on holiday by myself. While asking her lots of questions, I mentioned I was a computer programmer, drove a car, owned my own apartment and that I would like a Thai wife. I also said to Crystal that I was going to Pattaya the day after next.

The next day I went back and confidently asked Crystal if she would like to spend the night with me. She said yes. Crystal was a really nice woman but the sex wasn't great. For some reason she wouldn't take her top off and I found having the light on and the Thai TV blaring loudly disturbing. I would have liked to have had more intimacy.

The next day I went to Pattaya. My holiday package included a taxi to and from Pattaya which was about ninety minutes from Bangkok and seven nights in the Hard Rock Hotel. I didn't especially choose to stay at the music-themed hotel, it was part of the package I paid for the ten day holiday.

The Hard Rock Hotel was on the seafront road, a five to ten minute push in my wheelchair away from a load of bars and restaurants in Pattatya. The hotel had the best outdoor swimming pool that I've ever been in. The whole of one end of the pool was a gradual slope into the main body of the pool. It was made to look like walking into the sea from the beach. It allowed me to walk into the pool and when I got in deep enough I could put my crutches on the side, outside the pool.

Arriving in Pattaya on Sunday, I wasted no time in becoming acquainted with the afternoon and night life there.

I went twice into one of the bars in the first couple of days that had three girls in their twenties or thirties working in it. One of them spoke English, the other two didn't, but it didn't stop them trying to communicate with me. I didn't understand anything they were trying to convey!

After asking the girl who spoke English if there was a t-shirt shop nearby, she said there wasn't but she offered to take me to one on the back of her moped! Not being a fan of bikes I politely declined but it created a funny image in my mind and begged the question of where would my crutches go.

When I became bored of that bar I found a massage place and a nice woman, my age, called Holly who gave me a relaxing massage and her mobile number! The next day I tried calling Holly from a public street phone but I couldn't get the phone to work.

Prior to going to Thailand a couple of people told me to be careful of the ladyboys! I think they are easy to spot. However, as I was getting back into my wheelchair after using the phone, a beautiful looking lady came running across the road to help me. She looked so beautiful and seemed so eager to help me that I became suspicious that she could have been a ladybody! I wasn't going to take any chances. I became very defensive, and politely said I was alright and didn't let her help me.

As the staff in my hotel were nice people I went back there. As cool as anything, I said to the guy at the reception desk "I hope you can help me. My friend Holly said she would come and see me. I just tried to phone her from a public phone in town but it wasn't working, please could you phone her for me?"

The guy dialled the number and gave me the phone, I spoke to Holly and she came and spent the night with me! The sex wasn't great. My inexperience was evident, which made me feel inadequate. However I couldn't have been that bad because Holly told me to give her another call.

The next day was Wednesday and whilst sitting by the swimming pool, listening to my MP3 player, two girls in their late twenties, who had been sitting further around the pool, came over and chatted to me for ages.

Julia was from Kazakhstan but lived and worked in PR in Bangkok, whilst Helga lived in Russia and had come on holiday for a week with Julia.

They said they had arrived at the hotel on Sunday and had seen me sitting on my own over the last few days. The two girls asked me why I had come on holiday by myself and they were baffled as to why I didn't have a wife to look after me. I replied, "Women in England don't find me attractive."

The next day, after having spent ages talking with Julia by the pool again, she said that she and Helga were going to Walking Street which was a popular evening hangout place for tourists, with loads of bars, clubs and restaurants. Julia invited me to go with them.

The funny thing about that day was I had a pair of shorts on, which I normally wore with a belt as the button on them was a bit too tight for me to do up, but for some reason I wasn't wearing the belt.

Me: "Thank you for inviting me but I need to go and get changed first."

Julia: "You look fine the way you are."

I thought, 'Sod it, I'm on holiday" and didn't go back to my room first which in hindsight wasn't the best decision I've ever made.

A widely used mode of transport in Pattaya are the converted pickup trucks, which people sit sideways in the back of and hop on and off.

We took one of these to Walking Street. When I got out of my wheelchair and as Julia and the driver helped me into the back of the pickup truck, my shorts started to fall down!

Throughout the evening I kept pulling my shorts up. After wandering in Walking Street we went for a meal. Having been in my wheelchair for ages, I decided to walk into the restaurant and we sat out on the veranda at the back of the restaurant. I remember slowly hobbling past people eating their meals, scared that my shorts were going to fall down!

We had a good evening. I tried to pay for everything but Julia and Helga wouldn't let me contribute to anything.

In the pickup truck, returning to our hotel, Julia and I had a snog before she came back to my room and we had sex. She was an extremely nice girl and we were a bit drunk.

For the rest of the week I spent quite a bit of time with Julia - and Helga. Helga became resentful that Julia and I were spending so much time together. I can understand why Helga felt a bit irritated, having come on holiday to see her friend.

Saturday was the last full day of our holiday and we went on the beach that afternoon. Having really enjoyed jet-skiing when I had done it years earlier in Greece and Antigua, I became eager to do it again when Julia and Helga decided to do it.

However not realising how independent and able I am, Julia really didn't want me to go on a jet-ski, as she was scared that I would crash and fall off. Seeing how much I wanted to go jet-skiing, Julia said that if I didn't go jet-skiing she would have sex with me that evening which meant I stayed on the beach whilst the two girls jet-skied!

Saturday evening was the infamous Hard Rock Hotel foam party - where they fill a brick built enclosure, measuring about ten square metres and eight feet high, with bubble bath foam and people!

It was good fun and all went well until I became disorientated due to having foam in my eyes and was walking towards a wall. Seeing me and thinking I was about to walk into the wall and hurt myself although I would have felt the wall with one of my crutches, Julia pulled the back of my t-shirt a bit too vigorously, which made me fall over.

Seeing me fall shocked Julia. Speaking to her outside the foam enclosure, I tried to reassure her that I was fine and stable on my feet but she became frightened of me falling over. Julia told me to not go back into the foam party, before she went back to it.

Sitting there, hearing the loud music and lots of people having fun, I felt left out. Not liking it when someone tells me I cannot do something and wanting to show Julia that I was fine on my feet I went back into the foam party.

However it caused Julia and me to have a two hour argument. From her perspective I think the problem was that I had disobeyed her. However, I thought it was more of a communication problem and that she was scared of me falling over. I tried so hard to tell her that I am fine walking about everywhere.

The argument really upset both of us and needless to say, Julia didn't sleep with me that night.

The next morning Julia and Helga were leaving the hotel before I was. I went to reception, where Julia and I apologised to each other and made up, before I said goodbye to the two girls.

At home, I emailed Julia and explained how independent I am. I phoned her about once a week for the next couple of months or so.

I stayed in a disabled room at The Hard Rock Hotel. The bathroom had a walk-in shower but a normal tiled floor, which made it extremely slippery when wet, when walking with crutches. It caused me to fall over once, during my week's stay, where I whacked my knee on the floor. Upon complaining to the hotel, they put a large mat in the bathroom for me. The incident made me realise I could become a worldwide disabled hotel inspector!

Julia had an extremely good heart and she was protective and wanted to take care of me on holiday. She really touched me emotionally.

The reason why I have written so candidly about my holiday in Thailand is because it astonishes me how people I meet on holiday perceive me differently to the people I meet when I go out somewhere at home.

It amazes me how, almost effortlessly, in Thailand, I attracted three women, who then voluntarily slept with me. However, the point I'm making is not specifically about sex.

Most women I meet in England appear to be apprehensive of me and are unwilling to even have a proper conversation with me.

The difference between pulling and pushing (the law of attraction) and the fact that I am more relaxed and confident on holiday is a big factor.

But a large part of it is also due to acceptance.

Why are foreigners inspired by me when they see me in my wheelchair, having travelled halfway around the world? There is nothing difficult about sitting on a plane and having assistance on and off of it.

Why is it that British people try to avoid me when they see me walking past them?

Surely, I appear to be far more disabled, pushing myself in my wheelchair with my poor co-ordination, than I do walking with my crutches.

What struck me about the women I met in Thailand (and the ones in Antigua) and especially Julia, is they saw me as a human being. When Julia asked me why I didn't have a wife, I didn't quite know what to say.

Yes, I have Cerebral Palsy but why do most women not look past that and see me as a human being?

Jeremy Vine ran a weekly series on his Radio 2 show, where he invited inspirational people to answer the question 'What makes us human?' A few months ago I heard Alison Lapper MBE, an English artist who paints with her mouth because she was born without arms on the programme. Alison defined it extremely well. She said what makes us human is to love and to be loved, accepted and respected.

This is the most important point of my book because I get the impression that the people who call me an inspiration do not think about this.

The most basic human emotion is love. Everyone in the world needs it because it's the most fundamental thing in life.

When people see me walking around and doing everything I do and they think I'm an inspiration, do they consider my basic needs and desires as a human being?

For so many years, I have known that I haven't been physiologically fed. It's something that affects my confidence in everyday life - but I think people don't think or realise it about me.

I know what love is because I have loved two people (Rosie and Janet) very much. I overcome everything else in my life relatively easily. However, not having found someone to share my life with yet is the one thing I do not cope with well.

People know me as someone who is often laughing and joking, but I'm not like that when I'm at home alone. I wouldn't wish the pain it causes me on my worst enemy.

What really hurts me is that I have got so much love to give and I'm such a soft and gentle person, but people don't give me a chance to allow me to show them that side of me.

I think most people take relationships for granted and I have known so many people in bad relationships. It hurts me because I value people and relationships. People refer to their 'other half'. I feel like I'm half a person.

I often wonder how I keep going. It's due to my belief that I am going to find the right woman to share my life with. I am only human.

And now for something completely different!

Back at *Shh* in October 2009 I was still doing clerical work for Cath when someone in HR who was looking for another assignment for me, emailed me a role specification to work on a high profile external project. The role was for database administrators (DBA) with at least five years' experience. After reading through the specification I phoned the HR lady.

Me: "I'm not a DBA and I'm not qualified for this role."

HR lady: "Have the phone interview anyway."

As I never thought I was going to be offered the role, I wasn't worried about the phone interview and just decided to enjoy it. The two guys who interviewed me said they were so impressed with my "can do attitude" that they decided to train me up to be a DBA. Without even trying, I was offered the role! Ironically, the same strategy applies to attracting women.

After the formal part of the phone interview was over, they asked me if I would be alright spending a couple of days a week in Hemel Hempstead, north of London. Without thinking about it, I said I would be.

I didn't feel enthusiastic about doing the role but I thought it would be better than the boring clerical stuff I was doing.

Logistically, the office in Hemel Hempstead wasn't easy to get to. I still had my phobia of driving on motorways. At the time there were long term road works on the M25, which stretched for six miles. The motorway went down to two lanes and the left lane had steel railings which I was scared of crashing into, along one side. The right hand lane was a narrow lane. There was no hard shoulder and nowhere to stop for six miles. The speed limit was 50 mph but as I was so scared of not being able to stop I drove at 30 mph!

The funny thing is, I know that all phobias are psychological, irrational fears. Nevertheless, the twelve minutes it took me to drive through those road works were petrifying. I dreaded driving to and from Hemel Hempstead.

One time I went by train - it took two trains and having to get taxis to and from the hotel and office - it was more of a pain than driving to Hemel Hempstead. All I could do with driving on the M25 was feel the fear and do it anyway.

My team in Hemel Hempstead worked on the first floor of an old building. Once I arrived at the office, it took me fifteen minutes to walk from my car to where the team were located in the building. It involved going through no fewer than eleven doors! Additionally, in my rucksack I had my laptop and other things, which made it heavy to carry.

The team was actually split into two with five people in Hemel Hempstead and about seven in Leeds. I never met the people in Leeds including my line manager Reg, but the whole team had a conference call every Friday and the Leeds people sounded like a nice bunch.

The guys in Hemel Hempstead were good too, especially Ethan the team manager. He had a very stressful job. Not only was he in charge of the whole team but also, in technical terms, he was responsible for all of the databases.

At my Saturday afternoon job in the noughties

With Roy Stannard (2002)

Guayrapa newbies group (October 2015)

Potential cover photo
for Stairs For Breakfast
(thank you to Steve
Bell for taking it)

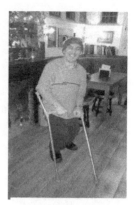

Me and my
AWESOME
hat (2015)

Entertaining an audience (2016)

I only type with my right hand when photos
are being taken!

Guayrapa (2017)

Minutes after my first live radio interview (2016)

Getting into my car
without being ran over!

Guayrapa (2017)

Ethan was always calm and he had a lot of time for me as in his eyes I could do no wrong. When I joined the team Ethan told me that it would take between eighteen months to two years for me to get trained up. It would involve going on external courses and he wasn't going let me on the live servers until I knew what I was doing. In the meantime, I had access only to the test and training servers.

The prospect of training didn't fill me with joy. The problem was I didn't see myself in the role in two years' time. But not being a quitter, I decided to try it for six months.

My visits to Hemel Hempstead soon reduced to once a month rather than every week. I spent most of my time doing online courses. I grappled with such things as how to install, configure, backup and restore a database. What I was learning wasn't invigorating stuff.

On the Friday conference calls, each member of the team took turns to say what they had done that week and what they were going to do the following week. When it came to my turn, saying, "I've just been doing online courses" made me feel a bit useless, as if I wasn't contributing anything to the team.

So I was given the responsibility of producing the tablespace report every morning. It was a five minute job running four scripts to produce some data, which I then copied into a spreadsheet and emailed to the team members.

I then progressed onto increasing some tablespaces. To explain, data in a database is stored in tables and the maximum size of each table is defined by its tablespace. Tablespaces needed to be increased as time progressed as users were entering data into the databases.

Whereas software development involves creativity, DBA work involves looking at data all day which is not very exciting.

When I went to Hemel Hempstead, Ethan always offered to carry my rucksack to my car for me, but I was reluctant to accept his help. It wasn't until I started writing my book that I consciously realised the main reason for my reluctance. When walking a long distance, I find it difficult to walk and to talk at the same time, so I didn't really want someone accompanying me.

On 1st November 2009 after just over seven and a half years of buying my flat for £100k, I made the last monthly payment on my mortgage. I paid my mortgage off so quickly by setting my monthly direct debit to £1k some years earlier and adding supplementary payments to it when I could. It gave me a real sense of achievement.

To be more accurate, what I did was pay down my mortgage, leaving it with an outstanding balance of £100. I didn't want to pay off my mortgage completely, as it would have incurred fees. I was now in the happy position of being able to withdraw money out of my mortgage with easy access up to about £100k.

I didn't know what I was going to do with the money but knew that having access to it was a good place to be in.

Over the years, I visualised my mortgage as if it were an iceberg surrounded by other icebergs of different sizes, melting at different speeds in the Antarctic. Left to melt away on its own it would take 25 years. However, chipping away at it means it will disintegrate a lot faster. I would like to apologise to Greenpeace because I feel, by paying off my mortgage so quickly, I have contributed to rising sea levels!

On 21st November Clare phoned and wished me a happy birthday. Clare sounded quite emotional in a way that I had not heard before. She told me that she and the kids had come over to England for a short break. The kids were staying with Rupert for a few days while she visited a friend up north.

What was unfolding was Clare and Rupert's separation during which time I assisted Clare financially and gave her emotional support. I felt like I was getting dragged into their separation, and it was making me stressed and unwell therefore I decided to detach myself from my whole family. In doing so I became more peaceful not being involved in any family stress. However I miss my niece and nephews, they know where I am and are welcome to contact me.

The timing was spooky I was able to assist Clare financially because on the 1st December I made my last mortgage payment. Christmas 2009 felt very odd. The family turmoil destroyed my confidence and the will to phone Julia again and I lost contact with her. Sad, but realistically with her living in Bangkok, our friendship wasn't going to go anywhere.

Rarely did I have any sick leave of work but I felt so stressed that I had a week off my managers Ethan and Reg were very understanding but when I returned to work I had even less motivation to become a DBA.

Another casualty was my friendship with Stuart because he didn't want to become involved in my families situation. We had been friends for over fifteen years and at times, he had felt like a father to me.Earlier,

I mentioned that I started going out in 2008 with City Socialising (CS). I carried on doing this throughout 2009 and 2010, going to a CS event two or three times a week and continuing to meet drunk women.

I did meet one nice woman who was ten to fifteen years older than me. We went for a platonic drink together a couple of times. She appreciated me for who I really am saying: "You are a really lovely guy. You will meet the right person for you sooner or later."

One of my motivations in writing this book is that I want to show people that you can achieve anything you want in life.

This is not a book on property investment. However, over the last few years, I have learnt so much from self-made property multimillionaires. I have gained knowledge about people, their mindset and the link between this and success. I have enough material to make a DVD or CD series with priceless information on how to be successful in whatever field you are in.

At a CS New Year's party in January 2010 above a pub in Hove I met Basil, as I was heading for the Gents' toilet:

Basil: "Are you interested in investing in property?"

Me: "I've never thought about it. I don't know?"

Basil: Would you like to buy an off-plan property in the Caribbean?"

Me: "No."

When I left the toilet, Basil was still there and he started to wax lyrical about buying an off-plan Caribbean property. I bluntly replied, "It sounds like a con, I'm not interested" and went back to the people that I was talking to prior to this.

Over the next month or so I met Basil again at a couple of CS events. The conversation returned to property and he said he ran a monthly property investment networking club in Brighton. My interest piqued, I went to Basil's next networking event in March.

The speaker at the event that month was Ruth. She spoke about the different ways you can buy property. It was an eye-opener and I found it interesting. There were about twenty people at the event. Some of them looked at me as if they were thinking 'What are you doing here?' At least that is what I was thinking! I didn't know anyone there apart from Basil and I was a bit shy. I heard people talking about HMOs and I didn't have the confidence to ask them what a House in Multiple Occupation (HMO) was. I felt a bit like a fish out of water.

One person there had curly blonde hair and looked about ten years older than me and a bit rough and ready. I thought, 'He's not going to make it in property'. I couldn't have been more wrong as he's been a successful property investor for at least fifteen years. He's my friend Neil Stovell and we've built a friendship based on mutual respect.

I spoke to Ruth at the end of her presentation and she seemed like a nice person.

The first phase of my property investment journey started here and ran through to September 2010. It reminds me of the expression: You don't know what you don't know.

After the first networking event I became friends with Basil. We spoke about property when we saw each other at CS events. I was fascinated about the different ways in which people can buy and make money from property. Basil and I met up for a bite to eat once a week when we would talk about property investment. Basil, however, could only be consumed in small doses as he was somewhat self-centred.

He continued to try to persuade me to buy an off-plan Caribbean property through Harlequin, for whom he was an agent. As he didn't seem to have all the answers and I was interested to find out more, I decided to look into it myself.

Basil suggested I read 'Property Magic' by Simon Zutshi who is one of the top mentors in the UK. I read it very quickly. It talks about how to find and buy a property directly from a vendor. It also underlines how important it is to be ethical when buying direct. If you are unethical and rip people off, you'll get a bad reputation and people will not work with you. The UK property investment community is relatively small and everyone knows each other.

I went to Basil's property networking club for the second time in April 2010 when I had a light bulb moment. I was watching a presentation on lease options and realised that property investment is a people business. The thought exploded in my head: 'property investment is the job that I've been looking for - because it involves people and numbers.'

I was more confident speaking to people at the second property networking event. Seeing my enthusiasm one person said to me, "You are a gift to the world" and "You're going to do very well in property because you've got good people skills". This was good to hear but I thought, 'I haven't done anything yet.'

Seeing that I was interested in finding out more about Harlequin and buying an off-plan Caribbean property, Basil arranged for Ruth, a Harlequin agent, to talk about it at a Brighton hotel. Basil managed to attract just one other potential investor to the presentation along with Gerald, an account manager who worked at Harlequin.

Ruth's Harlequin presentation interested me, but I was still very sceptical about the whole thing. Over the following three months I liaised with Gerald mainly via email, whilst doing due diligence on buying an off-plan apartment in St Lucia.

In early May I booked a week's all-inclusive holiday in the Dominican Republic. A couple of days before going on holiday Ray came to see me at home. Having heard me talking about Ray, Basil was keen to sell Ray a Harlequin property. I knew Ray wouldn't be interested in it but, mainly to keep Basil quiet, I invited Basil over as well to meet Ray.

At the time I wasn't very happy. I was still meeting drunk women at CS events and Mum was still very volatile as she had not accepted the situation with Clare and Rupert.

Ray had recently started writing a blog and when he came to see me he suggested:

Ray: "I think you should start writing a blog about yourself to help you find a girlfriend."

My immediate thought was 'What a silly idea. What am I going to say on it? "Hello, I'm Patrick and I would like a girlfriend…"'

Unenthusiastically, I replied "Yeah, maybe. I'll think about it."

Basil said that I would enjoy "Rich Dad Poor Dad "by Robert Kiyosaki and gave me the book to read on holiday. I started reading it on the plane to the Dominican Republic. I could tell from the start that it's a great book but I didn't get far with it on the plane.

Thomas Cook didn't upgrade me and I found myself sitting next to three eighteen year old girls, all a little naive. One of them didn't believe that Wales is part of the UK. Another became worried when she saw there was a bit of ice on the outside of the window. She thought it would be hotter at 37,000 feet than it was on the ground because, "We're closer to the sun up here!" I tried to educate them about these matters.

One of the girls didn't know how to fill in her immigration card so I helped her. This was a bit of a turnabout, because I usually ask one of the air-hostesses to fill mine in for me.

The three girls didn't stop talking all the way to the Caribbean, brushing their hair and putting on more and more make-up!

The Dominican Republic was one of the worst holidays I've been on. This was mainly due to the forty-two degree heat, much too hot to push myself in my wheelchair. The hotel staff weren't very friendly either, perhaps because I don't speak Spanish. Although in chatting to some of the women, I did pick up some words and phrases.

I met a load of Canadians who, by contrast, were friendly. It's easy to get drunk at an all-inclusive resort. One day, I sat at the bar with some people and we all had five Sambucas, which didn't seem to affect me at all! So the next evening, I went for eleven of them! I regretted it the following day when I felt as rough as a choppy North Sea ferry crossing!

My enduring memory of the Dominican Republic resort is sitting in the lobby and bar area reading 'Rich Dad Poor Dad'. It is by far the best book that I've read and I couldn't read it fast enough.

Seeing that I was engrossed in it, people kept asking me about the book. By the end of the week I was saying to people, "I'm going to make £1 million".

The book is about Robert Kiyosaki having two Dads when he was growing up. His real father which he refers to as *Poor Dad*, and his friend's father as *Rich Dad*.

Throughout the book, Robert Kiyosaki compares how Rich Dad thinks and does, to how Poor Dad thinks and does. Robert Kiyosaki also explains what Rich Dad taught him on how to be successful.

I've heard many people say that success is 95% about mindset (how you think) and 5% about action (what you do). I've known that to be the case for many years.

It may not seem it at first, but the mindsets of the two Dads are completely different:

Rich Dad thinks "The reason I am rich is because I've got three children to support."

Poor Dad thinks "The reason I am poor is because I've got three children to support."

I learnt so much from reading 'Rich Dad Poor Dad' and paraphrased, Robert Kiyosaki puts the case:

As a society we are brought up to do well at school, in order to get a job with good promotion prospects, work for forty years and then retire on a relatively low pension.

98% of people work for a company and make the company owner rich.

2% of people own a company and get someone else to run the company for them.

Successful people do the opposite to what 98% of the population are doing.

If you would like help from someone, help them first without expecting anything in return and then they will help you in abundance. This is reciprocity - I'll explain it later on.

However, the following are the most important things that I have learnt from Robert Kiyosaki about being successful in life:

- Success means building recursive streams of passive income.
- Opportunities of making money are all around you - you just need to spot them.
- Successful people take chances in life.
- The one key factor to being successful is *persistence*.

It was while I was reading 'Rich Dad Poor Dad' in the Dominican Republic that I realised that my future no longer lay in working for *Shh*. The book taught me the process of becoming rich. I knew I could do it - and that it would allow me to reach my full potential.

I also knew that working at *Shh* wasn't going to enable me to reach my full potential. That's why, before I had finished reading 'Rich Dad Poor Dad', I started saying to people "I'm going to make £1 million".

Since then, I have said on several occasions that what I want to do is set up one or more *recursive* streams of income.

It is far better to have several smaller 'pots' of income streams, rather than just one big pot. By having several pots, if something were to happen to one or two of them, you've still got your other pots of money. Were you to just have one big pot of money and something happened to it you would probably be screwed!

That is the process to making money. It's simple!

I grasped it immediately when I read 'Rich Dad Poor Dad'. I also realised something else in the Dominican Republic. I needed to find a good property mentor to teach me how I could buy an endless number of properties. I decided that the best way for me to find a mentor was to set up a blog and write about what I wanted to achieve and demonstrate my financial intelligence.

It was funny when I left the Dominican Republic. The plane was close enough to the terminal for me to walk out of the building to the plane. There were two sets of stairs onto the plane, one at the front of the aircraft and one in the centre of it.

There was no point in me walking past the stairs at the front to go up the middle stairs. Hence I went up the stairs at the front. Standing at the door of the plane was an air-hostess who watched me as I was walking up the stairs. I was quite out of breath when I reached the top and walked onto the plane.

Air-hostess: "Hello sir, don't worry about walking any further, you can sit in the front row."

Me: "Are you sure?"

Air-hostess: "Yes that's fine, we're not full in business class today."

Me: "Thank you, that's very nice of you."

Air-hostess: "Can I get you a drink?"

The flight home was nice and peaceful!

Not long after I got home I phoned my friend Ernie at *Shh*, who already knew that I was interested in property investment. Amongst much laughter, our hilarious conversation went along these lines:

Me: "I've just come back from holiday in the Dominican Republic, where I read a book called 'Rich Dad Poor Dad'. It's the best book I've ever read because it taught me how to make an endless amount of money. I have decided to make £1 million.

Ernie [laughing at me]: "Have you gone mad?"

Me [laughing my head off]: "No, I'm absolutely serious! I understand the process of how to make £1 million

Ernie: "How are you going to make £1 million then?"

Me: "By buying an endless number of properties and renting them out."

Ernie "You're mad! How are you going manage all of your properties?"

Me: "That's not important right now. My point is I know I can make £1 million."

Ernie: "I think you need to go and see your doctor because you're delirious!"

Me: "You don't think that I can make £1 million then?"

Ernie: "No!"

Me: "I know I can do it - and I'm going to prove it to you!

Me: "And another thing...I've decided that at some point I'm going to leave *Shh*."

Ernie: "You're absolutely mad! I think that holiday sun in the Dominican Republic has gotten to you! Listen, take my advice, stay working at *Shh* until you're fifty-five.

Me: "No offence but you're such the 'Poor Dad' character. You need to read the book."

Our humorous conversation continued for a while longer. Amazingly, Ernie bought the book from Amazon while I was on the phone with him.

I haven't spoken to Ernie for a few years, when I last did he said he had read up to page two of the book! Ernie started working at *Shh* in 1980 and he will probably still be there in 2080!

In May 2010 I purchased the domain SussexPatrick.com and by the end of the month I had set up my Wordpress blog. My second blog post included this joke:

*I would like to work at NASA because it really would be rocket science. However, the same could be said about working in a firework factory!*

The sub heading I came up with for my blog was 'I am the first property investor with Cerebral Palsy. This is my journey to one million pounds." There's nothing special about £1 million - I think it's just an eye-catching figure.

A couple of months after I started my blog, Clare called me on my mobile phone. Never will I forget that phone conversation, partly because I was sitting on the toilet at home when she called me!

Clare: "Your blog looks really good and I know you're going to do it [make £1 million]."

In December 2013 I published my one-hundredth blog post.

In June, when I told Ethan and Reg at work that I no longer wanted to become a DBA, they were very understanding. Explaining that I wanted to pursue property investment, I asked them if I could take a six-month sabbatical from *Shh*. It took a few months for them to investigate the possibility.

In the meantime, I was in a state of limbo at *Shh*, exacerbated by the policy that disabled people couldn't go on the bench to find another assignment. The only work I was allocated was to keep producing the daily five-minute table space report.

In early July, I took a rare Saturday off from doing the sports show when Ray invited me to an auto-response psychology workshop in London. Ray was still working with Colin, who was hosting the workshop. It sounded interesting so I went up to London with the two guys.

It gave me more of an awareness of how I and other people have a tendency to automatically respond to people's comments, without properly thinking about it first.

I never used to think that I was good at sales and marketing, but if you think about it we are all constantly 'selling' and 'marketing' ourselves with every conversation or interaction we have.

When it first came to working in pairs during the workshop, I made eye-contact with an attractive-looking African girl. It prompted her to come over to me and we spent the rest of the day working together. I thought Collette was a really sweet girl.

A week or so later, Ray invited me to a 'taster evening' in Croydon for a ten-week personal development course. Having been trained by Colin, the course was going to be run by three ladies, one of whom was Collette.

I thought it would be a fun and interesting course to do, one evening a week in Croydon and I really liked Collette! So I decided to do the course which started at the end of July.

During the evening I told Collette I thought she was really nice and I would like to go out with her. She just replied "Maybe..." Then at the end, when I was walking out of the hotel, Collette came up behind me, and without saying anything, she kissed me on the back of my neck. I thought it was a strange thing to do.

Since launching Splash FM the station hosts, 'The Garden Party' concert every July. As I worked on the sport show and I am a shareholder in MSH, I am given a ticket into the VIP marquee which includes complementary food and drink. Andy Sparsis of the Proto Restaurant Group, who owns several excellent restaurants in the area, does the catering and always puts on a good spread.

While I was sitting in the marquee at the concert in 2010 talking to Fergus, I saw Chris Copsey and we acknowledged one another. Having written to him a few times when I was a young teenager, asking if I could do some work experience at Southern FM, I thought about going over to Chris and saying hello and meeting him. However, I didn't feel the need to do so. He knew that I produced the sports show on Saturday afternoons. Not walking over and meeting Chris is something I would later come to regret.

When the personal development course in Croydon started there were about eight people on it. But over the weeks that number diminished. I did find it an interesting course. Some of the people on the course had gone through traumatic experiences earlier and were still affected by them.

My positive outlook on life enabled me to offer some words of wisdom and advice. They found me inspirational and I enjoyed helping them.

The other two ladies running the course were Helen and Anita; Helen was and still is about my age whilst Anita was relatively older than me.

I'm friends with Helen today. Her roots are in Ghana but she was brought up and lives in Croydon. I have said to Helen that she's my Ghanaian-Croydonian friend!

Helen and Anita were the more vocal coaches on the course than Collette. I found Collette wasn't as confident as her colleagues.

Over the weeks and months I sometimes phoned Collette in the evenings. She was happy to talk to me. She quite rightly said that in order for me to find a girlfriend, I first had to like myself. However, not long after Collette kissed me on the back of my neck she found herself a boyfriend called Russ on the internet!

Towards the end of the summer, I had spent over three months doing due diligence on purchasing an off-plan apartment in St Lucia from Harlequin. In doing so, I asked Gerald who was helpful, literally over a hundred questions. I understood the structure of the deal and I believed in it.

The purchase price of the property was £185k and I needed to put down £55.5k (30% of the purchase price) to buy it. Harlequin would pay me the monthly interest payments on my deposit until the property was built in a few years' time. At which point the property would be worth double the price I paid for it and I would be able to get a mortgage to cover the purchase price and all of the monthly interest payments from Harlequin.

I had spoken to many people about investing in Harlequin. Some people said 'don't do it, it sounds a con', others like Ruth said 'go for it'.'.

I had to make a judgement call. I had become a property investor and I wanted to take action and buy a property. Hence I chose to go for it. I knew there was a risk that it wouldn't come off but I was prepared to take a chance. I withdrew £55.5k from my mortgage on my flat and paid Harlequin the 30% deposit.

When I wrote a blog post saying I had bought an off-plan apartment from Harlequin, several people posted replies on my blog, saying Harlequin couldn't be trusted and that I had made a mistake. The negative comments didn't bother me because I believed in Harlequin and they were paying me the monthly interest payments.

My subsequent phone conversations with Ernie were hysterical. They were along the lines of:

Ernie: "You've made a terrible mistake, you're going to lose all of your money with Harlequin...!"

Me: "No I haven't, Harlequin are paying me my monthly mortgage payments and it's not costing me anything. I believe in it and am not worried...!"

Shortly after I bought my Harlequin property, Basil received a hefty commission from the £55.5k, part of which Ruth received. Although Basil didn't help me with any of the due diligence I had done, he was the person who introduced me to Harlequin.

Because I was so enthusiastic when I got into property and I thought I was going to be really successful, Basil was convinced I was going to become a Harlequin sales agent. I did briefly look into becoming one but decided not to do so.

One Friday evening, in summer 2010 when Basil and I were having a quick meal in Hove, he asked me if I would be prepared to give him half of all of the sales commissions I was going to make. It was an odd thing for Basil to ask me, particularly as I wasn't a Harlequin sales agent!

Me: "Alright then, if you want me to give half of my sales commissions, I would like half of the commission you received from my Harlequin property."

Basil: "No chance."

Basil was annoyed with me for arriving late at the restaurant. When I got there he was halfway through his meal! Basil walked out of the restaurant when I was still eating, and this marked the end of our friendship. It didn't disappoint me. Basil isn't anything like me.

I did consider buying a second Harlequin off-plan property but decided not to do so.

September 2010 was eventful in property terms.

My friend Steve Bell spotted a four bed, two bathroom, first and second floor maisonette for sale in Worthing and I put an offer on the property. It was a repossession and it had been poorly looked after.

As Ruth was the only (quasi) mentor I knew at the time, I asked her for advice. My plan was to refurbish the property and then to sell it and make about £100k profit on it. Although my offer to buy it was accepted someone else offered a higher price. I thought about making a higher offer but it would have tied up all of my available cash and there's was no guarantee on how much I could have resold it for.

The second time I viewed the property I went with my builder friend Dave. The stairs to the first floor of the maisonette were on the outside of the building. When I reached the first floor and inside the property, Dave was on the second floor and asked me:

Dave: "Have you been up here yet?"

Me: "No, not yet"

Dave: "You've got to come and have a look."

I was still slightly out of breath from climbing the first flight of stairs but in my eagerness decided to start climbing the second flight. As I put my foot on the first step, I could feel myself falling backwards. Instinctively I grabbed hold of one of the wooden banister posts. However it was rotten, and not strong enough to support my weight.

It was a surreal moment. I found myself lying flat on my back holding a little piece of banister post in my hand with the estate agent looking over me! This turned into a couple of minutes of embarrassment. Later, hilarity ensued and lasted for a few days.

I was keen to become financially free so I could leave *Shh*. I met Ruth for a coffee a couple of times. She asked me how much income I would need per month in order to leave *Shh*. I replied £2k.

Ruth said she knew a property sourcing company who sold refurbished two and three bed houses up north, as packaged deals.

A package deal is where you pay a property sourcer a fee to find you a good value property and who then helps you through the process of purchasing the property including setting up a mortgage.

Ruth said that I could take £40k out of my mortgage on my flat and buy ten package deals, which I could rent out. She said that each property would produce a net cashflow at £200, giving me a monthly income of £2k.

I was a bit dubious. One of my questions was:

Me: "If I'm going to have properties all over the north of England, how am I going to find good letting agents to manage each property?"

Ruth: "Don't worry, I'll help you find a good letting agent to manage each of them."

Following some consideration, I decided to buy one property and try it.

Ruth came up with a property and I started to purchase it. After she emailed me the illustration on it:

Me: "Is there a mistake here? It says the cashflow on it is only £117..."

Ruth: "The cashflow on some properties is lower than on others. The cashflow on the next one will be higher."

Me: "No, I don't want to do this anymore. I would have to buy more than ten properties to make £2k a month"

Ruth: "It's still a good deal..."

Me: "No, I want my money back please."

Ruth: "You've put me in a rather embarrassing situation. I've agreed to buy the deal now."

Me: "Well, you should have been honest with me in the first place...

Ruth: "You'll have to wait until I find another buyer for it."

Ruth soon found someone else and gave me my money back. Needless to say, I didn't work with her again.

In the first half of September, I received an email inviting me to The Wealth from Property seminar. Some of the UK's top property mentors were going to be there, so I took another Saturday off from the sports show.

The 18th September 2010 in London marked the beginning of the second phase in my property investment journey.

When I started out in property investment I felt like buying everything that came my way. I was like a kid in a sweet shop.

Knowing what I know now, my advice to people starting out in property investment is:

- Do not buy any properties for at least the first year. Spend the time going to networking events in your area and meet local investors.
- Educate yourself. Most people only know about making money from buying property and letting it out .There are so many smarter ways of generating cash from property
- Go to the Berkshire Property Meet. It is the biggest and best monthly networking event - and it's where the top property trainers and mentors hang out.

# Chapter 6

I wrote this chapter in 2012. I was thinking about writing a book at the time. Having only blogged about my property journey, I wanted to see how easy it would be for me to write a slightly more personal piece and how people would react to it. I knew it would make an excellent read. Enjoy!

***

In summer 2010, I went to a City Socialising (CS) get together at a bar on Brighton beach. It was a typically buzzing Brighton bar on a warm July Friday evening, with loads of people. I got there at about 9.30 and everyone was sitting in the patio area on the beach. I got myself a Corona and joined a group of CS people sitting at a long wooden table. I said hello to a couple of people I knew and there were loads of conversations going on.

On the opposite side of the table, slightly to my right was a girl I hadn't seen before. I listened to the conversation that Fiona was having for a minute or two and then she mentioned playing golf. This was my cue to tell my golf joke, which Fiona found very funny: "I've never played golf before but think I would score quite highly because I've got a good handicap!!"

We chatted for 30 seconds and as it was quite noisy, Fiona came and sat next to me and our conversation continued:

Fiona: "So what's wrong with you then?!"

Me: "I've got Cerebral Palsy - do you know what that is?"

Fiona: "I've heard of it, but not really...?"

Me: "When I was born, the umbilical cord was wrapped around my neck and I couldn't breathe for 4 minutes."

(This is one of the best and funniest things someone has ever said to me)

Fiona: "It was a bit stupid of you not to breathe for the first 4 minutes of your life!"

I thought: 'This girl is completely at ease with me.'

For the next three and a half hours we had an absolute laugh together. Fiona was thirty seven, lived in Hove, a single mother with 2 youngish kids, and worked in an old age home, but had worked in marketing in London. I bought her 3 or 4 drinks over the three and a half hours and I remember her drinking wine and lager. I had two Coronas as I was driving.

We talked to other people but Fiona always came back to me. She had a knack of insulting people but in a humorous tone - a sign that she had enough of talking to someone. I heard her say to a bloke who looked a bit like Jarvis Cocker. "Your green jacket doesn't go with your trousers. You look awful!"

Another bloke got: "You really don't know how to talk to women, do you?!"

I'm making Fiona sound horrible but I thought she was nice to me and I found her very funny.

I remember going into the packed bar with her and pushing my way to the front of the queue. Fiona shouted, "Excuse me, out the way, there's a disabled guy here!" Then as the barman put my card into the Chip & PIN machine, Fiona exclaimed, "He can't use one of them, he's disabled!" I guess the barman realised that I wasn't the most incoherent person at the bar!"

At about 1am we decided to leave and I offered Fiona a lift home. The bar was on the beach and there were two ways up to the promenade on the main road. On one side was the big slope I had used earlier, on the other were steps. I thought about which way to go for a few seconds. As we were slightly closer to the steps and because I always prefer a non-disabled route, I opted for the steps. It wasn't until we got in front of the steps that I realised how many and how steep they were.

Anyway, I went for it! I tried too hard because about half way up, I lost my footing! Luckily, I was holding onto the handrail but dangling, with a mighty drop below me! I remember thinking 'Oh no, what is she going to think of me now?' I kept saying my usual, "I'm alright...". Fiona was in no state to help me and said, "Come on, stop mucking around."

Somehow and, after a bit more dangling, I regained my footing and walked up the rest of the steps. I was feeling pretty exhausted as I reached the zebra crossing to cross the main road. I made eye contact with Fiona, hoping that she would go and press the button on the traffic lights. Fiona said, "Well go on then, go press the button..." So I did.

We got to my car and were about to get in when Fiona spotted the nearby casino.

Fiona: "Oh! Can we go to the casino?!"

Me: "It's late..."

Fiona: "Oh please, I've never been to the casino before and I really want to play the roulette wheel."

Me: "No, we both have to work tomorrow."

Fiona: "Please! I hardly ever go out."

Me: "I'm tired and want to get home."

Fiona: "PLEASE! I really want to play on the roulette wheel."

I thought 'She's a single mother and hardly ever goes out, I want to be nice to her and show her a good time. I've never been to a casino either, it could be good fun.' And with that thought, I had an influx of energy.

So we went to the casino. It took us about 30 minutes to register as new members because Fiona kept saying silly things and giving the wrong information. We then went upstairs in the lift, I bought some casino chips and we went over to the games tables.

Fiona on seeing a roulette wheel table: "ooh, look..."

Having stood for over 45 minutes I was feeling tired, hot and thirsty.

Me: "I'm really hot and thirsty, can we go and get a drink first?"

Fiona: "I tell you what [pulling a chair out for me at the roulette wheel table], you sit down here and I'll go get us some drinks.

Me; "Okay, thank you, could you get me a coke please."

I gave Fiona a £20 note. It was the smallest note I had left and I thought she would bring me back some change as she had done earlier. However, Fiona then decided to ask the female croupier some questions.

Fiona: "What's your name?"

The croupier (looking a little bemused) showed her nametag and said her name.

Fiona: "How long have you worked here for?"

Me: "I'm sorry..."

Fiona approached one of the players who was absorbed in the game: "How do you play this game then?"

Me: "I'm really sorry, I've only just met her this evening!"

Fiona turned to see that another player didn't have many chips on the table: "Ooh, you're not doing very well, are you?!"

This shifted the situation from mildly amusing to embarrassing and I had to do something.

Me: "I am so very sorry. Fiona, PLEASE can you go and buy me a coke."

And off Fiona went.

I started playing roulette and was lucky early on - I won £5 twice! Five minutes had gone by with no sign of Fiona. After about 10 minutes, I started to worry in case she was lying in a drunken stupor somewhere. I asked the waitress who was serving drinks at the table, (you're right, I didn't need to send Fiona to the bar at all!) if she could see Fiona anywhere. After a few minutes, the waitress came back and said, "She's okay, she's sitting at the bar drinking champagne." I thought, 'This isn't good.' By that stage I'd lost focus on playing roulette and had lost most of my initial £20 in chips. I felt an obligation to lose the rest before getting up and walking away (how my mindset has changed since!).

As I was walking to the bar, I saw Fiona sitting there, with a glass and bottle of pink champagne, talking to a bloke. The bottle was half full (I'm an optimist!) and Fiona was the only one drinking the champagne.

(It was about 2am)

Fiona (slurring her words): "I'm alright here, you can go home, if you like."

I wasn't going to do that. I felt responsible for Fiona. I had offered her a lift home and then taken her to the casino and I wanted to make sure she got home safely. And I liked the responsibility of looking after her.

I spent a few seconds listening to the conversation Fiona was having with the bloke. Fiona was insulting him in her unique way and he was making fun of her paralytic state.

Me: "Fiona, did you get me a coke?"

Fiona: "Ask the barman, he'll get one for you."

So I did. What Fiona didn't notice was that I also asked the barman to get rid of the champagne bottle.

Me (to the bloke Fiona was talking to): "Excuse me mate, do you think you could get me a chair, because a bar stool is a bit high for me?"

Bloke (his name escapes me): "Sure, no problem."

I then positioned myself between the two of them and started chatting with the bloke. He was on a stag do and had come to the bar to buy a round of drinks. It took me about five minutes to get the guy to leave the bar.

After ten minutes of talking to Fiona and trying to persuade her it was time for us to go, I realised I needed to try another tactic. Fiona kept saying "can we just stay for another drink."

I stood up in front of her, sitting on the bar stool, put my arms around her waist and gently slid her forward and onto her feet. 'Bingo!' I thought. I then started to guide her towards the lift. She kept trying to go in another direction. I kept saying "Come on, this way!" It felt like I was directing a small child.

When we were going down in the lift Fiona did say I was a nice guy and thanked me for looking after her.

When we got out of the lift I found myself saying "Come on, this way!" a few more times. The last person Fiona tried to chat to (and then insult) was the doorman outside the casino, but he wasn't having any of it!

I felt a great sense of achievement when we were both installed in my car.

Me: "Are you okay?"

Fiona (looking like she was semiconscious): "Yeah."

Me: "Where do you live in Hove?"

She told me the name of her road.

Me: "I don't know where that is. Can you direct me or shall I get my satnav out?"

Fiona: "Yes, I'll show you how to get there."

I started driving and within 30 seconds she was asleep! I pulled over and got my satnav. As I was driving I thought, 'I don't know what number she lives at. It's okay, when I get to her road I'll just wake her up.' Within 5 minutes I got to the start of her road and stopped the car.

(It was now 2.45am)

Me: "Fiona wake up, we're here."

No response.

Me (gently shaking her arm): "Wake up Fiona."

No response.

Me (Shaking her arm a bit harder): "Fiona..."

No response.

Me (Shaking her leg): "Fiona, wake up."

No response.

At this point I began to worry. For about 20 seconds I thought, 'Oh sh*t, is she okay? Am I going to have to take her to A&E?" And then she started snoring loudly and I knew she was okay.

As my car was in the middle of the road, I decided to find a parking space and think about what to do. Ironically, the only space I found was directly outside of a pub! My further efforts to wake her up didn't work, including shouting "Wake up!" shaking her again and turning up my radio as loudly as it would go.

I took the only option. I sat listening to the radio and waited for her to wake up. I thought about driving home and leaving her sleeping in my car. But she might have woken up and not known where she was, so that wasn't an option. Periodically, I tried to wake her up but nothing worked. If the pub had been open I would have gone there!

After sitting there with Fiona snoring away for three hours, at 5.45am, she woke up.

Fiona: (Surprised and innocent): "Oh, I live down here..."

Me: "I know but I don't know which number you live at...?"

Fiona: "It's further down [pointing straight ahead]."

I started to drive.

Fiona: "I'm really tired and I've got to be at work at 9.30."

Me: "Well, I've got to be at work by 2 o'clock and you've had three hours sleep more than I've had."

Nothing much else was said. When we got to her house, we swapped phone numbers and that was it.

I really felt like having a cooked breakfast but no cafés were open yet. I got home and had about four hours of sleep.

I texted Fiona the following day to see how she was. She said she had a very rough day at work and thanked me for looking after her.

We had several text conversations over the next couple of weeks and planned to meet up twice for a drink. On both occasions and at the last minute, Fiona came up with an excuse why she couldn't make it.

On text, Fiona suggested her life was hard as a single parent working full-time. She also said she was working extra shifts because she was taking her kids on holiday and needed the money.

I felt sorry for her and thought 'I bet nobody has sent her some flowers in ages and she would really appreciate it if I did' so I sent her some flowers. Fiona texted me the morning she received the flowers and said they were beautiful.

That evening I went for a meal in Brighton with a group of people. I was walking back to my car, after the meal, when my phone rang in my pocket. As I was a bit out of breath, I decided to leave it until I got back to my car. A few minutes later I discovered it was a missed call from Fiona, the first time she had called me. I phoned her back and left her a voice message. She texted me the next day saying she was going on holiday and would arrange to meet up when she got back.

\* \* \* \* \*

At the time of writing, that was over 18 months ago. She must be having a bloody good holiday!

If you remove the casino episode and the three hour wait for her to wake up, Fiona was just like many of the other woman I've met over the years.

When I told my friend Ray about Fiona a week later, he said, "She was just using you." It wasn't until I had stepped back from the situation that I realised it. Ray then said something that hit me like a brick: "You don't actually 'achieve' a girlfriend". Until that point I had used my 'I can achieve anything I put my mind to' mindset to try to find a girlfriend.

As I said at the beginning, I've learnt so much about myself over the last eighteen months and I have changed greatly. I've always held the belief that I am going to find the right person and now I know I don't have to do anything.

Doing the Progressive Master Class in November 2010 was a turning point. I made the decision there and then that my days of going out to meet drunken women were over. Focusing on property has made me much happier.

When I've been in relationships in the past I've been more confident and content. I've also known a couple of women who would like to be with me but I don't feel the same about them.

Another pivotal event was the three day Wealth & Lifestyle course I attended in December 2011. On the second day, Johnnie Cass asked the audience, "What is your greatest fear?" I put my hand up and then I thought 'What are people going to think of me?". Then I decided 'Sod it!' and said "Women rejecting me". Johnnie invited me up on stage and I thought 'what the f**k am I doing here, in front of about fifty people?!' He asked me some searching questions for a few minutes. I then said, "If people don't like me the way I am, it's their problem and not mine."

Having fifty people applauding me was a humbling experience.

Not that long after my encounter with Fiona, Clare phoned me. My sister never seemed to complain about anything and just got on with life. However, since her split with Rupert, perhaps as a result of spending time with Mum, she had become more negative.

Whenever Clare phoned me now, she went on a bit about her separation. It was bad enough having Mum using me as an emotional doormat and now Clare was doing the same thing. But she wasn't in Mum's league. I love Clare and did all I could to help her.

Whenever Clare or Mum contacted me they didn't really ask me how I was doing or just accepted my muttered answer, "I'm alright". Although I never told Clare about any of the women I met at the weekends, she knew I was going out and meeting them.

On this occasion, still feeling bruised by the casino debacle and cheesed off with Clare's negativity, I decided to tell Clare about Fiona. After my ten minute rant, encapsulating the whole episode and its aftermath, Clare was silent for a few seconds, before she came out with, "Well, there are plenty more fish in the sea."

Patrick Souiljaert

# Chapter 7

At 8.35am on Saturday, 18th September 2010 I arrived at a London hotel for the Wealth from Property event. I felt pumped up about the awesome day ahead.

While waiting to go into the event I bumped into Basil and Louise who I knew from Basil's networking event. Although Basil and I weren't really friends anymore we got on okay. I sat with them in the front row of the auditorium.

There were three to four hundred people in the audience and four speakers. Juswant Rai hosted the event. The speakers were in order of appearance:

- Sylvia Rai (Sylvia and Juswant run the Berkshire Property Meet)
- John Lee (co-founder of the Wealth Dragons)
- Rob Moore (co-founder of Progressive Property)
- Glenn Armstrong (Someone who inspired me to write this book)

Sylvia's speech was about the importance of having a positive mindset in order to succeed in life, in business and in property. It made me realise that property investment was the right thing for me to get into.

I specifically remember Sylvia saying that most people say they're going to do something, but then they never do it.

***If you really want to do something you will find a way, If you don't, you will find an excuse.***

What I remember from John Lee's presentation is him waving £20 notes in the air, saying "Who wants some money...?". He was also giving away books. I wasn't fast enough to get one of the £20 notes but I did get a book on lease options from him. As John gave me the book, he looked at me and said, "You took action!"

Rob Moore captivated me with his speech. In his pink and purple stripy shirt he said "Four years ago I was an artist and £30k in dept. Now I'm a multimillionaire...". I thought 'If he can do that, I can do it too - and I'm not £30k in debt.'

Throughout his presentation Rob was promoting Progressive's three-day masterclass, together with their other courses. He kept flashing up his Powerpoint presentation - which consisted of a white digital countdown clock in the centre of a plain black background saying, "You've now only got five minutes left to grab this special discounted offer."

The three day masterclass sounded brilliant. When the countdown clock got to three minutes, I picked my crutches up, put my arms in them and sat on the edge of my chair, poised to stand up, still intently listening to what Rob was saying.

When the time got down to one and a half minutes I thought, 'I can afford it. F**k it. I'm going to do it." I told Louise that I was going to sign up for the training courses. She replied, "Go for it, I know you're going to succeed."

I stood up and walked to the wide centre aisle. I had to get to the tables along the back wall of the hall to sign up. The tables seemed like a long way away at first, so I walked as fast as I could, nervous that I wasn't going make it in time. I did make it and paid £2.5k for the three-day masterclass and three one-day courses. It was a wise investment because I learnt so much.

I think the content of Glenn Amstrong's presentation was better than Rob's and John's. When Glenn set up his first recursive strategy, he set himself a goal to buy 52 properties in 52 weeks. He managed to get 52 properties in 48 weeks.

I met people all through the day and told them I was going to make £1 million. At the end of Glenn's presentation, I went to meet Rob Moore and said the same thing to him! I also said that I was really looking forward to the masterclass.

Two days later I went to the Berkshire Property Meet (BPM) for the first time.

The BPM is like no other property networking event. Each month there are over two hundred people there, from multimillionaires to people who are just interested in property investment. As property is a people business, it is full of genuine and nice people.

I hardly knew anyone there the first time, but it didn't stop me confidently walking up to people and saying "Hi, I'm Patrick, it's nice to meet you..." and I met such nice people.

I think the reason why I've always been very confident at networking and meeting people is because I spent so many years walking up to women in The Warwick and saying "Hi, I'm Patrick, it's nice to meet you..."

As a newbie at the September 2010 BPM, I met Sylvia and Juswant Rai, Glenn Armstrong and Simon Zutshi. Writing about it now, it was funny meeting Simon for the first time. Having read his book six months earlier I thought Simon was the god of property investing!

I remember apprehensively walking up to Simon and getting a little out of breath. I introduced myself and started to hyperventilate! Once I had overcome this, I told Simon a bit about myself and my goal to make £1 million. He replied "You would be an inspiration to my mastermind course."

Simon Zutshi was the main speaker at the BPM that evening. Before he started his presentation, Sylvia spoke for a few minutes about how to meet and network with people and the importance of having your own business cards and collecting other peoples'.

I remember Sylvia saying, "Don't just shove the business cards you collect into a shoebox at home, build a list from them. They then become your network."

That's what I did. My collection of business cards became an Excel spreadsheet. Then every time I wrote a blog update I emailed it to my network of property people and I still do it today.

When it comes to business cards, I believe that it's good to collect cards rather than just to give people yours, because then the onus is on you to contact the people that you've met.

This advice rings true: 'Your network is your net worth' – the people on your list will have skills and resources which are useful to you.

At the end of Simon Zutshi's presentation he offered one free place on his twelve-month mastermind mentoring programme. In order to qualify, you had to complete an online application form, saying why you deserved to win the free twelve-month mentorship. I decided to go for it.

I was so fired up by it that I filled in the application form when I got home at 1.30am! I spent most of the night on it, meticulously writing convincing answers to each question. I ended up going to bed at 6.30am!

It was disappointing when I didn't win the free mentorship place. Perhaps I wasn't offered it because I was honest on the application form, saying that I was already booked onto the courses with Progressive Property.

Since meeting Simon Zutshi for the first time in September 2010, I have seen him on several occasions. He always asks me how I'm doing. Whilst I highly respect Simon, I treat him like any other person.

There's nothing special about how multimillionaires look. What is special about self-made rich people is their mindset and their approach to making money. They love what they do and are contented without the impediment of stress.

On the personal development course I discovered that Collette was a bit of a saleswoman. She managed to get me to buy Colin's book by placing it in my hand. I must try that with my book! People find it difficult to refuse to purchase an item when they're holding it.

Having had quite a few phone conversations with Collette throughout the autumn, she invited me to a soul music night at the greyhound stadium in Hove one Friday evening. That afternoon she had come down from Croydon and was with a group of friends in Brighton who were all going to the soul evening. Collette was going to meet Russ (her internet boyfriend) at the greyhound stadium and then went back to his place in Lancing for the weekend.

Before meeting Collette at the stadium, she phoned me four or five times to arrange where and when to meet. She phoned so many times that it became annoying (in a nice way!).

When I met Russ that evening at the greyhound stadium, he appeared to be very bored, as if he didn't want to be there, with or without Collette. Russ didn't seem to be at all bothered by me hanging around with Collette.

While I was on the personal development course Mum sent me an email which I found upsetting. I was so stressed out that it caused me to vomit in a minor way in front of Helen and a couple of other people. I hardly ever threw up in front of people and it was an embarrassing experience.

I remember Helen saying to me "When you get an email from your Mum just delete it without reading it."

If it wasn't for my mum I wouldn't be as independent as I am and achieved everything I have. I am very grateful to her for this however sometimes I got the impression that she used me as a counsellor, which I found hard to deal with. My mum is essentially a good person but I got the impression that she lives in the past instead of the present.

On the personal development course I spoke of my desire for a girlfriend and about what I was doing in property. One of the other course coaches, the very intuitive Helen said that she was also interested in property investment.

Then one day before leaving to go to Basil's property networking club, Helen phoned me and said she was going to drive to Brighton (from Croydon) and come to the event as well.

The funny thing is, when I met Helen she said to me, "I'm here as your coach". Before this I thought she was interested in property investment. However now I speculated, 'Does Helen like me?'

The last weekend in October 2010 sticks in my mind. It was when I started Progressive's three-day property masterclass, one of the best courses I've ever done.

By that time, I had already written a lot of blog posts. Before attending the course I created a temporary front page for my blog, with the heading '**My goal:** Be the first person with Cerebral Palsy to be a self-made millionaire', with a photo of me in the main studio at Splash FM.

The page had hyperlinks to blog posts about me, my financial intelligence and what I had learnt in property so far. It took me ages to make the hyperlinks look aesthetically pleasing.

I thought the masterclass was my opportunity to find a property mentor for myself.

Progressive Property is in Peterborough, which is a three hour drive from Shoreham. I felt so positive about doing the masterclass that my two year old fear of driving on motorways simply vanished! I drove up to Peterborough the night before and stayed in the venue hotel.

There were about twenty people on the course. Whenever I go on a course I like to sit near the front. I'm not shy in asking and answering lots of questions as I like to be noticed and for people to realise that I'm not an idiot.

Rob Moore and Mark Homer, the two co-founders of Progressive Property, taught the course and covered a wide range of topics including mindset, success, how to read people (in life and business), psychology, marketing and property.

One of the very first things I remember Rob saying is there are two main ways of generating passive income; one is with property, the other is through internet marketing.

For some reason, I quickly established a good rapport with Rob and, throughout the three days, I often came up with some good retorts about what Rob was saying. I was the comedian on the course; making people laugh, building relationships. I felt in my element and was buzzing the whole time. I loved what I was learning and soaked up everything. My left index finger was busy typing notes on my laptop.

There are several reasons why self-made people become rich. One is that they love what they do. When you really love doing something, you will be successful at it.

Everyone has twenty-four hours a day at their disposal. Some people use this time more effectively than others.

On the Progressive masterclass Rob Moore pointed out that you should spend more time doing the things you love because you are very good at them - and less time on things you don't like doing and aren't very good at. I learnt the benefits of outsourcing things you aren't good at, because it gives you more time to do the things that you do well.

I have a cleaner who comes once a week, for example, because I find hoovering and cleaning the floor difficult.

On the three-day course, Rob lists ways of generating income. One item on that list is "Write a book on what you know." It planted a seed in my mind about writing a book. Two and a half years later, this book was born!

At first, I had the idea of writing a book on property investment. However, I thought, 'there are loads of books on property and the investment strategies aren't universal.'

This might be the most significant statement in my book because it defines you: **You create your reality**.

We all have a choice in life.

I can think that I'm not disabled and decide to not let my CP stop me from doing anything I want to in life and that I am going to make £1 million.

Alternatively, I could decide that walking and living independently is too difficult. I could choose to stop walking and stop doing everything I do, live my life in a wheelchair tied to a residential home for disabled people.

It was when Rob started talking about marketing and the fact that your brand is so important, that I came up with the strap-line 'I am the 1st property investor with Cerebral Palsy.'

I added it to my business card. I also incorporated the following into my email signature:

Perception is reality.

I might not be the first property investor with CP, but nobody has told me that I'm not. When I wrote the strap-line, I hadn't yet bought any investment properties in the UK. Nor does it matter that I don't feel like I've achieved much so far in life.

By marketing myself as the first property investor with CP, I am creating the perception that I've got 'expert status'.

Talking of perception, I have just been interviewed by the Daily Telegraph about mortgages. The newspaper contacted me after they found my blog where I wrote about paying off my mortgage in seven and a half years.

The phone interview lasted for about thirty minutes; I discussed how I paid off my mortgage so fast and how I've subsequently drawn funds from my mortgage to purchase buy-to-let properties locally.

I could have gone on for hours about mortgages and intelligent finance!

The interview I did is part of a series of features the Daily Telegraph are publishing, in association with Barclays Bank on mortgages. I'm one of the contributors in the series of articles.

The funny thing is, I don't feel I've achieved anything special!

During the masterclass I met Rodney and after a few conversations we decided to joint venture together. At the time I thought I needed to work with somebody because estate agents wouldn't take me seriously.

At the end of the masterclass Rob promoted Progressive's twelve-month mentoring programme, the VIP programme. It sounded ideal, so Rodney and I, along with other people on the course, signed up to it.

When I got home I was still really buzzing after the masterclass. I was feeling happy about what I had learnt and having signed up to the Progressive VIP, I wrote a blog update about the experience.

What I wanted to do most of all was set up a recursive strategy to enable me to buy one property per month. It's not a difficult target, once you have a strategy in place. For me, buying one property a month would have been success.

I made the decision that I was going to concentrate on property so I stopped going to City Socialising events. My experience with Fiona had convinced me that I was wasting my time. I was now going to property networking events and really enjoying meeting like-minded people.

Being on the Progressive VIP and their other courses, I drove to Peterborough fifteen to twenty times over the next fifteen months.

Rodney came to see me once or twice in November and we went to visit an estate agent together who I already knew from viewing the four-bed maisonette. After a few months of trying to work together, Rodney and I decided not to joint venture together, as we wanted to work in different areas.

I met Paul Ribbons at that November BPM. I will never forget Paul coming up to me and saying "I read your blog with tears in my eyes. It must be so hard for you to even get dressed in the morning." I found it touching and thought 'How did you know?!' Paul is very good at building a rapport with people.

After chatting, Paul said, "I would like to talk with you on the phone. I'm really busy for the next three weeks, can you phone me three weeks on Monday?" I agreed to phone him at 1pm on the agreed day.

November 2010 was only the third time I had been to the BPM but I had become a familiar face from giving my business card to people and my blog. I noticed people coming up to me, asking me how I was doing and calling me a real inspiration.

This was satisfying, but I found it odd because it prompted the thought, 'I haven't done anything yet. I haven't even bought one property.'

Back on the Saturday sports show on Splash FM, I used to discuss everything with Phil. After I was sacked from The Warwick, Phil switched to DJing there on Saturday nights. It meant we normally went for a meal after the sports show and discussed everything under the sun. The subject we seemed to talk about the most was me meeting women. I remember Phil saying "You're not desperate for a relationship but you do crave a relationship."

If you have read 'Stairs For Breakfast' you will no doubt remember that in 2010, I separated myself from my Mum and the stress it was causing me. It came to a head two or three days after my thirty-seventh birthday, when I went for a meal at a restaurant with Fergus and Phil. I was so stressed out by Mum's latest round of emotional blackmail that I wasn't able to speak or function properly.

After we had finished eating, the stress I was feeling caused me to vomit on the table, in front of Phil and Fergus and the other people in the restaurant. It compared with the embarrassment I felt when I peed myself in the classroom when I was ten years old.

Holding back tears, I kept saying to Phil and Fergus, "I'm so sorry...I'm really sorry..." they both kept replying "Don't worry about it...are you alright?"

During my vomiting period, I reached a point of no return where all I could do was to throw up. It was my way of releasing tension.

In the restaurant that day, I was so stressed that I told Phil and Fergus about what Mum had said to me which is something I never did because talking about it made me feel worse. In the process, I reached the point of no return.

It was the final straw. I had to take defining action.

I emailed Mum, told her what happened in the restaurant and I wrote "From this moment on, I have taken away your right to contact me. I am forbidding you from contacting me again. I will contact you when I'm ready to do so."

After sending that email I knew I had probably gotten through to Mum because she didn't reply to my email.

Then a couple of days later, I suddenly realised I was feeling relaxed and that I hadn't thrown up in the last two days. After sixteen years I now realised, due to her negativity, Mum was largely the cause of this problem.

The reason why I was now feeling so relaxed was because I wasn't thinking about my family's problems.

After sixteen years of vomiting several times a day, I stopped overnight. I had managed to get Mum to detach herself from me. It was something I had been trying to do since I moved into my flat in April 2002. It was a real turning point.

*Today, in February 2014, I still appreciate not throwing up.*

On Monday 6th December 2010, as arranged, I phoned Paul Ribbons. Not wanting to be too analytical, I called him at 1.05pm. The first thing he said to me was, "You're five minutes late!"

We must have spoken on the phone for about an hour or more. I found speaking with Paul very easy. He said nobody with my level of disability had ever been in property investment before. Paul said I had a quality that he didn't see in other people. I work hard in life and never give up.

Paul also said that estate agents would respond well to me and he offered to mentor me. I felt absolutely delighted. At the time, I didn't understand why Paul was so taken by me.

I have got a lot of time for Paul, in addition to teaching me lots about people, human behaviour and success, he is someone who has overcome adversity. His mother died when he was very young. He was bullied and didn't do well at school due to his dyslexia. However, it hasn't stopped him from becoming a self-made businessman and writing a book.

Paul really inspires me and I relate to him. He's a bit of a Dad to me now.

The following day, after speaking to Paul on the phone, I attended the Progressive VIP mentoring event for the first time.

At Progressive, the VIP evening consisted of a presentation, a one-to-one session with staff member James, a cold buffet and networking with twenty other people on the VIP programme.

I found the presentation interesting. It was by Daniel Wagner, an internet marketer. In the presentation he suggested how Facebook can be used as a marketing tool. Daniel said, "I have made millions of pounds using my laptop and I can work from anywhere in the world."

It's easy to summarise my experience on the VIP mentoring programme. For over a year I loved attending the monthly meetings. Driving to Peterborough every month, despite feeling physically tired from visiting estate agents and viewing properties, after each progressive evening I felt positive and re-energised.

For over twelve months I was frustrated with what I was doing. I wanted to find a recursive strategy which suited me. I was in email contact with Rob More virtually on a daily basis asking him if he could help me with a plan to make best use of my skills. However he advised me to keep viewing flats in my area. I must have viewed over fifty flats in one year. At the time I didn't realise the root of my frustration was that buying flats was not the right strategy for me. It was extremely physically demanding and I realised that I was never going to make £1 million buying flats. I got on really well with Rob but his strategy, while clearly great for others, did not work for me.

Rob's presentation at the VIP in January 2011 was amazing. It is one of the best mindset talks I have sat in front of. It was on people who take responsibility, and those who turn themselves into victims in life.

It was a light bulb moment because it taught me a lot. What I learnt is fascinating.

**Taking responsibility (Acceptance).**
1. People who take full responsibility for everything that happens to them in life
2. They don't feel hard done by or the need to blame others for their situation.
3. They feel in control of their life.
4. If they don't like something in life they feel empowered and change it.
5. They don't let the past control their future.
6. They think and act differently towards *external* sources (things around them which aren't under their control). It helps them to achieve positive outcomes.

**Being a victim (Denial)**
1. People who blame others for what has happened to them in life.
2. They think somebody else is at fault for a wrong-doing.
3. They believe people and their environment are against them.
4. They think they have no control over what happens in their life.
5. They like to apportion blame to other people because doing so justifies their circumstances.
6. They think external sources are the cause of their problems.
7. They believe they are powerless to change anything. This also allows them to not take any responsibility for the misery in their lives

8. They are often bitter, resentful, lost, and angry.

Here is advice for victims who want to turn themselves into responsibility takers:

- If it's not possible to change something in your life, accept it. Then you will able to move on.
- Blaming someone else for what's wrong in your life isn't going to change anything.
- You have the choice - accept responsibility for yourself or live in denial and be a victim.
- You stop being a victim when you start helping yourself.
- You have the power to change your life RIGHT NOW. You can change your life in an instant because it's just a decision you make.
- It comes down to you creating your own reality.
- Your outlook on life determines your success in life.

The following have helped me in my path towards success:

- Stretch and grow yourself by doing something that slightly scares you every day.
- If you want to do something but something is stopping you. Ask yourself "What's stopping me?"
- Motivate yourself. Make a 'to do' list every day and tick each item off when you've done it. This will give you a great sense of achievement and satisfaction.
- Making mistakes isn't a problem. It only becomes a problem if you don't learn from each mistake.
- You cannot fail if you never give up.

As you know, I'm a great believer in feeling the fear and doing it anyway because it makes you feel good afterwards. I also know that taking a chance in life leads to success.

# Chapter 8

Returning from the Progressive VIP on 4th January 2011 I was feeling buoyant, with a new lease of life and I started visiting estate agents in Worthing town centre, looking for my first buy-to-let property.

I had also spoken to Harvey at Progressive about him creating a lead generation website for me. Not being a web designer, I was hoping to outsource the whole thing to him. However, instead for two to three months I liaised with Harvey on the design and content of the website.

The 11th of January 2011 is a memorable date because something unexpected happened that day and it shocked many people across Sussex. After presenting the breakfast show, Chris Copsey went to the supermarket, where tragically, he suffered a heart attack and died.

*It's something which puts life into perspective. People should live in the moment and enjoy it. We come into the world with nothing and we don't take anything with us when we leave. It's the bit in the middle that matters. The important thing in life is being happy and for some, making a difference, because nobody knows when we are going pass away.*

The next morning, Paul Williams stepped bravely up to the challenge of presenting the breakfast show.

MSH set up a tribute webpage for Coppo and hundreds of people posted comments on it.

It is one of the rare occasions when people from rival radio stations came together. A few days after Chris' death Rik Scott did an excellent job hosting a tribute show. The programme included pre-recorded messages from presenters who had worked with Coppo since the early eighties.

Everyone who knew him said that Chris was a lovely guy and a real family man. This is the tribute I posted on the website.

*I remember Coppo calling me a megastar in 1984 on my way to school after I contributed to The Food Mountain. I owe a big thanks to Chris Copsey, as it was him who inspired me to want to work in radio. My thoughts are with his family and friends.*

In early 2011 Shh finally came back to me, to confirm that I could take a six month sabbatical. I replied "Thank you very much, I really appreciate it but I'm not quite ready to take it yet".

Psychologically, I had left Shh in May 2011, when I realised my future wasn't with the company. However, I wanted to hold on to my job and the salary for as long as possible. I didn't feel guilty for staying 'below the radar' because I had worked hard for the first four years at Shh. In the latter years, I had tried to find another stimulating role but it felt like nobody took my plight seriously. I enjoyed being a property investor, it's straightforward but a physically demanding task going into and building relationships with estate agents. The only type of buy-to-let (BTL) properties that were in my price range were flats, which involved a lot of stairs.

On 1st February, in another one-to-one with Rob Moore on the Progressive VIP, I was frustrated that I hadn't found my first property yet. The determination to do so reinforced by this meeting made me focus my mind on finding a flat to buy.

A couple of days later during my daily ritual of looking on Rightmove, I saw a first floor, two bedroom flat, on the market for £80k. The property stuck out like a sore thumb as it's rare to see two bed flats in Worthing at a price that low. From the description and photos on Rightmove, the property needed a refurbishment and it was in a large block of flats with comparables of £100k. I knew the flat would rent out for £650 per month. Buying it for £80k would be a good deal.

The property was on the market with one of the eleven estate agents I had already been into two or three times. When I phoned them, the next available appointment to view the property was in three days. It frustrated me because I wanted to view the flat immediately!

Three days later, I met Brett, the estate agent outside the block of flats. The stairs up to the first floor were really difficult for me to climb as its staircase had big lips! To explain why, my right foot gets caught under each step as I walk up them. The handrail was also on the right. Walking down the stairs is a doddle!

Viewing the flat felt weird but good. It had a tiny kitchen which was a concrete shell. The bathroom floor had been ripped out. The tiles around the bath looked fine but, oddly, the bath didn't have any panels!

I asked Brett a load of questions at the property. The flat was being sold by the family of an old lady who had recently died.

When I offered Brett £75k for the property, he replied, "We've already had an offer of 75..." I've always wondered if that was the truth or if Brett was trying to get me to offer more. So I offered £79k and it was accepted. The buying process of the property was simple, I had a good solicitor.

I already knew Worthing is a good area to rent flats. A few days after securing the purchase of my BTL flat, I phoned the council, spoke to the housing department, said I was buying a two bed flat and asked if they could recommend some letting agents. They gave me a list of four or five.

Having never spoken to a letting agent before about finding a tenant, I decided to phone the first agent the Council had recommended, Howard & Co.

I called them up and got through to Paul Howard. I explained the situation and asked Paul how long it would take them to find me a good tenant. He said about two weeks and that my flat would probably rent out for £675 per month. Paul sounded like a nice guy and I kept in touch with him during the buying and refurb process of the flat.

During the purchase, one afternoon, I arranged for five builders to come to the flat and provide quotes to refurbish it.

Feeling pleased that I had found and secured the purchase of my first BTL property I was eager to find another one. But it took me until December to find my second property.

Writing about it now, it's easy to sum up March to December 2011. It was a frustrating time.

For a while I kept on visiting estate agents and viewing flats but as the year progressed, I became more and more disillusioned. As property prices are slightly lower in Littlehampton than Worthing as it is nine miles to the west, I was looking in both areas.

I worked out that if I made £100 cashflow per month per flat after refurbishing and remortgaging it, to make a million I would need to buy one hundred flats. If I bought one in every ten flats that I viewed, I would need to view a thousand flats and negotiate a lot of stairs. With the prospect of having to view that many flats and that many stairs it made me realise that it wasn't feasible.

Before I do anything in life, I need to estimate how much energy consumption I will need to do it.

Just because I can climb stairs doesn't mean I enjoy doing so. Stairs just help me to get to where I want to go. Likewise with Computers, I am good with computers but I'm not a computer geek. A computer is just a tool that helps me in life.

Viewing flats in Worthing and Littlehampton didn't lead to a low enough accepted offer to enable me to get all of my cash back after the refurb and re-mortgage. Therefore it wasn't a recursive strategy.

One of the keys to my success in life has always been to set myself attainable goals and then break each one down to the nth degree into small steps. I even reduce a flight of stairs into individual steps!

Before starting each chapter of this book, I made a list to things to write about. In this chapter, these are the items I've already covered:

> New year - feeling free
> 11 Jan 11 - Coppo died
> Shh sabbatical
> Feb 11 - property number 1
> Paul Howard

And here are some of things I've yet to write about:

> Estate agents are people
> Worthing auction flat
> Focusing on one thing
> VIP - enjoyed like-minded people

Paul Ribbons - estate agent

BPM

When I don't have a plan it's difficult to set myself goals.

I got on well with Rob Moore and he really tried to help me. More often than not, I managed to have a one-to-one with him and I found his mindset sessions very good.

I enjoyed being on the Progressive VIP and being surrounded with like-minded people. I got to know extremely successful investors, who inspire me:

- John Philbin - one of the most genuine people I know.
- Brother and sister duo Kris and Jayne Carpenter - very successful investors
- Francis Dolley and his family - whenever I see Francis he tries to kick my crutches to de-stabilise me, so I put my crutches in front of his feet and try to trip him up! We have a laugh!
- Trevor Cutmore - if you think you're too old to get into property investment, Trevor started when he was a grandad.
- Steve Evans - the only blind property investor I know.

On the negotiation course with Simon Hazeldine, I discovered that I have got the mindset of a billionaire! No, it's not to do with making a billion pounds, but it is the reason why I never give up in life.

People with billionaire mindsets have ideas, visions and the belief that they can do things. They often don't know how they are going to implement their idea, but they keep going and overcome obstacles in the way until they achieve what they set out to do.

When I set myself the goal of making £1 million I didn't know how I was going to do it but I know I can do it.

Other people who have the mindset of a billionaire include:

- Bill Gates - who, in the 1970s had the vision that one day there would be a computer in every home.
- Ray Kroc was a milkshake machine salesman who had the idea of setting up McDonald's as a franchise corporation,

after he sold eight machines to a small restaurant in California run by brothers Dick and Mac McDonald.

- Richard Branson set up Virgin Galactic after he had the idea of doing tourist flights to space (and hopefully, back again!).
- Oprah Winfrey has certainly got a billionaire mindset.

Earlier in the book, I described how being rejected by women was like being in a boxing match, continually knocked down. The reason I keep getting back up is due to my billionaire mindset. I didn't know it, all those years ago in The Warwick!

Regularly writing blog updates helped me become known in the property investment community.

In 2011, I went to the BPM every month and soon became a familiar face there. Sylvia and Juswant always saved me a seat in the front row at the BPM. After I secured the purchase of my first BTL flat, I met a few cash investors who said that they would like to Joint Venture with me and told me to let them know when I found a good investment property.

Meeting and building relationships with estate agents wasn't difficult. Most of them found me inspirational because they hadn't met anyone like me before.

I took the view that estate agents are just people and treating them well and showing them respect, engendered good relations in return. When meeting an estate agent outside a property to view it, I always said, "Thank you for taking the time to come and show me this property." I remember one estate agent saying, "Wow - nobody has ever said that to me before."

She was an attractive lady, slightly older than me, and having never met her before, I joked and innocently flirted with her through the viewing. At the end of it she said to me, "You're going to do extremely well because you've got great people skills."

It's difficult to say how I went about building relationships with estate agents because it depended on their personality. I just used my instinct. I didn't keep count of how many properties I viewed in 2011 but it must have been between fifty and one hundred. I pretty much knew what offer I was going to make on the properties before I went to view each of them.

I recall meeting another estate agent outside a block of flats, waiting to view one on the second floor. I had spoken to the guy on the phone before but it was the first time we had met.

When he arrived, he saw me standing outside the building and asked, "Are you going to be alright going up the stairs? There are quite a lot of them…"

Off the top of my head I replied, "Yes, I'll be fine. I eat stairs For breakfast!" Hence the title of my first book, 'Stairs For Breakfast'!

In May 2011 I completed on the purchase of my first BTL flat. With quotes from five builders during the buying process, the refurbishment started soon after. Frank Sumner did it and it cost £3.5k.

The refurbishment consisted of refitting the entire kitchen and replacing the electrics throughout the flat, replacing the bathroom floor and bath panels and repainting the entire flat.

All the electricity plug sockets, light switches and light pendants were replaced. This is a simple and inexpensive way of modernising the flat for its revaluation for the re-mortage.

Towards the end of the refurbishment, I arranged for five letting agents to meet me at the flat to discuss finding a tenant. I limited each appointment to fifteen minutes and the agents came to the property in succession.

Amusingly, the only place where I could sit down was in the bathroom. I was 'interviewing' each letting agent whilst sitting on the toilet with painters and decorators milling around. The business had to be done somewhere!

It was then that I met Paul Howard and he stood out from the other agents because he was so sincere. I knew he was the agent to work with

A few days later, I met Phil at the property and he filmed a video. I did a piece to camera sitting on the toilet. Watching and editing that video was extremely strange.

My voice has always sounded perfectly normal to me. However, hearing myself on video, I sounded incredibly disabled, to the point where I found it hard to understand what I was saying. To my eyes, I also look very disabled on video.

How people see me and how I see myself are two different things. It puzzles me why I don't appear to be disabled when I see myself in a mirror. Having made a few videos now I'm more familiar with how people see and hear me.

Something happened in May 2011. At the beginning of the month I had another one-to-one with Rob Moore. Having been to see so many estate agents and flats, I was unhappy that I hadn't bought another property yet.

In a forty minute mindset session Rob helped me to go into 'the now' - living in the present moment.

He also gave me an action point to read 'The Power Of Now' by Eckhart Tolle. Not being someone who likes reading books, I don't think I responded very enthusiastically to that suggestion because, unexpectedly, a few days later I received the book in the post!

I spent about a month living in the present moment while the refurbishment of the flat was taking place. Everything in life was easy and effortless. I wasn't worried about anything, had loads of energy and my insomnia disappeared. I felt confident and happy.

Shortly before I completed on the purchase of my BTL flat, I mentioned to Phil that it would be good to make a video at the property. Phil said he had a pocket camcorder and would come along and film the video.

As the weeks progressed and the refurb started, Phil kept saying he hadn't had time to find his camcorder at home. Then on the third week of asking him to find his camcorder, I walked into Splash on the Saturday afternoon, extremely annoyed with him because I knew he still hadn't got the camera.

It sparked the only argument I've ever had with Phil. I remember saying to him, "All you care about in life is your family and your job". It was also the shortest argument I've had with someone because it only lasted a couple of minutes. However, the dispute took me out of living in the now.

I overcame the issue of not having a pocket camcorder by buying one.

Howard & Co found me a tenant within a couple of weeks. She was a single mother in her early twenties with a young baby. As Paul Howard said, the flat did rent out for £675 per month, and the tenants still live in the property today.

Out of the blue one afternoon in the first quarter of 2011, I had a phone call from my friend Helen from the personal development course. We had a two-hour conversation about religion. Christianity and faith are important to Helen and she wanted to know what my beliefs were.

I said that I had always been an atheist but, since starting my property journey, I had learnt a lot about people and about myself and it was changing my life in the sense that I had become more open-minded.

Me: "As an analytical person, I need proof. And since I can't prove or disprove that God exists, I'm open-minded."

Helen: "So at the moment you're at a crossroad...sooner or later you're going to have to decide which path to take."

Me: "Why...?"

Helen is a lovely person and I like our long phone conversations.

As my property journey progressed, I was blogging and meeting more people at the BPM, who saw me as an inspiration. Although I am always grateful for this, it really started to concern me because it made me think:

'I haven't achieved anything. I haven't found a recursive strategy yet. People see me walking around and know me from my blog updates. People have no idea what I've been through in life.'

This difference in perception, in how people see me and how I think of myself, is something I spoke to Helen about.

Me: "...I'm just a normal person and I haven't done anything yet. I've only used 10% of my full potential so far..."

Helen: "The fact that you inspire people without trying to do so is a real gift..."

Helen: "...Rather than getting frustrated by it, you should embrace it.

What Helen said is so true.

For a few months, I thought about Helen's words before defining my purpose in life:

*To help and inspire people and to reach my full potential.*

I feel that when I focus on the first part the second part will happen naturally. Inspiration works both ways. It has helped me to keep going over the last few years.

I think Helen was the first person who suggested that I write a book about my life.

In early summer 2011, after months of Shh asking me when I was going to take a six month sabbatical, I said, "I'm ready now". To my surprise they replied "We're no longer willing to let you have a sabbatical".

I've always believed that honesty is the best policy, but on this occasion my honesty hadn't helped me. I had been completely open about getting into property investment and it being the reason why I wanted a sabbatical.

With some justification, Shh were asking, "Why should we give you a sabbatical when you don't want to come back and work for Shh?" The answer: I wanted to become financially free before leaving my £30k job.

It was a shock and I worried about what do to. Had I said I wanted to go travelling, Shh would have given me a sabbatical.

I phoned KC to see if he could help me, but after I did the Progressive masterclass KC warned me, "You seem very excited, be careful. You'll get burnt and lose all of your money." So now he didn't want to have any part of me leaving Shh.

KC said to me "Why do you want to leave the security of a job for life?"

There wasn't a voluntary redundancy programme open at the time. I knew Shh weren't going to sack me so I decided to try to persuade Shh to offer me voluntary redundancy anyway.

I was liaising with a couple of people from the HR department and in one email I said, "I've got absolutely no motivation to work for Shh again, please could I be offered voluntary redundancy?"

A few days later, HR came back to me and said, "Yes, you can have voluntary redundancy."

It made me think 'Sh*t! What do I do? What do I do?'

I spoke to a three people about it:

- Phil said, "Take your money - you are going to be successful."
- Jack (who I sat with in the office and often helped, who is a very cautious person) said "You are so determined to succeed - go for it."
- Rob emailed "When you take action you will succeed."

It came to the point where HR said to me "Accept another project or leave". I decided to take a chance.

HR could have made me leave at the end of June but they let me stay until 31st July. Having worked for Shh for ten years, I received ten month's salary.

I knew that if I got into financial difficulty I could always rent out my spare bedroom.

In leaving Shh, I was forcing myself to become successful because I knew that I would never give up. I didn't say goodbye to KC. It's always been my intention to contact him again. In fact, I'm going to send him a copy of my book.

A couple of things made me smile as I was leaving Shh.

Firstly, I had managed to be made redundant when there wasn't a voluntary redundancy programme open.

Secondly, two months before leaving the company I was allocated a new manager, who I liked and who understood the situation and left me to my own devices. On the day that I left:

Manager: "It's a shame you're leaving because you've got so much potential."

Me: "That's the reason why I'm leaving..."

At the time, there's must have been a voluntary redundancy programme open in Jack's part of the business. A month before I went, he left. It surprised me because I thought Jack was going to stay until 2013, to reach forty years with the company.

I have just Googled KC. He left Shh in 2012. He's set up a photography company, donating the proceeds to charity. This is entirely in keeping with his personality.

In July 2011, I was scheduled to get a new Motability car but I couldn't find one that I liked. There was nothing wrong with the

Renault Mégane I had, so in reality there was no need for me to get a new one. The seats in the latest model Mégane aren't as comfortable as before and the other makes of car that I looked at didn't have cruise control as standard and were more expensive.

I phoned Motability and they allowed me to keep the car that I had for another two years. It only took one phone call.

Over the last three to four years, I have established the key elements to being successful. I'll outline them here because it will show you why I wasn't more successful in finding properties to buy in 2011:

**The key elements to success**

**Desire** - If you haven't got enough desire to do something, the chances are you're not going to achieve it. If you really want to do something, you will find a way to do it.

**Love what you do** - people are good at the things they love doing. All of the self-made people I know love what they do.

**Have a plan** - in 2011/2012 so many people said to me "If you fail to plan, you plan to fail".

**Focus on one thing** - even more people said "Focus on one strategy in one area".

**Keep things simple** - some people (including me) tend to over-complicate things. Successful people do simple things very effectively.

**Take focused action** - do what you say you're going to do.

Throughout 2011 I felt like a headless chicken, running around trying to find a recursive strategy which I could do.

I was visiting estate agents and viewing properties in Worthing, Littlehampton and Bognor Regis which is seven miles west of Littlehampton.

I was looking for flats to buy, houses for Paul Ribbons and properties for other investors. I also went to view a few houses in Brighton and Hove. Having found a property in Bognor, which potentially could be turned into an HMO, I went to view it again with Peter Fannon and Mandy.

I went to see Paul Howard about buying and converting a property he was handling into an HMO with the idea of living in one of the rooms and renting the other rooms, making it a cost-neutral property for me to live in.

I liked going to view houses for Paul Ribbons because the properties were wrecks. Some had subsidence. One property was an eight-bed house with severe water damage, following a burst pipe. The estate agent bought masks for us to wear inside the property. There was an absolute stench inside. I took my camcorder along and asked the estate agent to film it.

Had Paul bought one of the properties I went to see for him, I'm sure he would have given me a good finder's fee.

Frank Sumner also came to view a few flats with me in order to estimate the refurbishment costs on them.

With all this scattergun activity, I was consuming an enormous amount of energy and getting nowhere. It was physically tiring and demoralising. I ended up going out to see estate agents and properties no more than once or twice a week. It was extremely frustrating because I wanted to take great leaps forward but couldn't seem to move forward more than a few baby steps.

I motivated myself by targeting visiting 30 estate agents in 30 days in 2011. I went to 35 estate agents in 27 days. It may sound a lot but, as estate agents are often clustered together, I often visited five or six in one afternoon.

I went to an auction to bid on a two-bed flat I was interested in buying. A few weeks prior to the auction, I had viewed the first floor property. Frank met me there to estimate the refurbishment. There were lots of prospective buyers looking around the place at the same time. It was pouring with rain and there was an outside metal staircase leading to the flat, which made it slippery to climb.

I calculated that my maximum bid for the property was going to be £90k.

At the auction, there were only two other people bidding on the property. One of them was in the room, one on the phone. The bidding started at £70k and went up in increments of £1k. At £85k the phone bidder dropped out.

When it got to £90k, I put my hand up and thought, 'It's only another grand'. This is what happens to people at auctions. As an investor, you should never become emotional with properties and normally, I never did.

As I put my hand up and bid £95k, I thought 'Sh*t, I'm scared now!'

Fortunately, the other bidder bought the property for £96k. I was lucky.

Over the course of the year, whenever I saw or spoke to Paul Ribbons (usually at the BPM), he invariably asked me, "Why do you want to make £1 million?" He was trying to establish the reason for my desire.

I recited a litany of reasons, including:

- "Because I know I can do it."
- "So I don't need to work anymore."
- "Because I want to show all the people who have put me down in life that I'm better than them."

After each answer Paul replied, "No, that's not the reason."

This continued until one day, sitting with Paul in the bar at the Holiday Inn in Maidenhead, without really thinking about it, I came up with my reason why. We both knew it was the root of my desire. Paul replied "You've just made the hairs on the back of my neck stand up. I apologise. I understand now."

Strangely, Paul remembers the time and so do I but neither of us can remember what I said!

Perhaps it is too deep for words but I think the root of my desire is motivated by my feeling that I haven't achieved much in life so far.

I became well known at the BPM. As more people approached me repeating the 'inspirational' mantra and saying how much they liked my blog updates, I started to speculate on how I could monetise my blog.

I also realised that as so few people really knew my back story that it might be a good thing to set my tale down in a book.

When I set up my blog in 2010, I made the decision not to blog about my personal life or my family. My blog is about my journey to £1 million and I wanted my updates to be an inspiration without any negative context around them.

I wanted the book to be a personal account of my life. However, I thought, 'There's no way I'm going to include the incidents with Nathan and Freddie as they are far too personal.' If you are reading this and wondering who these people are, you will have to read my first book, 'Stairs For Breakfast'.

But on the other hand, I felt that without these incidents the book wouldn't make any sense.

For about a year I contemplated how to write an account that excluded Nathan and Freddie. I couldn't work out how to do it.

There was another downside to my high profile status at the BPM. An abundance of people who wanted to advise me. One of the reasons why my actions were so unfocused was that I was being influenced by so many people in my search for a recursive strategy. I felt overloaded with information and ideas.

At the networking events my confusion was being compounded because I would ask people that I respected "What strategy do you think I should follow?" and receive a variety of answers.

I decided to ask Glenn Armstrong for his advice on one occasion at the BPM. I had previously only spoken to Glenn briefly, and knowing that he is one of the top property mentors, it was as momentous as speaking to Simon Zutshi for the first time. Nervously, I walked up to Glenn and like once or twice before, became out of breath and started hyperventilating. Glenn advised me to send him an email - which I did.

More often than not I went to the BPM with Neil Stovell from Brighton. Many interesting conversations about property, people and life ensued on the way to and from Maidenhead. Sometimes we went in my car and Neil drove it.

Neil was driving my car on the motorway when the accelerator pedal dropped off. It was no big deal, Neil just pulled onto the hard shoulder and screwed the pedal back in.

Neil also often reminds me about the time when I fell over at the BPM and whacked my head against a fire door. Sylvia Rai saw me fall over and ran to get Neil. My head took over an hour to stop bleeding because I didn't sit still.

The first-aid staff at the hotel were very helpful and concerned about me. People suggested calling an ambulance, going to hospital and having stitches in my head. I said, "No, no, I'm fine, I'm fine, don't worry." At home the next morning, I had a shower and felt the bump on my head which wasn't a problem.

People who aren't used to me falling over tend to panic when they see me do it. There's no need to panic. When I say "I'm alright", I'm alright.

Falling over is part of my life and I know how to fall over without hurting myself. I instinctively put my hands out to protect myself. The only thing that is inevitable when I fall is that I will stand up again.

The reason I hurt myself at the BPM was because I didn't put my hands out to cushion my fall as I had my mobile phone in my hand. I was more concerned about not smashing my mobile than my head!

What people don't know is why I had my phone in my hand. Out of nowhere, I had just received a text message from Crystal, the masseuse I met in Bangkok. This was odd because it was the first time that Crystal had texted me since my holiday in 2009. She now tends to text me on Christmas day.

My fall was caused by my mentally drifting back to Thailand for a few seconds!

Over the last five years or so, my upper-body weight has become heavier as I have become more muscular, which causes me a slight issue when I fall. Falling over isn't the problem, it's summoning the energy to get back to my feet.

By early autumn 2011, I was tired of viewing decrepit old flats in Littlehampton so I widened my search to Bognor.

On Rightmove I found a ground floor studio flat for sale for £43k. This was remarkable as I had never come across a property so cheaply priced on the south coast. It had been on the market for quite a few months so I thought there must be a problem with it. I phoned the estate agent Amy to get some background.

I spoke to Amy on the phone and she emailed more information. I could tell that Amy was a pro-active person because she was always the one who answered the phone and she was extra helpful.

When I viewed the studio flat I discovered it was the size of a shoebox. It was just a rectangular-boxed room, with the 'kitchen' being a sixteen inch counter in one corner with a small shower room.

I met Amy at the property and afterwards she said, "Your blog is amazing, I've put a link to it on our blog."

Having seen the flat, I realised there weren't any comparables in order for prospective purchasers like me to get an idea of value. Prior to seeing it, I thought it would need a refurbishment, and then be valued at £50k. However, on inspection the flat was in good order.

I knew the flat would rent out for £500 per month. As I made an offer on most of the properties that I viewed, I offered £36k for the shoebox flat.

Having widened my search to Bognor, I found it was a better place to invest than Littlehampton. It was a more desirable place to live but property prices were slightly lower. Bognor is a dormitory for people who study or work in Chichester.

For the rest of 2011, I focused on Bognor rather than Littlehampton. In doing so, I built good relationships with seven estate agents there.

After my offer of £36K for the shoebox was accepted, I spent several months trying to find a way to buy it myself, and then finding someone else to purchase the property.

At first, I thought it wasn't a good deal because I calculated I would need to leave £7k in the property after buying it. However, Rob Moore advised me that leaving some money in a property is sensible, especially when the property has a high yield (the rental return based on purchase price). Rob advised me to buy the flat.

I couldn't get a mortgage on it, however. The size of the flat was below the prescribed dimensions of one mortgage lender, whilst another would only give me a mortgage on purchases of £50k and above!

I decided to find another buyer for the property in order to get a finder's fee. Two investors came from Kent to view the shoebox. They were surprised to see the actual size and rental return on it. But they decided not to buy the property because they didn't want to have to leave any money in the deal.

Through someone at the Brighton PIN meeting, I found Anita, who bought the shoebox with cash. I went to meet Anita and her partner at a café in Brighton Marina and I wasn't prepared for what happened.

Over a coffee and cake, Anita offered me a finder's fee of just £400. This jolted me because I knew a reasonable fee was £2-£3k. However I didn't have the confidence to say, 'No, £400 is not right...' I wanted to go home and double-check first.

After having done so, I phoned Anita and said, "I have checked and am not happy with a finder's fee off £400. Based on the return you will get, a finder's fee of £3k is a fair deal."

To which the ruthless businesswoman replied, "Well, you didn't say anything about it when I offered you £400 at the Marina."

Anita bought the shoebox for £30k in cash and paid me £400.

It taught me that no matter how nice a person you are, when it comes to business you need to be clear and clinical.

It wasn't until the third time I met Amy that I realised that I was 'pulling' her (attracting her without trying to do so). She found me and my property journey inspirational and she was keen to help me. She was in her thirties and attractive. However, I decided not to do anything about it as I was 'pulling' her, just by doing what I do. I always remained professional and focused on property when with her.

I was also keen to buy a large two bed flat in Bognor. The one I found had a low price because it was situated above a letting agent. The property had already had two sales fall through on it because of a complicated lease. I was monitoring the progress of the third offer on the flat. So I phoned the agent and asked hopefully, "Has it fallen through yet?!"

Sadly it didn't. A complicated lease isn't an issue when you have a good solicitor.

In the latter part of September I went to the Caribbean Island of St Vincent for a week. Having bought an off-plan property from Harlequin, it was a courtesy holiday, staying at their St Vincent resort.

I flew to Barbados, where the onward flight to St Vincent was delayed for five hours. I got talking to Tim, a semi-retired guy originally from Manchester, on his way back to St Vincent, where he had lived with his wife for several years.

Having built a large house on St Vincent, Tim also owned investment property in the UK and he was interested in my property journey. I sometimes hear from him as he's on my email distribution list.

One afternoon, Tim took me on the tour of the island and we had lunch in a restaurant overlooking the bay. It was a great memory to take back with me.

Another friend I made on that holiday was Ewan, who was part of the entertainment team at St Vincent. Originally from Texas, Ewan moved to the UK in the early eighties and lived in Hove, a mere ten minutes away from me. I've had a bite to eat with Ewan a few times locally.

St Vincent is a nice resort. I went there out of season when it was quiet. The local staff at the hotel were really friendly. One investor there on his free holiday, had purchased five off-plan properties from SwanfieldHarlequin, a case pf putting all his property eggs in one basket.

At St Vincent airport on the way home, the check-in girl put a disabled tag on my suitcase. Then as the plane landed in Barbados, the air hostess announced that due to excess weight, some of the suitcases had been left in St Vincent. She advised that if our luggage wasn't on the carousel, we needed to complete a form in order for our luggage to be posted to us at home.

Technically, the airhostess was correct in saying some of the luggage had been left in St Vincent. It later transpired that mine was the *only* one which had been brought over!

I bypassed the long queue of people moaning about not having their suitcases. It made me laugh. However, before I could join my Harlequin buddies in the executive lounge, I had to wait for over two hours until the check-in desk in Barbados opened. As the flight back to Gatwick wasn't due to leave for five hours, I don't know why the left luggage in St Vincent wasn't flown over on another plane. It was only a twenty minute flight.

The BPM in November 2011 coincided with my birthday. As I sat in the front row of the audience, Sylvia Rai got over two hundred people to sing happy birthday to me! It was a little embarrassing but I appreciated the recognition.

The speaker that evening was Glenn Armstrong and at the end of his presentation he offered me a place on his training course. I felt very humble.

Towards the end of November I knew the Progressive VIP competition to win either a Mercedes for a year or £5k was due to happen in December. I hadn't achieved much, having only bought one property, so I decided not to enter the competition.

In early December I viewed a small first floor, one bed flat in Worthing. It had been raining shortly before I went to see the flat and I needed new ferrules for my crutches as the ones on my sticks were worn and had lost their grip.

Walking up the path to the front of the property, I wasn't expecting the ground to be so slippery. I slipped and fell against two or three wheelie bins. The bins went flying and I landed on my back in dog mess which transferred itself to my t-shirt.

With a smelly t-shirt and a bleeding left elbow and hand, I walked up the steep staircase. The flat was a wreck and needed a complete refurbishment. The property was due to be sold by auction because the wooden bay window in the bedroom was rotten. The window frame was hanging by two wooden threads and supported by metal stilts.

Around the same time, Amy contacted me about a second floor, two bed flat about to come onto the market. She said the flat needed a refurbishment, the vendor needed to sell it quickly and was likely to accept a low offer on it.

I was the first person to view the flat in Bognor. As we walked around the flat, Amy ticked the items on my refurbshment sheet which needed doing. Then we sat down and priced each item. I gave Amy my calculator and we came up with my initial offer for the property. Amy, impressed, said she had never seen someone get to an offer price in that way before.

The property was on the market for £100k. I viewed the flat on a Thursday and made my initial offer of £81k the same day.

Confident that the vendor would accept a low offer, I mentioned the VIP competition to Amy and said I would enter if I got a low offer accepted on the property.

The next day, Amy phoned me and said the vendor had rejected £81k, so I made another offer of £85k.

The following Monday, Rob emailed me asking if I had secured a second property yet. I said I had been to see two properties and there was a possibility that I could get an offer accepted on both of them that week. Rob replied suggesting I enter the VIP competition.

Having phoned and left messages for Amy on Saturday and again that Monday morning, I was frustrated that she hadn't got back to me about my offer of £85k.

After receiving Rob's email I became determined to buy another property and enter the competition. In making that decision, something odd happened. My mind automatically re-set into living in the present moment.

Focused and feeling really confident, I decided that Monday afternoon to drive to the estate agents in Bognor and see Amy about the two bedroom flat. On my way to Bognor, I fixed my maximum offer on the two bedroom flat at £90k and resolved that, if I didn't buy that property, I would go for the one bed flat in Worthing.

As I parked outside the estate agents in Bognor, I felt a bit deflated because I could see through the window that Amy wasn't there. The only people in the office were two less empathetic women who I had only briefly spoken to on the phone before. Still living in the present moment, I sat thinking about what to do for a minute. I could see the two women staring at me through the window.

Walking confidently into the office, I said I had come to see Amy about my offer on the two bed flat and asked one of the two women when Amy would be back. She said Amy was on a viewing and would be about an hour, suggesting that I phoned Amy. I replied that I had already left Amy two messages without a response and said I would come back to see her.

I went to see a couple of other agents, before returning to see Amy over an hour later. However, she hadn't returned yet. I sat in the the estate agents for over half an hour. It was strange because normally it was a busy office and people there knew me and would talk to me. However, there were only a few people there that day and they all seemed to be avoiding me.

Then Amy walked in and virtually ignored me, before going into the back office. I knew something wasn't right because Amy was normally very talkative with me. It made me think 'What the hell is going on?'

I knew I hadn't done anything wrong. However, as I sat waiting on my own for a further fifteen minutes, I felt like I had. It wasn't a pleasant experience.

I guessed what had happened. When I had gone into the estate agents earlier, the two women assumed I was there to see Amy because they thought I liked her. I know she found me inspirational and probably spoke about me to her colleagues. Whatever happened, I always remained professional with Amy. I think it was another instance of people who don't know me, misjudging me. It's a shame that the estate agency manager wasn't in that day because he knew me.

Eventually, Clifford, the valuation guy appeared from the back office with Amy and came over to speak to me. I asked about my £85k offer on the two bedroom flat. Clifford said it hadn't been accepted so I made another offer of £90k. Clifford said he would phone the vendor with my new offer and then call me.

I complained about having been kept waiting for nearly an hour before I stood up to leave. Amy kindly moved a chair out of my way and opened the door for me. I left the estate agents thinking, 'What the hell just happened?'

When I had driven to Bognor earlier that afternoon I was feeling happy and confident. When I left Bognor I was deflated and furious about the way I had been treated - and no longer living in the present.

On my way home I received a phone call from Clifford. I pulled my car over and answered the phone. He said the vendor hadn't accepted £90k. I took the opportunity to have a rant at Clifford. I made it absolutely clear to him that the only reason I had gone to see Amy was because she hadn't returned my phone calls about my previous offer on the property. I think he realised that they had made a mistake.

The next day I emailed Amy and explained why I had gone to see her. She replied saying she understood and told me not to worry about it.

Ironically, the two bedroom flat in Bognor stayed on the market for about a year and the asking price went down to £90k!

Now that I had dismissed the Bognor flat, I went to view the one bed flat in Worthing for a second time. Here's where I made a few mistakes.

It would have been wiser to have viewed the flat with a builder because I was unable to see the extent of the damage to the bay window in the bedroom. One of the walls in the lounge also had damp damage.

After viewing the property, I went home, did some calculations, and phoned the estate agent manager before going to see him about buying the property.

Coincidentally, the property was being sold by the same estate agency that I bought my first BTL flat from. Most of the people knew me there but the Manager was new to the branch.

The second error was in seeing that manager and making it too obvious that I was very eager to buy the property. I offered £62k to buy the property, to which the manager replied, "The vendor won't accept anything under £64k." Without further discussion, I agreed to buy the flat for £64k.

I would have been much wiser to wait until the property went to auction. However the auction was after the VIP competition.

Writing about it now, it hurts me because I acted out of character. I was buying the property out of emotion and not common sense. I was so determined to buy a second property, enter the VIP competition and to win it.

Nevertheless, I had secured my second property. I didn't have much time left to make a video, which was part of the rules in order to enter the competition. I went over to Splash in midweek and Phil helped me make a humorous off-the-cuff video.

Twelve people entered the competition and everyone on the VIP mentorship programme could then vote for one of them. Having been on the VIP for a year I was well known in that community.

In the week leading up to the Progressive Christmas party, when the competition winner would be announced, I was very active blogging every day, drumming up voters. People said they were going to vote for me and I really thought I was going to win the competition.

On the evening prior to the winner being announced, people were coming up to me saying I had done so well throughout the year and that I was a shoe-in.

I was so convinced I was going to win, that when the winner was announced and it wasn't me I was deeply disappointed. I didn't even come second.

People were used to seeing me being positive, laughing and joking. After the winner was announced, I sat very quietly for up to an hour.

John Philbin was concerned about me.

John: "Are you okay? I've never seen you like this…"

Me: "I'm alright, I'm just very p*ssed off. I've worked *so* hard over the year and I don't feel like I've achieved anything."

Success for me would have been to find a strategy to enable me to acquire one property per month. Over the last year, I had been running around trying to find the right strategy for me but hadn't found it. At the same time, I had been to see numerous estate agents and properties  and tackled a huge number of stairs.

Not winning the VIP competition felt like all my efforts had been wasted. I felt like I had run out of steam.

Writing about it now, the huge efforts I made to win one small competition seems odd. However, it wasn't about winning a Mercedes for a year, I would have opted for the £5k. It   wasn't really about winning the money either. For me it was about recognition,

Later on, at the Progressive Christmas party, while sitting at the hotel bar with John Philbin and Kris Carpenter, they were surprised when I told them how much property prices were in my area.

When I told them about my two flats in Worthing at £79k and £64k, and those prices were hard to come by, they said, "You can buy a three bed house for 40k in Leeds...!"

Both John and Kris said I was being too hard on myself, something I heard from many quarters in 2011. They suggested I go up to Leeds to look at the market there and consider working with either one of them. I thought it was a good idea and planned to do so in early 2012.

The conversation with John and Kris convinced me not to go and view flats anymore.

Building relationships with estate agents takes commitment and consistency. In 2011, I had the former but not the latter.

Estate agents will point you in the direction of a good property deal if you go and see them often enough to stick in their mind.

With over forty estate agents in Worthing, physically, it wasn't feasible for me to go visit them all regularly. And at the time, I wasn't focused enough on one strategy and one area.

With hindsight, I would have had more success if I just focused on Littlehampton. There were only four estate agents in the town centre and I could have gone to see them one afternoon a week and phoned them with the same regularity. But then, there were thirteen other estate agents on the outskirts of Littlehampton..

Buying flats wasn't the right strategy for me.

A few days before Christmas in 2011, Amy emailed me after I sent her a Christmas card. She said she really appreciated the card and that it was a lovely act on my part. I nearly asked Amy if she would like to have a coffee with me but decided not to in case she said no. She emailed again later that afternoon, to let me know that it was her last week working in Bognor because she had been promoted to another branch.

I received a phone call from Howard & Co one morning around the same time, saying the tenant had been moved out of my two bedroom flat in Worthing because it had been flooded by the flat above it! I thought, 'Great! What the hell do I do?'

Howard & Co were extremely helpful and the 'flood' wasn't as bad as I initially thought. My tenant moved back into the property after three days. Also the leasehold company put dehumidifiers in the flat, which made me think that the leak had been caused by a building maintenance issue.

In 2012 I started to practice ascension meditation. This calls you to observe your thoughts rather than believe that your thoughts are what you are. I also learnt a lot about how the mind works.

One of the main roles of the mind is to protect us. It acts like our defence mechanism and constantly monitors potential danger. The mind is like a library storing harmful experiences. When it comes across a similarly harmful scenarios or their originators, it alerts us: "Danger, I don't like this...". This is why we have so many negative thoughts.

Most agree that all fears and phobias are derived from past experiences and learnt behaviours.

The mind loves having problems to solve because these keep it busy. The mind is also highly critical of the things we do. Some people refer to it as *our little inner voice.*

The mind is an oxymoron! It's very good at creating problems so that it has got problems to solve!

All in all, the mind is a pretty negative thing which produces negative thoughts.

I don't remember where I learnt the phrase, *You are not your mind.*

It might be from 'The Power of Now', in which, after explaining how the mind works, Eckhart Tolle teaches how to become *The watcher* of the mind's thoughts.

I am now very aware of my thoughts and why they occur.

Eckhart Tolle also says that some people set themselves goal after goal and don't spend time living in the present moment. They don't enjoy what they have already achieved because they are always striving to achieve more. Until I started writing this book, that was me.

A tiny percentage of the population have heard about living in the present moment and an even smaller number of people are actually doing so. Getting into the present moment takes practise. Meditation, something I leant in 2012, enables this and I'll explain more in the next chapter.

I'm not dedicated when it comes to meditating and don't often practise it at the moment. However meditating every day enables you to greatly control your thoughts. The beauty of living in the now is, it stops the mind from creating problems for it to solve and therefore eliminates negative thoughts.

I'm not a meditation guru either, but it is widely believed that meditation is healthy for your mind and body.

I firmly believe that in order to be successful in life, you need to surround yourself with like-minded and successful people.

I stopped watching the news on TV in 2012 because it's so negative. I'm still interested in current affairs. I hear the news on the radio and choose what to read online every day. I just don't spend half an hour of the day watching 'bad' news anymore. It helps me to maintain a positive mindset.

I'm still a charitable person and I like helping people. I can help people more effectively the more positive my mindset.

# Chapter 9

Ever since December 2010, as a result of seeing Daniel Wagner's presentation on using Facebook as a marketing tool, I had been thinking, 'How can I make money from the internet?'

After Daniel said "I have made millions of pounds using my laptop and I can work from anywhere in the world", it made me think 'If he can do it, so can I' but I didn't know how.

A year or so later, I saw Daniel Wagner at the BPM and we had a brief conversation:

Me: "How can *I* make money from the internet?"

Daniel: "Tell your story."

I didn't think much about it at the time, but subconsciously, it got me moving closer to starting my book. I was still trying to work out how to write it without including Nathan or Freddie. Strangely those two incidents now seem somewhat insignificant.

In January 2012 I went to Leeds to see John Philbin and Kris and Jayne Carpenter. This entailed three train journeys and I hadn't slept at all the night before because I was worried I would miss my first train, which left Shoreham at 6.30am.

When I arrived at St Pancras station and went over the road to King's Cross for the train to Leeds, I discovered that, due to a fault on the line, there were literally no trains, so I went back to St Pancras and caught a train to Sheffield.

John kindly came to pick me up at Sheffield station and he also gave a lift to the woman that I had sat next to on the train.

That afternoon John took me around a number of houses and I remember feeling really tired. The following morning was spent with Kris and Jayne, before returning to Shoreham in the afternoon.

Leeds was very interesting, as were the houses John, Kris and Jayne purchased. John invests in south Leeds whilst the brother and sister team invest in the north of the city. You can buy a three bed house for £40k in Leeds, (at least you could in 2012) and it's a city where the buy, refurbish and remortgage strategy works well.

Kris and Jayne were inspiring because they've got their strategy sorted. Not only do they source properties for their portfolio but they also package deals for other people as well as owning a letting agency. Kris and Jayne are dynamic and young, being no more than thirty at the time.

I was envious of Kris and Jayne (in a positive way) because they've got a recursive strategy which works well.

John is older and has been an investor for longer than Kris and Jayne. In consequence, he was more relaxed than them and not so busy chasing deals. He also had two other businesses to run.

When I got home, I agonised over who to work with because they are all good people. I decided to work with John because he was offering me more of a 50/50 JV structure. He would source properties for me to buy and I would help John with the numbers and spreadsheets. Kris and Jayne had just offered to sell me packaged deals.

However, when John found me a property and I thought about buying it, I thought 'I've done nothing to buy this property'. I didn't feel it was an equal JV structure or that I was pulling my weight. It seemed too easy. John is such a genuine person, I felt he was just trying to help me.

John was one of the people who often said that I was being too hard on myself.

I remember saying to John, "This is too easy…it's not part of my challenge of making £1 million.'

At the time, I felt like I had something to prove. In writing this book, I no longer feel like I've got anything to prove.

In hindsight, it might have been wiser to take that opportunity to work with John as we shared the same values. However, I still have the option of doing this in the future.

Since getting into property, I haven't ever regretted things I have or haven't done. I've tended to look forward and I've just kept going.

I feel I started on a journey four years ago. I've had to plot my own path and I have learnt from my mistakes. Through writing this book, I can see several ways forward.

Several people have said to me, "It's not the destination that's important, it's the journey that matters." I understand what they mean. Enjoy what you are doing and live in the present.

Having bought my second BTL flat under an auction contract in early 2012, I completed the purchase in January. The refurbishment cost £6K and Andy and Debbie Kime did an excellent job, including restoring the bay window. Howard & Co found me an Indian couple with a small baby who were great tenants.

This first floor property has a very steep staircase with no handrail to hold on to. However, as usual I found a way to tackle the stairs and have made a couple of videos of me doing so. You can see these on my website: **www.StairsForBreakfast.com**

The one bed flat isn't very big for three people. Hardworking Indian families sometimes choose to do this in order to save money and send it back to their family in India.

Rob Moore was the speaker at the BPM in February 2012. He talked about how to attract potential JV partners who have money to invest. It was a memorable presentation because it taught me the difference between 'pushing' and 'pulling' women.

Like many speakers, Rob liked to walk the width of the audience and I was sitting in the front row. At one point Rob said, "You don't want to go up to someone, all full of yourself and say to them. I've got this great deal - would you like to invest with me...?"

Then Rob asked the audience, "Do you know someone who's a bit full of themselves?"

I was in a seat directly in front of him. I piped up. "Rob Moore!" It made over two hundred people laugh spontaneously and halted Rob in his tracks. The timing could not have been better and it was my best ever heckle! At the end of the presentation, Mark Homer came over to congratulate me on it!

Rob is the only speaker that I used to heckle but he always reacted well... A comedian is nothing without an audience!

Feeling frustrated towards the end of February, I phoned Ian Lawson. Ian was a highly experienced investor in Brighton, and I thought he would be able to advise me. I had been thinking about phoning Ian for ages but, reluctant to ask for help, it was some time before I called him.

I had met Ian three times before at local property events and seen him do a talk about how he and his girlfriend Faye had gotten into meditation. After building a passive monthly income of £10k, he and Faye went on holiday around the world for four years.

Although they had worked hard building this, Ian was unable to 'switch off' on holiday. His mind was constantly active, thinking about work.

While Ian and Faye were travelling, they got to know a really relaxed guy. Intrigued to know how he achieved this, Ian asked, "What's your secret?" He replied, "I'm living in the present moment' and he introduced Ian and Faye to ascension meditation.

So impressed were they by this methodology that they themselves became qualified teachers of ascension meditation.

The phone call with Ian went like this. I said, "I feel like I am on a hamster-wheel and I'm not getting anywhere."

Ian replied, "You're still looking into which strategy suits you best, and that's no bad thing". Knowing Ian worked with Glenn Armstrong, I mentioned that I was looking forward to doing the training with Glenn soon.

Hearing my frustration, Ian suggested I went on the next two-day meditation course that he and Faye were running. I thought 'I'll give it a go' and agreed.

In early March I went to the Progressive Super Conference. The main keynote speaker at the event in 2012 was Bob Geldof. His speech was very interesting. I didn't realise he had such a track record in business and property.

Afterwards, we had the chance to meet Bob Geldof. I nearly fell over myself to do it!

When I reached the front of the long queue of people waiting to meet Sir Bob, I put my right hand out to shake his hand too abruptly and I started to fall forwards!

Bob: "Oh, don't fall over!"

Me: "No, I won't!"

After regaining my balance, I gave Bob my business card which I was holding in my left hand.

Me: "It's nice to meet you."

Bob: [Looking at my business card] "How do you say your surname?"

Me: "Sue-lee-art."

Bob: Foc that! Why don't you call yourself Murphy?

He made me laugh!

I was then asked to move along swiftly.

Towards the end of March I drove to Milton Keynes and attended one of Glenn Armstrong's two-day weekend courses.

On the first day, Glenn said to me, "I have had a look back at your recent blog updates. You're in a state of paralysis and you don't know what to do." That told me a lot about Glenn. He went on to say, "Don't worry, I'm going to sort you out. I need to get to know how your mind works first."

One of the things I like about Glenn is he tells it like it is. When I mentioned my frustration over not finding any potential Rent2Rent houses in the BN2 area of Brighton, he replied, "Well, obviously you were looking in the wrong area to do Rent2Rent!"

Then at the end of the course Glenn asked me, "Are you going to come back to do the next course?" Over the next couple of months I did all three of Glenn's courses (free of charge):

The courses were held in a hotel and on the Saturday evening, Glenn and his team had dinner with us students. Chatting to Tony who works for Glenn, he said that he and Glenn had commented on the determination they saw in my eyes as I was walking towards them earlier that day. I felt like pointing out that one of my eyes is rather lazy!

I made a number of friends on the three courses, including Elizabeth who lives in London.

In mid-April I did the two day ascension meditation course. This form of meditation is designed to enable living in the moment. The book 'The Power Of Now' talks about living in the present but it doesn't really explain how to do it.

Through meditation, I'm now more aware of how the mind works and the thoughts it produces. Ascension meditation is extremely simple but it requires some dedication. On the course Ian and Faye advise you to meditate for twenty minutes, three times a day - when you wake up in the morning, before your evening meal and before going to sleep at night.

Like most things in life, meditation gets easier the more you do it and you feel the benefits. People who meditate daily say it becomes effortless.

I have spent sporadic but productive times in the present moment. It's a great state to be in. One of the benefits is an upsurge in productivity. But regretfully, I'm not disciplined when it comes to meditating. I find it difficult to do on my own and much easier in a group environment.

Like me, people tend to meditate immediately after doing the course and then drift a little. The sensible arrangement is that after paying to do the course the first time, you can then redo it as many times as you like. Ian and Faye and other leaders regularly hold meditation evenings just because they want to.

Over the last couple of years, I've redone the course once and have been to a few evening sessions where I came up with the line, "My mind is far too busy to meditate!"

During one of the meditations the first time I did the course, I found myself with tears rolling down my face. Meditation cleanses the mind. But the reason for my tears was the realisation that my desire to become successful (and to make £1 million) is so strong, it is ingrained in me.

I set myself a goal to make £1 million and I still want to achieve it. But my ambition was to set up one or more recursive strategies and that is still true.

However, this has evolved over the last four years. I now want to make a difference in the world.

Can I remind you of my purpose in life? To help and inspire others and reach my full potential.

A few days after started the meditation course, there was a knock on my front door which subsequently propelled me into internet marketing.

When I opened the door, my neighbour Bruce was outside holding his laptop asking, "Can you help me with my computer?"

Bruce is about sixty, and a person who tends to keep himself to himself, we had only said a passing hello to each other before.

Bruce came in and I helped him with his laptop. He wanted to know how to increase the text size in Firefox. We then chatted for a while before Bruce said:

Bruce: "I'm into something you might be interested in."

Me: "What's that?""

Bruce: "It's something to do with advertising on the internet. I don't know much about it but Larry, who lives on the other side of the complex, signed me up to it. I'll ask Larry to come and see you about it."

It prompted me to look into the system that Bruce was talking about. It was a web advertising company operating an affiliate programme. After watching a few of their videos I started Googling affiliate internet marketing and realised it's about driving people to websites.

I remembered that about a year ago, I had watched three or four video webinars by Jo Barnes on creating Facebook fanpages and I visited her website 'The Social Networking Academy'.

After a bit more Googling, I found a video of Jo Barnes interviewing Chris Farrell. Captivated, I watched Chris discussing success being about mindset, taking action and feeling the fear and doing it anyway. He said he procrastinated for years before teaching himself internet marketing and starting his business.

I remember Chris Farrell when he was a radio presenter on Heart in London.

The video led me to his website, 'Chris Farrell Membership'. It was then that it struck me.

Sitting at my desk I thought 'I've been busting my ass trying to find the right property strategy for the last two years when the thing that I've been looking for is staring me in the face. I can make £1 million on my laptop doing internet marketing.'

The sequence of events that evening was triggered by Bruce knocking on my door. He said the reason he asked me to help him was because he often saw me on my computer as he walked passed my window.

Over the next few days I looked closely at The Social Networking Academy and at Chris Farrell Membership. Both websites teach people internet marketing through a series of online training courses. Jo's site is aimed at people who have already got a business and who want to promote it using internet marketing, whereas Chris' site is aimed at people who are interested in starting an internet marketing business.

The other thing which appealed to me about Chris' site is his step-by-step style of teaching. This is significant because it suits my analytical mind and learning new things logically. I'm also the type of person who finds reading user guides beneficial.

After Bruce asked Larry to come to see me we went through the user guide until I fully understood the affiliate programme. I signed up under Bruce and put some money into it.

Larry and I got on well from the start, as we have the same can-do mindset and sense of humour. Larry has always been active and entrepreneurial. Now in his mid-sixties, he lives most of time in southern Spain. A few years ago, he bought over a dozen BTL flats as packaged deals in the north of England and, to date, he has never visited any of the properties.

Moving from property investment into internet marketing is something I thought about carefully. After all, I had spent the previous two years learning property investment and had put a tremendous amount of effort into it. Changing direction wasn't an easy decision.

By the time I went on Glenn Armstrong's third course at the end of May, I had already decided to learn internet marketing. I spoke to Glenn about diversifying and he thought it was a good idea.

Despite this, at the end of the property course that weekend, Glenn invited me onto his monthly Mastermind mentoring programme, free of charge. Wanting to focus on internet marketing I politely declined his kind offer.

I changed my email signature to include 'I am the 1st property investor & internet marketer with Cerebral Palsy'.

Over the first half of 2012, I felt less need to contact Rob Moore. I didn't go to the Progressive VIP again and didn't email Rob anymore. I think Rob was pleased that I was focused on one thing and learning something that I was passionate about.

The first training course I opted to do on Chris Farrell's site was how to create videos using Microsoft Powerpoint. I wanted to see how good Chris was at teaching something that I had previously found difficult to grasp. I had tried to use Powerpoint at university and at *Shh*. Not being an artistic person, I had always found it boring and thought that Powerpoint was too arty-farty for me.

Chris Farrell's teaching style is very straightforward. All you need to do is copy what he does in the training videos. It couldn't be simpler.

In creating a primitive Powerpoint video, it gave me the idea of making a much more elaborate video. I had a definite vision of what I wanted to create and I put the video together diligently over the course of a month.

The video is about mindset. How I learnt to use Powerpoint, my journey to date and what I want to achieve. I narrated the video and at the end, I built a pictorial representation of me learning internet marketing in order to help people and make money.

As I wasn't very confident speaking on camera, my narration took some editing. I find making an off- the cuff video, with someone else filming it, a lot easier to do.

I made the opening sequence of the video as my last task, backed with a fifty second edit of

Vangelis' 'Chariots of Fire'. The video was completed by the end of June, coinciding with the run-up to the Olympic Games in London.

I knew I had made a powerful video and was surprised with how easily I had grasped Powerpoint. I emailed my video to the

Patrick Souiljaert

support team at Chris Farrell Membership. Surprisingly I received the following response from Steve Dutton of the support team.

*Hi Patrick,*

*Glad this helped and your video is excellent. It is always refreshing to see people taking steps to use the skills they have and have learned to get creative and make something totally original.*

*I have passed this ticket over to Chris's assistant Tricia so that she can let Chris see your work.*

*Good luck in your endeavours and I'm sure you will be in the 3% of successful people who apply themselves no matter what obstacles are placed in front of them.*

I then received an email from Tricia, followed by an audio message from Chris Farrell. He said that he was extremely impressed with my video and that he had refunded the subscription I had paid for the first month and given me a lifetime's free access to his membership website. Chris also mentioned inviting me to speak with him on stage!

I was taken aback. I thought I would just get some positive feedback.

You can find the video on my website: **www.StairsForBreakfast.com**

When I included the video in a blog update I received very positive feedback. I had met Raj Shastri once at the BPM in 2011. When Raj saw the video, he emailed back advising me to send the video to Oprah Winfrey and do everything in my power to get onto her TV show.

It prompted Raj to come and meet me again at the BPM. In chatting to him he said, "If you've got the desire to make £1 million you will do so." I often say inspiration works both ways and Raj is one of the people who inspires me.

In June 2012 the radio sports show I produced on Saturday afternoons ended. The programme was dropped when Phil decided to not present it anymore. After working on Saturdays for eight years Phil wanted to spend more time at the weekends with his family. In 2003 I never thought it would last nine years. I would like to return to radio one day.

When the programme ended, Phil and Allan said I could do some work on Selector, the music scheduling database instead. But working on Selector wouldn't have been as much fun as pressing buttons in a live studio environment! I let it go by as I had just gotten into internet marketing and decided to focus on it.

I have learnt a lot from Chris Farrell. People would ask, "I want to make loads of money in internet marketing and become really successful." His position is that the key to becoming successful and making lots of money is to provide a product or service that adds value to people's lives. You can apply this to any industry. In essence, internet marketing requires a database of people who are interested in what you are doing.

As a result, I created StairsForBreakfast.com to go with my autobiography. In subscribing to my network you will receive a free gift from me. I will also email you updates on what I am doing and how my journey is progressing.

Over the last few years I've built a small list from meeting people at property networking events, and when I write a blog update I receive positive responses from them.

In early September, after my friend Elizabeth purchased lots of tickets, we went to the Paralympic Games. Elizabeth is such a good person. She's always doing things for people.

The evening before going to the Games, I drove to central London and stayed at Elizabeth's flat. Before Elizabeth went to bed she said to me, "We need to get up at five o'clock in the morning because we have to collect some people and give them a lift to the Olympic Park." Surprised, I exclaimed, "Five am!" However she generously didn't wake me up until 5.45!

The Olympic Park was awesome and scootering around it made it even better. We watched athletics and wheelchair rugby. The rugby seemed like a rough game, with people ramming each other and wheelchairs tipping over. I thought about entering the weight-lifting event! It was a good day and the atmosphere in the athletics stadium was great.

Something I haven't written much about is my falling over because it is just part of my life. It's difficult to say how often I fall over but on average it's probably about once a month. I lose my balance far more often. I can sense it, almost as if in slow motion and usually I just regain my balance again.

When I fall over I instinctively know how to protect myself by putting my hands out. When I fall backwards, I put my head forwards. Grazes and bruises are common but I've never really hurt myself, apart from a unique fall on 24th September 2012.

If I were to try and recreate it a thousand times, I don't think I could. It's a fall which put me in hospital for four days and which debilitated me for five months. The fall affected me mentally more than physically, although I was badly hurt. I haven't experienced anything like it before or since.

It happened at home at around 2 o'clock in the afternoon. I had just made a cup of tea in my travel mug, which I can carry around my flat and had placed it on my desk in my lounge. As I was about to sit down at my computer, I noticed a box of hay fever tablets. The box had been sitting on my desk for months.

Before sitting down, I decided to put the box of pills onto the shelf, which is about sixteen inches to the right of my desk. It's not a high shelf and directly below it is a low unit for my TV and hi-fi. The action was one of those things that are so quick and easy, you don't even think about it.

I picked up the box with my left hand and walked a few paces to my right. Standing in front of the TV, I reached out and put the box on the shelf. My left arm was in the hoop of one of my sticks which was raised off the floor. I was balanced using my right arm in the hoop of my other stick. Although my right hand wasn't holding the handle of the stick, I'm perfectly used to balancing with my right arm on my stick, while doing something with my left hand.

However, I was standing a fraction further away from the shelf than I should have been. Consequently, the box of pills was half hanging off the shelf. Without thinking and rather than taking a tiny step forward, I leaned a fraction further forwards and pushed the box onto the shelf with my left hand. In doing so, I reached a tipping point and my right arm slid off my stick.

As I started to fall forwards towards the shelf, the stick on my right started to freefall and it collided with my right hip. Consequently, it pushed my body to the left. My instinct told me that I was going to fall to my left and so I put my hands out on my left hand side to cushion the fall. I fell into the sixteen inch gap between my desk and TV unit and smashed my nose on the wall.

Having fallen over hundreds of times, this was the first time that one of my sticks had collided with my body and pushed me in the opposite direction. Because I was already leaning forwards before I started to stumble, the fall happened so quickly that I couldn't do anything to avert it.

When my nose hit the wall with some force, three things went through my mind:

'I wasn't expecting that to happen.'

'Wow...that hurt.'

'I feel like I'm going to faint.'

I then crumpled to the floor and both of my arms became trapped underneath my body. The stick which had been on my left arm ended up between my right arm and my body. Between the position of the stick and the weight of my body, my right arm was under tremendous pressure.

Although I didn't faint I was powerless; the outside of my nose was bleeding and I started to get pins and needles in my arms and hands. Ordinarily, I would have rolled over onto my back but there was no space to do so. I was caught between my desk and the TV unit.

My hands were trapped and I didn't have the strength to move backwards out of the gap. I kept thinking, 'I'll be alright in a minute, I just need to get some energy back.'

Between three to four o'clock that afternoon, Frasier was coming to see me about internet marketing and Larry was coming over at three.

I kept thinking 'I need to get up and clean up my nose before Larry and Frasier arrive'. I could feel the handle of the stick pressing down on my right arm and the pins and needles getting progressively worse. I thought, 'It's only pins and needles, it'll disappear when I get myself up'.

It took me half an hour to reverse myself out of the gap that I had been lying in. I crawled over to one of my sofas, and kneeling in front of it, I put my arms with severe pins and needles in them onto the sofa. I spent a further thirty minutes pushing down on my arms, trying to stand up.

It was only at that point that I got my mobile out of my left trouser pocket and called neighbours for help. I called five people and none answered their phone. Then Steve phoned me back and came over. Shortly after, the other four people arrived, including Larry. I was a mess. The cut on my nose looked bad but it was only a superficial scratch.

When I sat down my right arm was at a right angle, almost as if it were in a sling around my neck. It wasn't painful, I just had severe pins and needles in both arms down to my fingers.

After a few minutes I went to the bathroom. The really strange thing was, when I stood up, I wasn't able to straighten my right arm. It meant that I wasn't putting my right stick on the floor. I kind of hobbled to and from the bathroom on one stick.

I kept saying "I'll be alright in a minute!"

Larry stayed with me and the other four people left. Then Frasier arrived and Larry and I went through internet marketing with him. Larry did most of the talking, but in my dazed and weakened state I couldn't do more than utter the odd sentence!

Frasier stayed for about three hours. I phoned my doctor's surgery as the pins and needles was still severe and my right arm was still at a right angle. The doctor I spoke to didn't know me and she speculated that the pins and needles were due to anxiety - to which I replied, "I don't have anxiety!"

The doctor phoned me back a couple hours later, in advance of visiting. In the meantime, following Larry's and Frasier's advice, I had called for an ambulance to get checked over by A&E. Because I wasn't classed as an emergency, the ambulance took over four hours to get to me. The paramedics who took me to hospital thought my nose was broken. I was more concerned about the pins and needles down my arms.

It must have been about 9pm when I arrived at the hospital. I didn't have to wait long in A&E before I was seen by a junior doctor, who looked like a teenager and thought I may have broken my right elbow or shoulder. The x-rays revealed that I had no broken bones. I was then wheeled into an annex-ward for people who need to stay in A&E overnight. However, it was such a constant hive of activity that it was virtually impossible to get any sleep.

The pins and needles lasted for over twelve hours and slowly mutated into a really itchy pain. My fingers in both hands became so painful that I asked for some painkillers. I found it soothing putting my fingers on the cold metal rails, either side of the bed.

At about 5.30am the junior doctor came to see me. My right arm was resting over my chest.

Junior doctor: "Why are you holding your right arm like that?"

Me: "I don't know...because it's comfortable..."

I tried to straighten my arm out but wasn't able to do so.

Me: "My fingers are also really painful...What's wrong with me? What have I done?"

Junior doctor [before walking away]: "I don't think there's anything wrong with you."

It wasn't until the ward lights were turned on at 6.30 when I realised that my fingers were swollen. They were so bloated that I couldn't grip anything.

Later that day, the hospital wanted to send me home but unable to grip anything, I was unable to walk. During my four day stay in hospital I was seen by five doctors. None of whom seemed to know what was wrong with me or what to do with me. One doctor thought, in hitting my nose against the wall, I had sustained whiplash and had damaged my neck, the reason for the pins and needles in my arms.

I endured two sleepless nights in the A&E ward before I was moved onto another ward. A few hospital physios and occupational therapists assessed me but I had no treatment on my right arm. I was given painkillers and anti-inflammatory tablets every four hours, which didn't help in ease the swelling.

I phoned Shirley the community physio, who has supplied me with new crutches and ferrules over the ten years or so, and she came to visit me the day before I went home. Shirley was shocked to see me in the state I was in. The cut on my nose looked bad and I could only just grip my crutches by then. It wasn't easy to straighten my arm enough in order to put my right stick on the ground. To do so, I had to walk ever so slowly.

Shirley thought that I should have stayed in hospital for a few more days. However, it wasn't a nice place to be in and I had already decided that I was going home the following morning. In addition to picking me up from hospital, Larry also visited me one afternoon.

When I got home, on Friday, I thought 'I'm at home and I'm back to normal now.' However, my body said, "I'm not!" and I fell over twice within a few hours. I was walking too fast and wasn't putting my right stick down properly.

Getting undressed that night was incredibly difficult. I wasn't able to hold either leg up with my right hand in order to take my shoes and socks off with my left hand. It took me over an hour to get undressed. In the hospital, the nurses had helped me with my shoes and socks, as the bed was too high for me to do it myself.

I was really looking forward to having a nice hot shower. Only to discover there was no hot water as the hot water timer had stopped working.

The next morning I had great difficulty getting my clothes on. Fortunately, my cleaner Ann arrived and she helped me.

For the next few days, my neighbour Bruce helped me with my shoes and socks.

Every time I tried to hold each leg up with my right hand, my leg slipped through my fingers, as if it was covered in butter. My arms, hands and fingers were still very swollen. Not being able to straighten my right arm was the biggest problem because it affected my walking and balance. I had to do something. And I still had no hot water.

On the Monday morning, I phoned my doctor's surgery and explained the situation. I thought the receptionist was going to say, "Dr Smith can come and see you three weeks on Wednesday" but instead she replied "Alison will be with you within the next two hours". And she was.

Alison: "It must have been some fall you had..."

After I explained what happened.

Alison: "You're unique because you're so independent and I want you to regain your independence."

Me: "All I need is decent physio, two or three times a week for a month and I'll be fine."

Alison: "I think you will need to go to a specialist CP rehabilitation centre" - and mentioned a place in Middlesex she knew of.

Me: "I don't mind where, I just want to get back to normal as soon as possible."

Alison said she would investigate and get back to me. In the meantime, she would arrange for some emergency homecare, to help me get dressed and undressed.

Having been my GP since 1984, Alison told me that she was due to retire at the end of 2012. It surprised and disappointed me because she was a great doctor. Alison said that I was one of the patients who she admired the most.

The next five months were amongst the most stressful and frustrating times of my life.

In the first two weeks after coming out of hospital I had visits from numerous physios, occupational therapists, social workers, homecare people and others who all came to assess me. Even someone from the fire brigade visited me.

Having been independent since I was a kid, it was weird needing carers to help me get dressed and undressed. It was something I didn't like but had to accept.

Another problem was I had lost all confidence in walking outside. When I tried to do so, my right arm became rigid with fear and, consequently, I wasn't putting my right stick on the ground. My lack of confidence also affected driving my car. At first, I didn't have the dexterity to wrap all of my fingers around the hand control lever and my arm would tighten up, meaning that I couldn't operate the lever to accelerate. At least I could still brake with my left foot!

One of the people who came to see me at home was Shirley, the community physio from the neurological team. She tried to stretch my arm but it was so tight she couldn't do so. She thought that I needed a botox injection to relax my arm.

From what I saw when I was in hospital, nurses are stretched and work hard and it annoyed me that some patients were rude towards them. There must be some aspects of the NHS which function okay. But the treatment I received from the NHS, after I came out of hospital, was totally inadequate and lacked common sense.

About a week after Alison came to see me she emailed me, "There's a rehab centre in Chichester but there's a waiting list for it and unfortunately you're not a priority."

Maybe I should have made an absolute fuss with Alison to get me into the rehab centre, but I felt so demoralized at that early stage.

As Shirley didn't normally visit patients in Shoreham, I was assigned to Debra, another neurological community physio, who came to visit me with Abi, a trainee physio. Debra found it virtually impossible to stretch my arm and advised Alison that I needed a botox injection.

I researched botox injections and they sounded dangerous. They cause side effects and botox doesn't provide a cure, it just masks the problem. People who rely on botox as a muscle relaxant have botox every few months.

This exemplifies how NHS doesn't work. Cerebral Palsy is a neurological condition caused by brain damage at birth and so I was seen by the neurological community physio team. However, virtually all of the patients they treat are older people who have had a stroke.

Patients who have had a stroke need gentle exercise to regain functionality of parts of their body. The neurological physios do not have the expertise to treat someone with CP like me.

My muscles are strong and powerful stretches are required. It reminded me of the early nineties, when I went to the neurological physio department at my local hospital to have my hamstrings stretched.

From the start, I knew, through no fault of her own, that Debra didn't have the expertise to treat me. What's more, she only came once a week for 15-30 minutes. You can imagine my frustration.

For the first two to three weeks out of hospital I fell over so many times, making my injuries worse. I sustained more carpet burns than a carpet factory on fire! I was in regular email contact with Alison, who got me an 'emergency' appointment with a consultant in Chichester. The 'emergency' appointment was in six weeks' time!

If that wasn't bad enough, my natural resilience was being tested to the limit in other ways too by other events.

My home phone and broadband suddenly went down due to vandalism, which took over a week to be fixed. In the meantime I connected to Bruce's wi-fi.

One of the falls I had was in my bedroom. To get up, I kneeled in front of my bed and used my arms to push down on my mattress. In the process of standing up again I hit my mobile phone in my trouser pocket on the side of the bed and broke the screen!

I could still use my mobile but the screen wasn't working, and nor was my home phone. I couldn't walk or drive anywhere to go and buy a new mobile. I thought 'What do I do? The solution was to buy a new handset from Ebay.

It took about three weeks for my hot water to be fixed. At first I didn't know if it was a plumbing or electrical problem. My cleaner, Ann recommended a plumber who said I needed a new timer and he recommended an electrician.

The electrician fitted a 'new' timer and I paid him £60. When I realised the water still wasn't heating overnight. I called the 'Basil Fawlty' electrician back, who said it was a plumbing problem. The plumber came back, tested the 'new' timer and confirmed it wasn't working, when the 'Fawlty' electrician returned on the Sunday he refused to accept that the timer he fitted was faulty!

I ended up buying a new timer online and after phoning his boss a couple of times the Fawlty electrician came back and fitted it. I later heard that he had been fired!

Seeing my frustration with the NHS, Bruce recommended a neighbour, Dermot, a sports injury masseur who Bruce had met at the onsite jacuzzi. Not knowing his address, Bruce put a note on Dermot's car, asking him to phone me.

Two weeks after I came out of hospital Dermot came to see me. After hearing about my unique fall, Dermot knew why my right arm wasn't straightening up. He said that after I fell over, the muscles in my arm were under so much pressure from my stick and bodyweight that they were in shock and had tightened up.

Dermot said that I had injured the right side of my body from my shoulder down to my fingers, and the right side of my ribcage. Dermot was good, he knew his stuff and he wanted to help me.

When he first came to see me my arms, hands and fingers were still swollen. After massage, the swelling disappeared within three days. Dermot came to see me twice a week and after eight days he had stretched my right arm straight. Having been seen by so many people from the NHS, it was a real relief to get proper treatment.

Three to four weeks after coming home from hospital, I was managing to get myself undressed again. I only needed help in the mornings to get dressed. No matter how hard I tried I wasn't able to hold my right leg up with my right hand, in order to get a sock over my heel.

The more I tried to put my right shoe and sock on, the more frustrated I became. The effort of trying to hold my leg up caused my right hip to ache. This developed so gradually that I didn't realise that it was due to me trying so hard. Although Dermot had managed to straighten my right arm, I wasn't able to straighten it myself. I still had dexterity issues with my right hand and my confidence wasn't improving. In the end, I didn't regain my independence until early February.

Dermot, as well as Debra and Abi, were visiting me every week. Dermot was very helpful, massaging my arm and leg and advising me to improve my balance by placing my right stick out to the side more. He also advised that I should re-train my brain to hold my stick slightly differently with my right hand, as it would help my wrist later on in life.

In October something important happened. Paul Ribbons sent an email invitation to a webinar he was presenting, entitled 'A life without limits'.

There, Paul spoke very candidly about his life and success. He talked about his Mum dying when he was a baby, being brought up by his stepmother, coping at school with dyslexia, how he got a job in an estate agency, when people said he couldn't do it, and how he ended up managing the place. All this before he became a property trader.

It was a really open and inspiring presentation. I don't recall why Paul suggested writing a book. Maybe it was because this was something he had done.

However I do remember Paul saying, "Write a book and put everything in it. It's a way of wiping the slate clean."

When Paul said that, I realised that I *could* include the incidents with Nathan and Freddie in my book. At the end of the webinar I wrote on the feedback form, "Thank you Paul, you have inspired me to write my book", which Paul read out.

From that moment, I thought more and more about my book. It prompted me to write a series of blog updates (between November-February) about my unique fall and the struggles I was going through. Not having blogged about any personal matters before, I wanted to see how easy it would be for me to do it. It also helped to reduce my frustration.

In November, Larry drove me to see the consultant at Chichester Hospital. I had to provide a urine sample. On the way there I suggested buying some apple juice to fool the urine tester.

However, when we got to the hospital, I was bursting for a wee and asked the staff for a specimen pot.

Picture the scene:

I was standing at the toilet, with my trousers and boxer shorts around my ankles to avoid the consequences of an overspill. I was using my right hand (and stick) to balance, holding the little pot in my left hand. I didn't know which to do first. A tiny wee in the pot or my main wee in the toilet. I was concerned that once I got going I wouldn't be able to stop. For the record, I did the tiny wee first and was in perfect control at all times.

Waiting to see the consultant, I realised that Larry was holding my urine sample. As I didn't want to hold it, I decided not to raise it. Talk about taking the piss.

The consultant saw me for about half an hour. He asked me a few questions, examined my limbs and ordered some x-rays. He suspected nerve damage in my right arm and referred me to have my nerves tested.

Ten days after this, I received a copy of the letter he sent to Alison, confirming my referral for nerve testing. In his letter, the consultant said, "Patrick's CP might have gone downhill this late in life." I was thirty-nine years old!

I think the consultant needs educating. Cerebral Palsy is not a progressive disability and it doesn't shorten life expectancy. On the contrary, I become better able to do things as time goes on.

In November Dermot went on holiday to Thailand for two months and Debra was on sick-leave for five weeks. Abi, the trainee physio, came to see me once a week. She was pro-active and nice. To try and solve putting on my right sock and shoe, we came up with all sorts of things to rest my foot on. However, the counteraction of having my foot elevated makes me lean backwards and I wasn't able to reach my foot to put a sock on it.

My friend, the retired engineer Peter Fanning, even built something out of wood for me to put my foot on. Nothing worked. As time went on I was getting closer, but no cigar. This increased my frustration.

In autumn 2012 my two flats in Worthing increased the stress level. Ever since my first BTL flat suffered a leak from the property above it, both properties had added to my distress.

The leasehold company had supposedly taken responsibility for the leak by putting dehumidifiers in my flat. They also cleaned the carpets. But there was damage to the walls and ceilings in the hall, lounge, bathroom and kitchen.

From then on, the leasehold company told me they were going to get the damage repaired. They said they didn't want to claim on the buildings insurance because they had already done so on other flats in the block.

In the autumn the leasehold company changed their stance. They now said it was my responsibility to get the damage fixed. Having had so many exchanges with them, I sent an email of complaint to the freehold company.

This was a mistake. I received a letter from the Head of the freehold company saying I didn't have the right to rent out the property and I was in breach of the lease.

I phoned and, very calmly and politely, apologised for my complaint. Then I just listened to what he said. In order to rent the flat out, he said I needed a deed of variation to my lease, which the freehold company would charge me thousands of pounds for. He advised me to seek legal advice. I said I wanted to work with him and was going to sort the situation out.

It raised my stress levels but I resolved the situation. I got legal advice from three sources, the best being Bernie Wales who knows UK leasehold and freehold law like the back of his hand. I wasn't in breach of my lease. The freehold company were quoting part of one of the clauses, out of context.

Bernie gave me excellent advice: "Don't do anything and wait for them - the freehold company - to take action against you, and then react." He also advised that the next time the freehold company accepted ground rent from me, they forfeited the possibility that I was in breach of the lease.

Once I had paid the ground rent in February 2013, I knew that I was in the clear. It didn't stop the freehold company chasing me up a couple of times. I just replied. "I've sought legal advice and I'm not in breach of the lease."

The storm I had accidentally created was mainly due to a lack of communication. At the time I didn't know that the leak was caused by a washing machine pipe in the flat above. This meant the owner of that property was responsible for the damage to my flat, not the leasehold company. It turned out that the damage was minimal.

I got the lounge ceiling repainted in order to have the property revalued. Having it revalued at £100k was a good result. In buying and refurbing the flat, I put in £35k. When it was re-mortgaged I received £28k.

Near the start of 2013, Bernie Wales went to assess the remaining damage and wrote to the leasehold/freehold company on my behalf. I've met Bernie a couple of times at the Brighton PIN. He's just the person you need for negotiating the terms of lease extensions.

Another mistake I made was after the tenants moved out of my flat. I became impatient when Howard & Co hadn't found me another tenant within a month and I decided I would find another agent to source a tenant for the property.

Having spoken to Mandy, an experienced Worthing investor who I met at the Brighton PIN, I asked for her advice. She recommended an agent called Henry. I arranged to meet him at the flat.

Not being able to walk or drive properly, Larry came with me and showed Henry the flat. Soon enough Henry found me a good tenant.

My doubts began when Henry came and pressed me to let him take over the management of my two bedroom flat from Howard & Co.

In November I went back to Chichester with my neighbour Steve to have my nerves tested. It wasn't a pleasant experience, as it involved having a series of electric shocks and needles in my arm.

The guy who carried out the tests didn't have the best people skills. Talking to his assistant nurse as if I was stupid, he declared, "Why have they bloody referred him for nerve testing...it's obvious there's nothing wrong with his nerves."

Agitated, my arm tensed up completely. The guy thought my arm was rigid due to my CP. It was easier for me to say nothing about it.

Ewan, my Hove friend who I met in St Vincent, was concerned about me. I was still nervous about walking outside.

My perception was different to how Ewan saw it. I knew I was going to make a full recovery and regain my confidence, whereas Ewan thought I had lost my independence. He has a non-identical twin brother who is disabled and dependant on people. Ewan's view was that, "It's not a problem that you can't put your shoes and shocks on." I disagreed, "It is a problem"!

I know Ewan relates to me a little like a brother. He really helped me by clearing out my spare bedroom. For ten years it had been used as a store room and was full of junk.

In December, because of my hip ache, I went to a local chiropractor a few times. Ewan met me at the chiropractor twice as he was interested in the treatment the chiropractor was providing.

As a theatre actor and director, Ewan works around the UK, often for several months at a time.

Although inconvenienced by the fall, I was able to continue with the training courses on Chris Farrell's site.

In December 2012, after nine weeks of carer-based help to get dressed, the NHS decided I wasn't entitled to funding anymore. They pronounced that this was because I needed "too little help".

I felt abandoned, mortified that I now had to pay someone to put my shoes and socks on. I was desperate to be self-sufficient and was nearly there. Glenn Armstrong helped me when he said, "Be grateful you are in a position to afford somebody to help you."

Rarely do I get so stressed that I shout at someone. After not seeing me for six weeks, Debra returned from sick-leave. Abi briefly brought her up to date as I tried to put my shoe on and I mentioned my aching hip.

Debra, who was still standing at my bedroom door, observed glibly: "I think the problem is with your back..."

It was such an idiotic thing for her to say. Out of frustration I shouted, "You don't understand the problem. Would you like to see the dent in my hip?" It brought a tear to Abi's eyes because she identified with my frustration.

After I had apologised for my outburst, I laid on the bed. Debra got me to move my right leg a bit and she said: "I'm baffled and don't know what to do."

She then went on to say that she had a bad back and had to live with the problem and that I might have to live with my hip ache. A case of someone creating their own reality.

Me: "I'm going to make a full recovery."

Debra: "I'm sure you are."

When Debra came to see me a week later she said the neurological community team had done everything they could for me. She admitted that she didn't normally treat people with CP and didn't have the experience to help me recover. If only Debra had admitted this three months earlier, it would have helped me to receive proper treatment and saved a lot of time.

The last thing Alison did for me, before she retired at the end of 2012, was arrange an outpatients' appointment at the rehab centre in Chichester. Ewan came with me in early January. I was seen by an experienced physio who was authoritative in a nice way, but no consequent improvement materialised. Ewan stayed with me for a week that month. This was a massive help.

After meeting my friend Helen on the personal development course in Croydon in 2010, we remained in contact. We normally speak on the phone every few months. Our conversations last for a couple of hours and cover everything under the sun, with a lot of humour.

Helen does contract work as a business analyst and likes to travel. She visits her family in Ghana once or twice a year. My CP isn't an issue to Helen and I know she finds me stimulating company. Our phone conversations often include quite a bit of flirting with each other.

I said to Helen that she's got a really good voice and several times I've suggested that she could succeed as a voiceover artist. Her response was always, "You're just chatting me up..." Then after a recent trip to Ghana, Helen told me "Someone asked me if I had ever considered doing voiceover work, because they said I've got a good voice!"

In our phone conversations over the years, I've felt like Helen and I are in a telecoms sitcom. Several times Helen has hinted that she was going to come to see me and I've offered to go and meet her in Croydon. I kept thinking 'If Helen really wants to see me, she'll come and see me'.

Religion is very important to Helen. The fact that I'm not a religious person is an issue that means our conversations have remained almost entirely on the telephonic plane.

I met Helen once in 2012 at the BPM. Beforehand, she told me she might be going to it with a friend. I didn't see her in the bar at the start so I thought she wasn't there. I bumped into her and her friend after the presentation and we spoke for literally two minutes. Helen said they had to get back to Croydon because they were both working the next morning. I think Helen was pleased to see me, as she was blushing a bit!

Near the end of 2012 I phoned Helen one evening. To my surprise, she said she was going to come to see me either on the Sunday coming or the next one. I took this with a pinch of salt and thought about confirming the visit in an email. However, I was in a pull rather than push mode at the time so did nothing about it. I waited in vain for the visit.


It is far better to create your own product or service in internet marketing because you have total control over it. There are reams of affiliate multi-level marketing products online offering handsome returns. Not all of them are viable products or systems. My friend and neighbour Larry is an entrepreneur with good people skills. When he was living in the same complex, we put money into a couple of these online affiliate marketing systems, which didn't fully pay out. Larry's attitude was, 'you win some, you lose some'. I haven't heard from Larry since he moved away. He is someone I respect and I am sure we will meet up again in the future.

One of the things I've discovered about myself in the last four years is, that in order to be successful it helps when I'm focused on one thing. My priority is to finish writing this book, find a good editor and publisher and then promote my book like hell, or rather, like heaven!

In early 2013 I phoned Helen. At the beginning of the conversation she apologised for not coming to see me as she had been busy. I said it didn't matter and we proceeded to have

our usual two hour conversation. Then at the end of the phone call Helen said, "Don't forget, we've still got a date..." I thought 'what is she on about? I don't like playing mind games, I much prefer people telling it like it is.

Having known Helen for nearly three years, I decided to take a chance and give her a little *push* - mainly to see how she would react and what she would say. A few days later I phoned Helen and said that I liked her. She said she was surprised and flattered, but persisted in being evasive.

Helen is lovely but she is also an analytical person and two people of this inclination don't go well together. Since then, I've been happy just being friends with her.

Helen has said she would like to have kids but hasn't found the right person yet. In my comedic way I advised her, "You'd better hurry up and find the right person then!"

In the first week of February I finally overcame my unique fall when I regained my independence by putting on my right shoe myself. It happened after I thought, 'Before I fell over I was putting on my shoe without thinking about it.'

What started out as a physical problem due to my arms, hands and fingers being so swollen, mutated into a psychological issue. I was terrified at the thought of losing my independence. My state of mind was working against me. I became so agitated that I was tensing up my right arm and leg. Once I relaxed my body, putting my shoe on became simple again.

Do not underestimate the power of your mind.

October 2012 to February 2013 was a bad time. I was letting people and things frustrate me. My unique fall taught me a valuable lesson. Rather than spending an hour trying to get myself up and in the process, putting so much pressure on my right side, I should have freed my left hand, got my phone from my pocket and called neighbours for help sooner. Had I done so, I wouldn't have sustained such severe injuries.

By February, I had completed most of the training courses on Chris Farrell's site and I needed to come up with a product to sell. I didn't have one and I wasn't sure what my niche was. At the same time, I was contemplating writing my book. The off-putting thought was, 'It's such a mammoth thing and it will take me too long to write it.'

Around the same time, another serious issue started to unfold...

# Chapter 10

A couple of days before I regained my independence, my monthly interest payment from Harlequin failed to arrive. It made me think, 'Uh-oh...'" Ever since summer 2010, when I purchased my off-plan property in the Caribbean, I had received my interest payment at the beginning of each month.

I phoned Harlequin and asked to speak to Gerald, the sales rep who I had dealt with in 2010. The receptionist told me Gerald had left the company and said that another salesman would call me back.

It became obvious Harlequin weren't in a healthy state when I found a couple of articles online claiming the company were having payment problems. Following an article in a national newspaper, Harlequin sent a statement to investors, saying the article was grossly misleading.

My worries weren't eased when I received an email from an investor, who had found the blog post I had written in 2010 about my Harlequin investment. She enquired if I was still receiving my monthly interest payments. When I phoned she said Harlequin had stopped her payments two or three months earlier.

When I didn't receive any money from Harlequin in early March, I knew I had to do something. I decided to make a video about my experience to help other investors. I decided to create a powerful video, and perhaps even turn a negative situation into a positive one.

It took me a couple weeks to make and in the process, I spoke to Paul Ribbons about it. I also spoke to Paul about my book because I had made the decision to write it. Having thought about it for 30 months, it got to the point where I thought 'F**k it, I am going write my book.' I wrote the first few hundred words of Chapter One in March.

Towards the end of March I uploaded my video onto YouTube.

I emailed my video to a few people at Harlequin. The only comment I had back about the video was from one salesman who observed, "Do you believe that creating adverse publicity is good for you and all the other investors!"

A few days after uploading the video, I discovered that someone who had been following my blog (the video wasn't on the blog – but such is the power of social media), had created a thread about me on a property forum website claiming, 'I was a very real casualty of guru-ism'!

You can tell it's a misleading thread from its title! I think the guy who did it thought he was acting with good intentions. However, the thread grew to seven pages and hosted false information. It is full of people speculating about me not being very bright! I find it weird how people who don't know me, feel able to write about me!

I was pushed by the forum owner into writing a piece on the thread defending myself. Paul Ribbons wrote a couple of nice things about me on it and set the record straight.

After seeing the thread, Glenn Armstrong emailed me and asked if I was alright. Glenn offered to pay my mortgage for me, which blew me away. After thanking him, I said I had lost a few hundred pounds of income per month but could cope. Glenn gave me his mobile number and advised me to contact him if I needed any help. I told Glenn that I had decided to write my book.

I considered asking the forum owner to delete the thread about me. Instead I posted a link on it, inviting people to buy my book.

I don't like my Harlequin video because I resemble a 'victim'. However, it makes me smile because to date it has had over 2,200 views. I had made a powerful video.

Usefully, the ability to make powerful video will help me to promote this book!

In April, I started writing my book in earnest, typing up to five hundred words per day (all with my left index finger). After seeing my video, I was contacted by a couple of Harlequin investors. They believed that I should mount a campaign to get my £55.5k deposit back.

I'm sure that if I really went for it I would get my deposit back. I had visions of me turning up at Harlequin's office with a camera crew. Instead I decided to write the £55.5k off. When I invested in Harlequin in 2010 I knew there was a possibility it could all go 'belly-up'.

I spent a month emailing and phoning people at Harlequin to ascertain the likelihood of getting my money back, I also attended an Investors meeting in London hosted by the Chairman of Harlequin.

Getting my deposit back would have involved a lot of work. It would have been draining and caused negative energy. Writing my book, on the other hand, is empowering and constructive, which creates positive energy. I don't want to be portrayed as a victim.

Losing £55.5k, some people would give up. Not me. It has made me even more determined to succeed. Harlequin ceasing to pay me the interest payments gave me a useful kick in the ass to write my book.

In times of despair, clarity often prevails. Just over a year after starting it, I've nearly finished my autobiography.

One of the keys to being successful is not how you celebrate your successes. It's about how you deal with the disappointments.

When I told Glenn Armstrong that I had decided to write my book he asked me to email him a synopsis of it. He then advised me to email him a daily count of words written. What a brilliant way to help keep me motivated. I wish I had Glenn's brain!

As I am slow at typing I thought about dictating the book into a voice recorder and having someone transcribe it. However, I don't think I would have ended up with such a good book. My pedestrian typing gives me more time to think about what to write.

I also considered promoting 'Stairs For Breakfast' by blogging bits of it while writing it. I decided not to do so, mainly because I suspected my mum was reading my blog. I didn't want to give her cause to contact me or hassle me about anything that she didn't like. In order to write this book successfully, I didn't need additional stress from my family.

Once I had written the first chapter, I got into my stride and became progressively more determined to write an exceptional book. Ultimately, my autobiography is not an achievement until I have finished it.

Reminded that I was due a new car in summer 2013, I phoned Motability and asked if I could extend my contract again. As the car was now five years old, Motability would only extend the contract for a further six months. It meant that I was going have to order a new car before the end of 2013.

Having a keen sense of humour, I've often thought about going to a laughter therapy group. In the summer I Googled and found one in Hove and went along. It was hilarious!

There were about ten of us, sitting in a circle. At first I found the exercises so strange that they made me laugh out loud! Laugher is contagious in that environment. My laugher made other people laugh, which made me laugh even more. Also my ironic off-the-cuff remarks added to the hilarity.

The laughter group was run by Philip Evans, who's an undertaker and a (live) people person. Philip met his girlfriend Sallie at the group. I'm now friends with the couple. Whenever we meet up we turn into comedians and come out with a succession of one-liners! Philip and Sallie are such good people.

By going to the laughter therapy group I discovered Meetup which is a website for anyone to find or organise social face-to-face groups and events in their local area. Consequently, I've joined several Meetup groups in Brighton and Worthing.

When socialising with a new group of people, what I've found is that I am more comfortable in smaller groups, where everyone talks to everyone else. In bigger groups (above twenty people, for example), most people tend to stay away from me because they see me as being very disabled.

Of course, the way I feel also comes into it and I mix better where I know there are like-minded people. I'm confident meeting property investors at the BPM who know and respect me.

Over the summer I began emailing Debbie, the disabled woman I met on a dating website. After emailing each other for a week we spoke on the phone. We had a thirty minute conversation and it went well. Afterwards, Debbie said she wanted to talk on the phone again but we never did.

Instead, we spent the next four weeks emailing one another. I found it a real chore, having spent hours writing my book during the day. We didn't 'gel' that well but Debbie kept saying she wanted to speak on the phone again. Then in the week before she went on a family holiday, she said she was going to call me on three occasions but said she had been too busy packing for her holiday and had run out of time! Then she asked if I could text her while she was on holiday! I decided not to do so.

A couple of weeks after Debbie's holiday I emailed her this:

*Hi Debbie*

*How are you? I hope you had a good holiday? I'm sorry I didn't text you.*

*When we first started emailing each other we both said that honesty was very important to us and all I can be is honest with you.*

*I think you are a nice person and I would like to get to know you better.*

*I was hoping we could talk on the phone rather than email.*

*I know you were unwell for a few weeks (and that's fine). I was a little disappointed in the week you went on holiday because you said you would phone me on three occasions, but you didn't. It hurt me a bit. When you asked me to text you on holiday, it just reminded me of the many women I met over the years, who just wanted to text (or email) me and didn't want to talk to me on the phone.*

*Talking on the phone is a lot easier for me – and it's a much nicer way to get to know someone.*

*Also please understand, I get physically very tired from typing my book.*

*Would you like to speak with me over the phone?*

*Patrick*

I'm glad that she didn't reply to it.

In early August an extremely stressful situation started to develop. It came about after the tenant in my one bed flat had moved out of the property at the end of May. Letting agent Henry didn't like the competition when I also instructed Howard & Co to find me a new tenant. I think it inspired Henry to find me a tenant instantly, and he did so within a few days.

I remember the afternoon when Henry phoned me about Liam. Henry said he had rented a property to Liam before and that he was working full-time. However, Henry went on to say Liam wasn't great at managing his money and therefore his employer would be paying his rent for him, out of his salary.

I didn't know what to do. Larry had come to see me that afternoon so I asked him what he thought and he said to go for Liam, so I did.

Writing about it now, I feel like holding my hands over my face in shame! At the time, having lost the monthly payments from Harlequin, my income consisted mainly of the rental cashflow from my two flats, so I was eager to find a new tenant.

A month into the tenancy, I was concerned when Liam's rent arrived three days late and it became a problem in August when there was no sign of his rent.

My frustration had got the better of me and I made a mistake. Henry was not very helpful in trying to get Liam to vacate the property without having to take him to court. In frustration, I said to Henry that I was not going to allow him to find me another tenant once Liam left the property. It would have been better to keep him on my side and to make it worth his while to get Liam out. Instead it felt like Henry was doing everything he could to make my life even more difficult.

It was clear that Liam knew tenant law and what his rights were and I followed the legal process in getting him evicted with Duncan's help and advice.

Glenn Armstrong assisted me in asking Duncan (who works for Glenn) if he would do the Section 8 for me. Duncan was extremely helpful and once the Section 8 was submitted in early

October, it was a weight off of my mind. Two weeks after Liam was served with the Section 8 with no sign of him vacating, Duncan applied for a court hearing, which took place in early December.

Meanwhile in September, I had a couple of other problems to overcome. Not receiving any rent from my one bed flat meant that my monthly outgoings were more than my income. I had £3.5k in savings and I had to get a new car by the end of the year.

I decided to sort out my car first. As there was nothing wrong with the car I had at the time I would have been happy to keep it for longer. I knew the down payment on a new Renault Mégane was £2k and my hand controls would cost £300-400, I wasn't in a position to spend most of my savings on a new Motability car.

When phoning Motability I explained my financial situation and asked them if I could keep the car I had for a bit longer. As it was over five years old, they said no and suggested I applied for a Motability grant for a new car. I was put through to a lady in the grants department.

After explaining my situation to the lady, she said she would post me an application form, and asked me why I needed a car with a proximity card. She then said that I would need a letter from my GP to justify it. I explained that that might be difficult as Alison had retired at the end of 2012 and I hadn't been to see my new doctor yet.

I asked her, that as I was on my own and unable to write clearly, whether I could go through the application form with her on the phone. She said no. Asking her if I could complete the form online or by email I also got a "No". No matter how much I pleaded with her to help me fill in the form on the phone, she wasn't going to help me. I remember her saying "We haven't got that facility here, sorry...", before she ended the call.

Half an hour later, not happy with the outcome of the call, I phoned Motability again. This time I was a bit more assertive and said, "Hello, I hope you can help me - I need to apply for a grant for a new car but I live on my own and I've got nobody to help me fill in the application form. Is there someone there who can complete the form with me over the phone?" The receptionist replied "Bear with me, I'll see if I can find someone who can help you." I was put through to James in the Grants department. He said he could help me complete the application and asked if he could call me back the following day, when his office would be quieter.

James already had most of the information he needed when he phoned me back the next afternoon. He asked me, "Why do you need a car with keyless entry?" I explained, "When I had cars with a normal key I couldn't turn the engine on and off with my right hand. I did so with my left hand, which was a bit difficult." He also asked what hand controls I needed.

The phone call lasted under ten minutes and it couldn't have been easier. Afterwards, I emailed James a couple of bank statements. Three days later, he emailed me to let me know that my grant for a new Mégane had been approved! In the middle of other things not going well for me, I felt like I had achieved something.

However, I had forgotten to ask James if Motability would pay for the hand controls to be fitted. I thought I would be pushing my luck a bit but I phoned and got put through to someone else in the Grants department, who said, "Don't worry, Motability pay for the hand controls anyway." It surprised me because I've always paid for the hand controls myself in the past. We concluded it might have been something that Motability had introduced in the last five years.

A week or so after getting my new car, I received a cheque from Motability for £450. They call it a bonus for handing back the previous car in good condition. That *is* something new that they've introduced! I emailed James and thanked him again for his help. He replied wishing me good luck with my book.

There is no doubt that my communication skills and a bit of persistence helped me to get a grant for a new car. However, having to apply for a grant, made me feel more worthless. I never had any financial difficulties before leaving Shh.

When I left *Shh*, I knew that if I ran into financial difficulty I could rent out my spare room for £100 per week. The blocking factor for me since I moved into my flat in 2002 was my fear of rejection. I don't mean my fear of being rejected by women in a romantic sense. It's the way I am sometimes ostracized by people who don't know me.

I thought 'people see me as being very disabled and they won't want to share a flat with me.' I know I need to change the way I think and surround myself with sympathetic, like-minded people. However, I do appear very disabled and I have confronted this all of my life. It has had a psychologically debilitating effect on me. When people get to know me, they see that I'm a really nice guy.

At the beginning of September 2013 I knew I had to create more income speedily. Therefore I phoned my neighbour Barbara who has had lodgers for years and asked her what furniture I needed to rent out my spare room. Occupying the room was a good quality hi-fi system that my dad had paid for in 1987. I had recently advertised it for sale for £50 but hadn't received any response.

I then looked on Freecycle for a chest of drawers and a chair. Having never looked on the giveaway website before, I spotted a wanted ad for a hi-fi. I phoned the guy up and said, "I've got a stereo you can have."

It pained me to give away such a good piece of equipment, but I needed the space.

When the guy came to collect the hi-fi, he was so pleased when he saw it he asked me "Is there anything you need?" Being a regular Freecycler, the guy collected the chest of drawers and chair I needed to rent the room out!

On 25th September I published a blog post, which included the following:

*I have been busy writing my book. That's the good news.*

*The bad news is my finances aren't great.*

*I've got a non-paying tenant in one of my two flats.*

*The last few months have been stressful.*

*Do I regret leaving my £30k job? No – it was boring and not enabling me to reach my full potential.*

*Do I miss my salary? Yes!*

*However it's good to take chances in life. I'll get out of this current situation because I overcome everything. It's what I do.*

It was an unusual blog post for me to write. However in writing about it, I was forcing myself to get out of my financial hole.

*Interestingly, a few people offered to lend me some money, including my good friend John Potts.*

Then on 1st October Barbara emailed me, asking if I was still looking for a lodger because she was moving to Eastbourne and her lodger Tod needed to find somewhere else to live. Barbara brought Tod over to meet me and he moved into my spare room towards the end of October. Tod likes the fact that he has an en-suite shower room. When he was living with Barbara, she was always telling him to clean the bathroom after he used it.

Todd was studying for a commercial pilot's license. Tod saw me as really old whilst I thought he was a lazy and irresponsible twenty-one year old kid. However, he was very quiet and I hardly knew he was there. When he wasn't at college or out with his mates, he stayed in his room. He also went home to the Midlands every few weeks.

Before Tod moved in, Barbara advised me what Tod was like and she said that I had to be tough with him, otherwise she said, "He'll walk all over you". However, I didn't want to be the type of landlord who was always telling Tod to do things.

I've learnt that I should have been tougher with Tod from the start. There are two things which Tod didn't excel at: 1) Paying his rent on time. 2) Cleaning his room. He rarely visited the kitchen either. He seemed to live on takeaway burger and chips. When he didn't have to get up early for college, he got up in the mid-afternoon or early evening!

Barbara is a good person who doesn't stand for any nonsense. When Tod moved in Barbara said to me "See how it goes with Tod, if you don't like him, give him a week's notice and find another lodger."

Then when Tod started being problematic, Barbara advised me, "Get another lodger, it's easy..." I know Barbara was right.

However, in order to write my book I needed peace and quiet and that's what I got with Tod.

Yes, I had to remind him to pay his rent every four weeks and to clean his room but I knew how to handle him. If he quibbled over the rent payment, I threatened to disable the wi-fi! He knew that I would have told him to leave if he really annoyed me.

I tolerated the situation because I think people will be put off by my voice, when they phone about the room. I'm only human.

Barbara offered to help me and I might ask her to take the phone calls for me in the future. She's a good judge of character and she'll tell the people about me.

In November, with my fortieth birthday approaching, I became a bit down for a few days. During my teens, twenties and thirties, I thought I would be married and doing well by the time I reached forty. The fact that I had left *Shh* to make £1 million and was in a financial mess wasn't helping either!

I phoned Paul Ribbons who advised me, "You need to put your fear of rejection behind you." What he then said was also so true: "You are choosing to feel the way you do at the moment." Paul observed that a nurse would love to be with me and half joked that I should go to a pub where nurses hang out. I've always found nurses attractive.

I started looking for some more Meetup groups to join. I found a workshop day on the law of attraction, and in one of my daily word count emails to Glenn Armstrong, I mentioned that I was thinking about going to the workshop.

In response to my email, Glenn sent me an A4-sized inspirational poster, containing many lines, such as:

*This is your life.*

*Do what you love, and do it often.*

*If you don't like something, change it.*

*Open your mind, arms and heart to new things*

The line which resonates with me the most is:

*If you are looking for the love of your life, stop; they will be waiting for you when you start doing things you love.*

Although I didn't go to the law of attraction workshop, I've joined some other Meetup groups and go out regularly. I get a buzz telling people about my book as they seem to be inspired by me and say they can't wait to read the book. I also love speaking to people about mindset success.

Around my birthday I went out four evenings in a row and organised a nice restaurant meal with some good friends.

The court hearing to evict Liam from my one bed flat was in early December. I thought I knew where the Magistrates' Court in Worthing was. Upon arriving outside what I thought was the court, I realised that it was in fact Worthing library! I cursed, 'Sh*t, sh*t, sh*t, where's the court?'

I knew the court was nearby so I carried on driving and spotted the court building round the corner.

After going through the airport-like security, I got to the right waiting area in the court. With twenty-five minutes to spare, I 'checked-in' with the usher. We were both puzzled that my name wasn't on the list of hearings that morning. However, when the usher went through the list I recognised Creative Lettings, as it's one of Glenn Armstrong's companies. I realised that it wasn't under my name because Duncan had submitted the Section 8 and court application online, as I explained to the usher.

There were about twelve other people sitting in the waiting area and Liam wasn't one of them. As expected, he hadn't turned up. I got chatting to a woman and mentioned why I was there and she found it a bit strange when I said, "I'm quite excited to be going to court!"

However, when the usher called "Creative Lettings versus Liam Bloggs" I became slightly anxious, more out of anticipation than nervousness. My anxiousness caused my right arm to tense up which made the fifteen yard walk to the courtroom difficult. Despite my saying I was alright, the usher wanted to carry my bag for me.

By the time I made it into the courtroom, I was out of breath and slightly asthmatic. The courtroom was an office with a number of desks put together, forming a large rectangle table with a jug of water and some glasses in the centre of it. The lady judge was sitting at the far end at the head of the table.

As I sat down halfway along one side of the table and faced the judge, she was a bit concerned that I was out of breath. After the judge asked the usher to pour me some water, she asked me "Is there anything we can get you to make you more comfortable?"

Being a quick-witted person, I was tempted to say, 'Some coffee and biscuits would be nice..."but instead I said, "No thank you, I'm fine. I'll be alright in a minute when I've got my breath back."

The consequences of my right arm tensing up may sound funny but it's something which really annoys me. It makes me appear much more disabled than I am and my arm never tensed up prior to my unique fall in 2012. Fortunately, I'm overcoming the issue as my confidence is increasing.

The judge was slightly perplexed about the case being in Creative Lettings' name. Once I explained the situation she was happy to proceed.

I went to court armed with a load of printed emails chronicling Liam's misdemeanours. When the judge had read though the wad of emails and asked me a few questions and as a result of Liam's absence from court, she ordered a notice to be served, giving Liam fourteen days to vacate the property. It was the best possible outcome and I thought it was a piece a cake!

When I go to Worthing on a property matter I often have a cooked breakfast in my favourite café afterwards. As I did so on that day, I phoned Duncan to let him know the outcome of the hearing and thanked him for his help.

Sixteen days after the hearing, I went to check if Liam had vacated the flat. Having misled me so many times over the previous five months, I was expecting him to still be in the property. On my way over to Worthing I wasn't thrilled by the prospect of walking up the stairs and knocking on the front door of the flat.

When I arrived and as I was getting out of my car, I couldn't believe my luck. I saw a guy who lives in one of the other flats walking out of the building. I rushed over, explained the situation and asked if he would knock on Liam's door. He was a bit reluctant at first but did so, as I waited outside. After about a minute the guy came back out and said, "Liam said he's going to come down and speak to you."

Before long Liam appeared. Despite not having met Liam before, our conversation unfolded:

Liam: "I'm moving out tomorrow…"

Me: "You had until yesterday to vacate the property. You know that."

Liam: "You emailed me two weeks ago tomorrow and said I had two weeks…"

Me: "I specifically said in the email that you needed to move out by yesterday's date."

Liam: "Well I'm moving out tomorrow."

Me: "What time? What time are you moving out tomorrow?"

Liam [shrugging his shoulders]: "I dunno…"

Me: "As I have said to you before, I don't believe a word you say."

Liam [walking back into the property]: 'I'll email you tomorrow…"

After thanking the neighbour who was standing by me, I went to the Magistrates' Court office where a clerk completed a bailiff's form, in order for me to get possession of the property.

As it was just over a week before Christmas the clerk informed me that there was a two-week 'eviction amnesty' and the bailiff was now off work until 6th January. Knowing a seven-day notice needs to be served before an eviction takes place, I realised I wouldn't get possession of the property until at least mid-January.

Liam did email the day after I met him and claimed he wasn't able to move out yet because "…at the weekend, I paid for someone with a van to help me move, the last I heard from them is that they had a flat tyre and I haven't been able to contact them since…"

At least his excuses were entertaining.

I left the bailiff a voicemail asking him to phone me, but the reply took until after the 6th January. The bailiff informed me that he had served Liam with the eviction notice but, due to the backlog, the eviction was on 22nd January. The bailiff also confirmed that I had to organise a locksmith to be there. I also arranged for two other people to attend the eviction ten minutes afterwards to give me a quote for cleaning the flat.

I thought Liam would vacate the flat a few days prior to the eviction. I arrived twenty-five minutes early on the morning, followed soon after by the locksmith and two bailiffs (a guy in his sixties and woman in her forties/fifties). We met the helpful neighbour who said he hadn't seen Liam for a couple of days.

Although we suspected that Liam had vacated, I found it funny that we stood on the stairs chatting for ten minutes until the allotted time to enter the flat. As one of the bailiffs said, "Liam might be out shopping and could return to the property."

Liam wasn't in the flat but he had turned it into an absolute pigsty. Apart from loads of rubbish, there was furniture and lots of clothes scattered everywhere. As there was no need for me to see the disgusting mess I didn't go up the stairs

The bailiff advised me that I had to give Liam a reasonable amount of time to collect or claim his belongings. Ambiguously, when I asked how many days was reasonable, the bailiff said it was up to my discretion.

I felt I deserved a cooked breakfast afterwards. In speaking to Jason, the café owner, he offered to clean the flat and we agreed on £200!

Back home, I emailed Liam to tell him I now had possession of the property and gave him four days to collect his stuff. He said he wanted to pick up his belongings but then didn't get back to me.

When Ann saw the state of the flat she didn't want to clean it, saying it was a two-person job. So Jason and his girlfriend cleaned and cleared the flat. Afterwards, Jason told me that the rubbish had filled ten bin bags.

Leaving beer cans, vodka bottles, pizza boxes, clothes and other rubbish everywhere is one thing, but abandoning pornographic magazines and used tissues is quite another.

Since going to the laughter therapy group in summer 2013, I have joined other Meetup groups and regularly go to events such as restaurant meals and stand-up comedy. I am known at Meetup events as a writer with a sense of humour – and for providing comedians with heckle material and easy laughs.

In mid-February I went to a Meetup meal with thirty others. There was a tragi-comic end to the evening in the wet and windy weather. As a number of us left the restaurant, Imogen said goodbye to me before she went to get a taxi with a few people.

My car was parked about twenty-five yards away on the other side of the road. I was walking with Marion who had organised the meal. The weather was wild and Marion was concerned that I might fall over. Before I crossed the road, I said to her "Don't worry, I'll be fine." Marion was watching me walking to my car from the other side of the road.

As I reached the front of my car, a heavy gust of wind blew me off my feet and I fell backwards towards the pavement. Marion panicked and ran across the road. I didn't hurt myself and was fine. Imogen asked "Are you okay?" I replied, "Yeah, I'm fine. I'm just having a lie down!" Marion and someone else helped me back onto my feet.

I started going to her Meetup events in 2013. She now knows not to panic if she sees me falling over!

When I fell over, it was windy but I think I wouldn't have fallen had my right arm not been tense, causing my right stick to be up in the air.

In late summer of 2013 I also started sailing with Sailability, a charity for disable people. It came about after I saw Mike Green when I went to 'The Duke' pub to see Steve Bell play in his folk band. I've known Mike and his wife Judy for years. I first met Mike during his brief spell managing the Harbour Club when Steve and I had a laugh playing bingo!

I've been to The Duke a few times recently and find it strange. Twenty years ago it was a pub for people in their late teens and twenties who enjoyed loud indie bands. Now, it seems to be an enclave for the over-sixties who like folk music!

Mike Green has been sailing all of his life and is a sails-maker. When I saw him in the pub he thought I would enjoy sailing, so he introduced me to Sailability and came along with me the first time I went.

I went sailing three or four times in 2013 before the season ended. On the first couple of occasions I went in a little Access boat. On arriving at the sailing club the third time, one of the organisers asked me "Would you like to go out on your own?"

I replied "I don't really know what I'm doing yet but I'm up for it!"

Before getting into the boat I glanced at a flag to see which way the wind was blowing.

I was doing a good pace along the river, although a bit concerned about the boat leaning from side to side now and again. Then my boat came to a stop, for no apparent reason.

People were whizzing past me. I thought, 'what are they doing that I'm not?' I decided to follow one of them, but I only got so far before my boat stopped again. I was going round in circles and saying to people "I don't know what I'm doing!"

After seeing that I was struggling, Katie, an experienced sailor, decided to teach me. She was very good and I learnt a great deal. She also said, "Don't worry about the Access tipping over. I've tried my hardest to capsize the boat and haven't managed to do so."

I then went up and down the river and leant over as much as I could! I was on the river for two and a half hours and people said I did really well. Mike took photos of me.

In April 2014 when the sailing season started, knowing that it is virtually impossible to capsize an Access boat, I did my utmost to try and tilt the boat as much as possible. When people saw me do this they thought that I must be crazy, but with the belief that the boat won't capsize, I was perfectly safe and it gave me a buzz. To this day, I'm still learning the ropes, as some of the time I find myself going round in circles! Sailing is just something I do every few weeks.

In regaining possession of my one bed flat, it took two months to sort the property out, which involved a lot of time and expense. After Jason cleaned the flat I went up and saw it and discovered that Liam had smashed a window and broken the hinges on it – another thing to fix.

Then I put the flat on the rental market with Howard & Co.

In order of occurrence, the carpet started smelling so it was cleaned.

Then the heavy rain came and damaged the lounge wall and bedroom ceiling.

Then the roof had to be fixed which involved going to the flat and liaising with the leasehold company.

Then dehumidifiers were placed into the flat to dry it out.

Then the bedroom and lounge were redecorated – by Jason. However the lounge wall hadn't absolutely dried out yet so the wallpaper wouldn't stick to it!

Then I discovered that the electric radiator, attached to the bedroom wall, had disappeared so it had to be replaced. Phew!

Howard & Co found me a good tenant who moved into the flat mid-March.

I learnt a lot from my mistake of going to Henry. It's much wiser to work with a good agent, who fully references prospective tenants. Dealing with Liam and Henry, when they didn't want to co-operate, was extremely stressful.

Liam said he was going to forfeit his one month deposit a long time before he actually did so. Even then, when Henry received the money from the tenant deposit website, it took him a while to transfer the money into my account.

Earlier on, I mentioned I was taking steps to regain my confidence to stop my right arm from tensing up. I started going to an Emotional Freedom Technique (EFT) Tapping Meetup group in Brighton. EFT Tapping is similar to cognitive behaviour therapy and involves thinking positive thoughts while tapping certain points on the body.

When I arrived for the class I found I was the only attendee! The EFT trainer Stephanie, said that she had recently taken over running the group and needed to advertise it. She was very good and it was good being the only one there.

Interestingly, even though she hadn't met me before, by the end of the two hour session Stephanie with great perception said that I am too hard on myself and that I should be proud of what I have achieved so far in life. Over my four years in property, many people have said the same thing to me,

I know I have achieved a lot but it's a drop in the ocean compared to what I know I can achieve. Writing this book has helped me. I have become more relaxed and content with myself and I think my book will be my greatest achievement to date.

The nearest I could park my car to the EFT Tapping group was on the other side of a busy road. There was no pedestrian crossing nearby and, ordinarily, crossing wouldn't worry me because when cars see me standing on the side of the road, they stop.

However, crossing the road, on my way to the tapping group, my right arm tensed up so much that I was holding my right stick horizontally in the air. It wasn't easy walking across the road just using my left stick and I walked so slowly that I nearly made it onto a couple of the Radio 2 traffic bulletins!

Stephanie said regaining my full confidence is about taking small steps. It's no coincidence that I have expressed my journey as taking steps to regain my confidence - it's how my mind works. Crossing the road and walking back to my car after the session was much easier as I was putting my right stick on the ground. I did become a little anxious when I was standing in the road because I couldn't see if any vehicles were coming around the corner! I felt great when I made it to my car.

I know I am going to regain my fearlessness in walking and driving. It's a question of feeling the fear and doing it anyway.

Patrick Souiljaert

# Chapter 11

Y ou can probably detect that it is nearly the end of the book!

It is now April 2017, three years on from when I wrote the previous chapter. Ascension meditation has become part of my journey and everyday life. When the weekly Brighton ascension group started in May 2014 it really helped me with my meditation practice. It also motivated me to go to Guayrapa, the ascension meditation retreat in Spain.

My first impression of Guayrapa was everyone's mental picture of a prison camp. The dining room had long wooden tables and benches and everyone queued to be served food on metal plates and bowls! When I asked for a black tea with two sugars, I was informed, "There's no sugar here"!

One of my initial thoughts was 'I'm not going to last two weeks here...' However, I actually ended up extending my stay to a month, the whole of October 2015. I was desperate to stay for the month of November but as the retreat was fully pre-booked I had to return home on 31st October.

Before I went to Guayrapa, I thought the retreat was on top of a mountain and that it wouldn't be too difficult for me to get around it. The reality is that the retreat is on the side of a mountain and it was far too steep and widespread for me to get around it on my own.

The first week in Spain was tough for my old self. I thought, "I'm independent, I don't need any help..." But I did need people's help. All of the ascension teachers are excellent and Satta taught me a great lesson when she said to me, "At home you're independent, but here you need people to help you. Let go of not wanting to be helped. You inspire people and people like to help each other. By not allowing people to help you, you are not serving."

Patrick Souiljaert

Once you let go of something which is bothering you, it doesn't bother you anymore. Hence when I accepted that I needed help getting around, it was easy and joyful.

On the second day at Guayrapa, I fell over walking down one of the steep slopes. Not being able to get myself up again I just sat on the ground knowing that someone would be walking past soon and would help me up. In the distance George saw me and came over and asked if I was okay? I replied, "I'm fine, I just need help getting up". George and I quickly became great buddies as it was our first time in Guayrapa and we were both in the newbies group, which was great fun. Not least because Manyu was our teacher and one of the funniest guys I have ever met.

Satta assigned two teachers called Maitreya and Prakasha to help me get around the retreat during my month there. George also took it upon himself to help me and we became like brothers. After the first week I started to really enjoy my time at the retreat. I had three main people helping me around and getting my food at meal times.

My thirty five year old wheelchair was too archaic to cope with the steep, mountainous terrain, so Guayrapa hired a new wheelchair for me to use during my stay. However, I still needed two or three people to get up and down the mountain.

Consider this: You are not your thoughts and they are not real. Have you ever reached out and touched one of your thoughts? Point to where your thoughts are! Thoughts are just what we have been pre-conditioned to believe. Ascension is about observing thoughts rather than identifying with them. When you attach yourself to your thoughts, they seem to be real but in reality they don't exist!

Ascension provides unbounded inner peace. The more you meditate the more you live in the moment and the more inner peace, love and joy you experience. Ascension is also about serving people. People naturally enjoy helping one another.

The programme at Guayrapa consists of two meetings a day and extended periods of meditation. It is amazing what happens at a retreat with eighty to one hundred other people, all there to meditate and experience more peace, love and joy. Some people use ascension to overcome serious physical pain. Ascending for six hours a day made my walking smoother and easier. The mind and body are connected, so when the mind relaxes, the body relaxes.

For the first week I fell over twice a day but as I became more relaxed, I stopped falling over. Being me, I was vocal in the meetings and soon became a quasi-star of the retreat.

To help people in my everyday life, I get them to close their eyes and count their thoughts. By counting your thoughts, you're not identifying yourself with them and they pass through your mind quickly. One of my favourite sayings is, "It's just a thought...".

On the last day of my stay in Guayrapa in 2015, I had the following exchange with Satta:

Satta: "Are you going to be back next year?"

Me: "Absolutely!"

Satta: "Anything you need, we will make happen."

Knowing that the food at Guayrapa is mainly vegetarian and salad and that Satta reads the registration forms, in my application to go back to Guayrapa in 2016 I decided to state the following under dietary requirements: "In order to maintain my upper body physique, I need a daily 16-ounce steak for lunch, cooked medium to rare."

When I returned to Guayrapa in September 2016, Manyu presented me with a couple of steaks for lunch one day. I must be the only person who ever got to eat steak at Guayrapa and it was delicious!

Satta arranged for Mahan to be my personal assistant for the month and he was excellent. I nicknamed him 'My-Hand'! I didn't need any help getting around the retreat, he mainly got my food for me at meal times and did my laundry. As with all the teachers at Guayrapa, I was able to talk with Mahan about what I was experiencing when meditating and we got on well.

George and I organised to go back to Spain at the same time in 2016 and this added to the magical experience of the retreat.

Guayrapa is a six month course in mastering inner peace and being able to choose to be present in whatever situation you are in. At the end of the six month course you also become an ascension teacher. When I went to Guayrapa for the first time in 2015 it was not my intention to become a spiritual teacher. I have been told that I will make a great ascension teacher and no doubt I will complete the course and become a teacher in the next couple of years.

In 2016 I hired a mobility scooter from a local shop and took it with me to Spain, thus I was able to get around Guayrapa independently and eliminating the need for a wheelchair. Being well travelled, it was the first time that I have been through an airport without a wheelchair and without any assistance. It felt so liberating.

'Stairs For Breakfast' has given me a platform as a public speaker. It's important to do the things you love in life and I have found that speaking in front of people is something I am naturally gifted at and love to do. My Cerebral Palsy is a gift because I don't see myself as being disabled. I am using my disability positively to help and inspire others.

When I took the momentous decision to leave my job for life at *Shh* in 2011 I was convinced that I was going to make £1 million in property. I haven't done that yet. Instead I've had to find my own path and it has led me to where I am today.

I knew I was setting myself a challenge back in 2011 but I didn't think I was going to find it as difficult as I have done. The main reason for my struggles over the last seven years is because my actions have been so scattered, desperately searching for a recursive strategy that suits me.

In 2012 Glenn Armstrong was partly right in asking me "Why are you trying to do property? You don't even like property..." and it's true, I don't enjoy viewing countless properties, dealing with neither tenants nor maintenance issues. However property is a people business and I have great people skills. The last seven years have however taken a lot out of me.

Success is also about desire and as you've no doubt gathered by now, my greatest desire is to share my life with someone. In 2014, I felt I had met the woman of my dreams but it didn't materialise. For over two years I felt like I was on an emotional rollercoaster ride, asking myself 'Are we or aren't we going to get together?' She seemed to be pulling me towards her with one hand and pushing me away with the other. Ironically, since then I have become a more peaceful person, I'm off the rollercoaster now. Funfairs have never really been my thing anyway!

My meditation practice says 'When you let go of everything, what you need comes to you'. My journey over the last few years has been more about inner peace and loving myself than about making money.

Property investment and internet marketing are still two key parts of my vision. One of the keys to success is creating a product or service that adds value to people's lives. Another is doing something you love.

After publishing 'Stairs For Breakfast', I did a few radio interviews and it was an amazing experience. Despite my 'I can do anything' mindset, I never thought I would speak on the radio with my CP-affected voice.

It was easy getting onto BBC Sussex. I emailed them a press release about 'Stairs For Breakfast' and they phoned me and asked if I could do a live interview on the breakfast show the following morning. As I hadn't spoken on the radio before, I felt a bit daunted by it but I knew it was going to happen anyway. At 7:30pm the night before, I got a phone call from Graham Torrington's producer asking if I could do a fifteen minute pre-recorded interview that evening. "Yes", I replied". She went on to say that Graham presents an evening radio show across the BBC in the Midlands.

At 9:00pm the producer called me and after we spoke for a couple of minutes she put me through to Graham who interviewed me on the phone for fifteen minutes. It was an amazing experience, I wasn't at all nervous. You can hear the interview on the Publicity Page of my website.

The following morning at 7:30am my friend and neighbour Laura came to pick me up and we drove to BBC Sussex in central Brighton. Laura is a radio journalist I know through working in radio and as she works for the BBC in Brighton where it is difficult to park, she offered to give me a lift. The pre-recorded interview I did the previous evening was a good warm up for the live interview. I felt a little nervous on the way to Brighton but, once again, when I walked into the studio the live interview was a natural and amazing experience.

Another piece of radio I have done was with my friend Ray who invited me to be his guest on his weekly show on the community station Seahaven FM. I was his guest for the two hour show and we had a great conversation with me picking all the music on the show. I was so relaxed and it is one of the best things I have ever done.

I have also done a couple interviews on local TV. However, another amazing experience was when I was filmed by ascension teachers Greg and Sally who were making a documentary series on how ascension has impacted people's lives and communities around the world. Greg and Sally came to Brighton with a film crew and they filmed me in my car as I drove to Devil's Dyke, where I then did a piece to camera. Being filmed by Greg and Sally is one of the best things I have ever done. I loved it, when I woke up that morning I didn't know I was going to be filmed driving my car but when the film crew suggested it to me, I just felt the fear and did it anyway.

Something which has taken me a lot of time and persistence recently is applying for an Access to Work Government grant to employ a full time PA. When I completed the initial online application form, I was given only five days to complete a business plan. Having never done a business plan before, I found a template online and spent three days completing it. After speaking to the Access to Work advisor and emailing my draft business plan I received a letter in the post advising that my application had been declined. I went through the appeal process and knew I had to submit a business plan that Access to Work would accept. I realised that there must be an organisation that helps disabled people obtain an Access to Work grant and I found *Start Ability Services*.

*Start Ability are excellent, they sent me a straightforward template and helped me complete a business plan and business case.* It took me six months, an appeal and two business cases (the typing of these, ironically, has given me RSI!). I have been working with Felicity, my PA for the last three months and it has transformed the way I work and live.

Felicity is excellent, but it has taken a couple of months for us to work effectively together. This is because when Felicity started I was delighted but unprepared, thinking, 'now what do I do'! Then I realised that Felicity can help me do property and organise speaking events. This led to a load of scattered activity, going to visit estate agents one day, seeking speaking events the next.

I know I work most effectively when I focus on one thing at a time. Therefore, for the last month Felicity has helped me edit this book and as you can see it's nearly done! Felicity has also contacted organisations such as Round Table, Rotary and the Lions Club to offer my services as a speaker.

At the end of writing this book, I will start the self-publishing process and start promoting it. It will give me a platform from which to speak to people and organisations about what has gone into it. I also want to manage property and Felicity can do the leg-work for me. We just need to establish a property strategy and where to do it.

I have also contacted Kaleidoscope Investments, who give disabled people guidance with their start-up businesses. Having approached them for assistance and spoken on the phone, they are impressed with what I am doing. They have invited me to a training day in May. I feel this is an exciting opportunity and it will help me with the next stage of my journey!

I have been told that I am a pathfinder. No, not an aircraft sent ahead to locate and mark the target area for bombing. Instead, I'm a person who tracks ahead and shows others the right path.

Having written two books myself, I hope I have demonstrated that you can achieve anything you want to in life. All you need is a full tank of desire, self-belief and persistence.

I hope you have enjoyed reading this book as much as I have enjoyed writing it. If you have please go to: **www.StairsForBreafast.com** and leave a 5-star review. It will help this book to make a difference to the world.

You can also watch short videos of me and sign up to my network. In return, I'll email you a free gift and keep you updated on my progress.

# What's Next...

It is now April 2018 and I've done half of the six month course at Guayrapa.

I'm much more peaceful and happier person than I have ever been. Also the more I ascend the easier it is for me to walk and talk! When the mind is relaxed the body relaxes.

In September I'm returning to Guayrapa to complete the course and become an ascension teacher. It will enable me to travel the world helping people find the happiness I have found.

I've recently made a video about my experience with ascension meditation. It's the best video I've ever made.

You can watch the video by going to

**http://stairsforbreakfast.com/videos**

Public speaking and property investment are two things I want to do more of.

My desire at the moment is to spend the summer promoting my books and going back to Guayrapa in September.

In February I got a new flatmate called Nick. Conincedentelly, he has been interested in meditation for years but never commited to a particular practice before.

We have been meditating together in the evenings for the last seven weeks.

Three weeks ago we went to Oslo for the weekend because Maitreya and Dhama Raj were hosting a First Sphere course. It was very funny and the best First Sphere I've attended.

Nick is finding ascension powerful and says it's the thing he's been searching for all his adult life.

Patrick Souiljaert

# Thank you Maitreya

After meeting him at Guayrapa in 2015 we have stayed in touch via email and Skype.

There are certain people who really understand me and he is one of them. We have a strong bond and are like brothers. He has really helped and advised me over the last two and a half years.

Not only is he a great ascension teacher, I can rely on him if I have a problem and need advice.

When I went to Guayrapa last year Maitreya was there and got me food at mealtimes and did my weekly laundry for me. And he is going to be there to help me when I go back in September.

We like telling people stories about each other and I have a few about Maitreya!

This is an anecdote, from Guayrapa last year, that he likes telling even more than I do!

It wasn't uncommon for Maitreya to get food for me first and then for him to go and sit at another table (with only room for six people per table). However on the day in question Maitreya sat with me twice.

At lunchtime we sat with four other people, one of whom was 'Scott from Scotland' (a golf instructor and one of my roommates). As the conversation was about golf it gave me a cue to tell my golf joke, which got a good laugh.

Then at dinnertime, Maitreya was sitting opposite me and we were at a table with three or four people, who had just arrived at the retreat. We hadn't met them before and English wasn't their first language.

After we had introduced ourselves and asked them where they were from, Maitreya (thinking it would make a good icebreaker) quietly said to me "Tell your golf joke, it's really funny...!"

I thought 'I'm so bored of it and I'm eating', so I replied "No, I can't eat and talk at the same time. You tell it..."

After pausing for a moment, Maitreya turned to the rest of the people on the table and piped out "I've got a joke about Patrick......Why does Patrick like playing golf so much?......Because he's got a good handicap!"

The look on the new people's faces was one of horror and confusion. They were speechless!

Not knowing what to say or do Maitreya reiterated "...It's a joke...". He looked at me as if to say 'Help me out of this hole I'm in..."

So I put my hands over my eyes and started pretending to sob, saying "How can you make fun of someone who's disabled?"

Still speechless, the new people looked even more horrified and perplexed. They probably thought 'Who are these strange people and where have we just landed?"

I'm sure Maitreya just wanted to run away! But he continued trying to recover the situation, scrambling "No, no, it's okay, he's joking..."

He then went on and tried explaining what a handicap in golf is (without much luck)!

I was just enjoying the moment.

And that's how Maitreya got his reputation as someone who makes fun of disabled people!

Come September I'll have three months of this kind of thing!

I love spending time with my 'brother'. He's not all bad. He's good at selling my books for me. And being an author himself, he has helped me self-publish this one on Create Space.

Maitreya has written two books under the name Oliver Seligman. *The Broker Who Broke Free* and *No Rest for the Wicked.*

I've read them and they are both GREAT reads. The latter is a laugh-out-loud book.

Patrick Souiljaert

You can buy both of my books directly from me via **www.StairsForBreakfast.com**. They make excellent gifts for people and I'm cheaper than Amazon!